The Eagle: From A Chicken Run to the Sky

The Eagle:
From A Chicken Run
to the Sky:

A Woman's Walk of Faith

By

DR BETTY SIBONGILE DLAMINI

iUniverse, Inc.
New York   Bloomington

iUniverse books may be ordered through booksellers or by contacting:

iUniverse
1663 Liberty Drive
Bloomington, IN 47403
www.iuniverse.com
1-800-Authors (1-800-288-4677)

Because of the dynamic nature of the Internet, any Web addresses or links contained in this book may have changed since publication and may no longer be valid. The views expressed in this work are solely those of the author and do not necessarily reflect the views of the publisher, and the publisher hereby disclaims any responsibility for them.

ISBN: 978-1-4401-8443-7 (sc)
ISBN: 978-1-4401-8444-4 (ebook)

Printed in the United States of America

iUniverse rev. date: 11/19/2009

Dedication

I dedicate this work to my mother, MaRosie, two sisters 'Mbusane' Busisiwe and 'Zomdibaby' Zanele and most of all my three stars, Sibusiso, the blessing, Nqobile, the victorious one and Mazulu, the heavenly celebration. I call you ministers of the gospel. Always remember, eagles beget eagles. There shall be no more loss in my territory and there shall be no limits! The sky is not the limit, but a domain where we ought to soar higher and higher with absolutely NO LIMITS!

Contents

Foreword

This book will renew your hope for the future and propel you into your destiny. It will help you resolve issues that may have been suppressed and celebrate your strength. It will show you how to overcome your past challenges and place you on a pursuit to live lavishly, to love vicariously and to never again be a victim but a victor!

It enables you to be more than a conqueror, overcoming all barriers, exhibiting freedom, releasing inner healing to personnel issues, quantum leaps over past failures, hurdling over obstacles into your fabulous future. "For I know the plans I have for you, declares the LORD, plans to prosper you and not to harm you, plans to give you hope and a future" (Jeremiah 29: 11).

As a gifted and talented forerunner from Swaziland (Africa), going all the way to England, and called to America, God's humble servant to humanity, exhibiting strengths, exemplifies excellence in communication with .various ethnic culture groups. She's a builder of bridges over international waters. Transparent in her life and ministry, she shows her strengths and communicates her failures so that others may be healed with God's Love. To appreciate her gifts, God has allowed us to read this special book for special individuals. Never settle for less than the best.

Her character builds nations and we get to benefit from her strengths. I am proud to be her friend and asked to foreword this awesome book. In advance I give innumerable applause for you choosing the right book to enhance your life and assail you into success.

I speak the blessings of the Lord, the empowerment of His Word, the comfort of His joy and the peace that pulls it altogether. I speak promotion to expound in deep wells of his anointing and power. May you become a cistern of His wells of salvation and walk in his path of determination to finish your race that has been set before you. Ladies and gentleman, it is my stoop privilege and honor to present to you, Author, Friend, Professor, Humble Servant, Educator, Tenaciously walking in dominion authority throughout the world, Best Sellers for Betty... my Lovely Friend, Dr. Betty Dlamini (PhD).

By Reba Loftlis Dallas, Texas USA

Acknowledgements

My sincere thanks to everybody that has made me the person I am today. If I was still looking at life from a natural perspective only, I would be thanking only those who have intentionally built me up by nurturing, teaching, correcting, encouraging, protecting and providing for me. However, I now look at life, more from the higher spiritual realm than natural perspective, so I will thank even those who intended to harm and destroy me. I will bless them and pray that they get the blessing of the Apostle Paul who had a license to kill believers, but ended up preaching the Good News to gentiles. I joyfully express, that what Satan, the chief adversary had intended for destruction has turned out to be my refiner, bringing my best shimmer.

To all my true brothers and sisters who are children of the King of kings, I am thankful to you because you accord me a real sense of belonging to our Father's family even whilst still here on earth. I am thankful to every person whose name or initials feature in this testimony, for without you the story would not be the same. Your contributions in my life are invaluable. To you all, precious readers, who took time to read the very first draft full of what I call 'weeds', I want to express my heartfelt gratitude. The call was sent to many, but only you responded. Dr Amon Chizema, Comfort Mabuza, Fabienne Douf, Francis Lukhele, Pastor Rosie Jarvis, Dr Sarah Mkhonza, Dr Sibongile Mtshali-Dlamini, Thandazile Dlamini, Thuli Mamba I have no suitable words to thank you enough. Zodwa Mkhonta, young as you may be, you literally drove me to getting to the finishing point by your continually asking for more! To Dorah Dlamini, Ellen Chizema, Hazel Zungu and Julie Afiari your comments were invaluable. Dr Emily Cheserem, Jean Ndlovu, Thabani Motsa and Zanele Dlamini, thank you for taking time to cross those 'T's and dot those 'I's when I could not do it at all by myself. Prophetess Reba Loftlis, Dr Betty Bramble and all of you, readers encouragers and editors I think God handpicked you to stand strong and perform the duty of committed midwives, making sure that I give birth to a 'healthy baby'.

To you intercessors, I want to say God, who sees in secret will reward you publicly: Mama MaRosie, Anti Phindile Ground, Phephile Zwane, Nqobile and Sbusiso, you did not read, but I felt your presence in prayer all the way through. I want to let all of you, my spiritual fathers and mothers know how much I value you and your counsel in my life. Regardless of the distance for some of you, I continually hear your voices: Pastor Matthew Ashimolowo –"There is a winner inside you!" Pastor Yemisi Ashimolowo – "What are you waiting for?" Pastor Biodun Yola – "You shall be discovered... God is doing a new start!" Pastor Dr Dipo –"I am going higher! Higher! Higheeeer! ...The future is bright!" Prophetess Reba –"It is your uniqueness! You are unique!" Ms Jeannie Callis –"You are a blessing;" Dr Murdock –"Finish what you start!" Dr Gumedze –"Let us pray Betty Mntanami." Dr Smalley, I have no words to express what you have done to me through your Church-On-The-Phone sessions, especially the School of Writing. Well, to you Joe Dodson, always remember, if ever there has been a time you made someone experience joy, it is the day you sent the email "Betty, Good news..." It is good news indeed because you have made the publication of this book possible without causing me any stress. Blessed is the hand that gives than the one that receives!

Most of all, I thank God who loved me and sent His only Son to die for me. It is through that love, Agape, that I am who I am today. Your Royal Highness, King MDM, you are an audible voice that God uses in my life and for that I stay indebted!

Testimonials of "The Eagle..."

Betty's life story 'The EAGLE' is an exciting, inspirational and challenging autobiography. To read how God has guided her through seemingly insurmountable challenges starting from her beginnings in Swaziland to where she now works as a Professor in the US is to see the miraculous hand of God at work in one woman's life. I encourage you to pick up this book, discover her testimony and afterwards you will be stirred up to go and be best YOU can be! **Dr Emily Cheserem (Med.) London, England**

This is an amazing story of God's faithfulness ... through it all. Your faith will be spurred on to greater heights when you read this book, **by Jean Ndlovu, Leicester, England**.

Betty is a practical and credible author who uses everyday experiences to describe her closer walk of faith with the heavenly FATHER. She is a prayer warrior and intercessor who has great passion for happy marriages. The eagle is a must read for singles, married and divorced people from all walks of life, as it explores the issues taken for granted in relationships, by **Ellen Chizema -Leicester England.**

I find this book remarkable and it will appeal to both believers and non believers. It deals with the practical challenges of life and how to overcome. What came to mind immediately I finished reading was Jeremiah 29: 11 "For I know the plans I have for you," declares the LORD, "plans to prosper you and not to harm you, plans to give you hope and a future. The book affirms that scripture and it is not about what is appealing to the eyes of people, but what God sees and what He says, **By Julie Afiari, London, England.**

What the author went through in life as we learn from THE EAGLE is a true testimony that Christ lives, listens, provides, protects, restores, forgives, heals, fulfills His promises and above all He is everything to us. The book demonstrates how God stands by those who fully trust and obey Him. The book also practically demonstrates the verse in Isaiah 40:31, which states that those who wait upon the Lord shall renew their strengths, they shall mount up with wings like eagles, they shall run and not be weary and they shall walk and not faint, **By Zodwa Mkhonta Wolver Hampton, England.**

Reading this book and digging down into memory lane, I can only say "Phenomenal" a true manifestation of God in us. There is still a race to be run and victories to be won, **By Mfundo Nkosi, Cosmo City – Johannesburg, South Africa.**

The Eagle is an inspiring book worth reading. It clearly shows God's power in action and that God has a good and perfect plan for each individual, which manifest the minute you say agree to take a walk of faith with Him. The book demonstrates that even though there are trials and challenges along the way, if you hold onto God, He will bless you and take you into greater heights. I urge both youth and adults to purchase and read this book because it is a book that demonstrate the life changing power of God, **by Thabani Motsa, Royal Swaziland Sugar corporation, Simunye, Swaziland**

About the author

Dr Betty Dlamini's ministry has a wide coverage, including being a teacher, singer, actress, playwright, poet and fiction writer. At the time of this book's publication she was a professor at Indiana University (Bloomington), USA. She has published over forty-four independent works which include short stories, plays, play-screen and a Siswati novel that won the Macmillan 2008 Grand prize. Dr Dlamini believes that each individual person has some excellence that is incomparable. She bases her philosophy on the fact that God has a part of Himself within each person which can flourish and be raised to the best level when that person reconnects with God and stays in constant alignment with God's will for their lives. She believes this glorious reality can get distorted if people try to be whom and what God did not intend them to be. This distortion normally results from external pressures wielded by other people. She identifies herself with an eagle that enjoyed being an eagle for a short time when young, got lost and tried to live as a chicken whilst living among chickens, but finally broke free again and started soaring in the skies as eagles are meant to do! As a captive that has been set free she deems it her assignment to inspire other people not to lose their track and be the best they can be! Thus she named her ministry, Best Brand Ministries.

Sis Betty, as I call her, is an inspiration to me. From the time I first met her, I have known Sis Betty to put God first in everything she does. She is a woman who does not allow me to 'sleep', because she makes me realize how valuable I am as a woman. She constantly teaches and reminds me of what I am worth in the eyes of God, my father. Irrespective of the age difference, each time I call her I always want to listen to what she wants to say to me, for she speaks the truth and the word of God. Not only does she speak, but she gives an ear to listen. This *eagle* has been set by God to fly high. This is demonstrated by her actions, her talk, her faith and her defined purpose, according to God the Almighty. She is one person who always says: "I know I can make it...I know that I can, no matter what may come my way...My life is in God's hand. I just want to agree with her that the God we serve is a living God. God is using her to bring my life closer to him each and every day. The way I speak with my heavenly father das drastically changed through sis Betty. I believe you will be blessed by *the eagle* the same way as I am, By **Faith Zodwa Mkhonta, Wolver Hampton, England**. **In the 28 years** that I have known Betty, I know I can come to her with any challenge because she will give me advice based on biblical principles and at the same not being judgmental. Through my friendship with her, I have learnt that being a Christian is a lifestyle; it is personal and that you can talk to God (pray) at any time, even while walking or driving. Betty is a very genuine person, with child-like faith in God and that is what I have also become, by **Hazel Busisiwe Zungu Mbabane, Swaziland**

Betty is someone I feel privileged to know. She is an inspiring woman of faith and practices one hundred percent what she says. I have appreciated her encouragement and support in my life as a pastor's wife, by **Pastor Rosie Jarvis, Leicester, England**

Sbongile, my lovely sister; not only is she a rock, she is a shining star that keeps getting brighter and brighter ..., by her baby sister **Zanele Woods, Chelmsford, England**.

Prologue

Different groups of people, ranging from the young to the elderly are talking everywhere,

"Have you heard the latest news?"

"What news sister?"

The second woman halts and puts down her grocery bags whilst wiping her sweaty forehead with some Kleenex tissue...

This kind of conversation is found in emails, telephone and drink outings. Now, walk with me through the imagination's eye and see a more organized gathering of people assembled together. The majority of them look a bit disappointed and others only portray eagerness and readiness to hear what the 'guilty' person has to say for herself. History seems to be repeating itself here. If you analyse the situation carefully, you will find quite a number of similarly 'accused' ones in the Bible.

There was a man who had spent almost a lifetime lying down with infirmity because he claimed that no one was there to assist him get into the healing pool whenever the angel came to stir the pool. After Jesus had come and spoken to the man He healed him by telling him to stand up, take his pallet and go. The man did as commanded and received his healing. It was a Sabbath, so the Pharisees did not like that. They did not care how much the man had suffered, what mattered to them was keeping the Sabbath. He was accused for a miracle that occurred on the Sabbath day!

Another young man who had been blind from birth was healed by Jesus. Jesus spat to make a paste of mud, smeared it on the blind man's eyes and told him to go and wash his eyes. The young man obeyed and received his sight. Hearing about this, the Pharisees did not like it at all. To them, what mattered most was keeping the Sabbath day. They accused the Healer of being blasphemous. When they cornered and interrogated the healed man he told them that he did not know who his healer was, or whether He was blasphemous or not; all he knew was that he was blind but then could see.

Today, as I deliver to you this word of testimony, I do not have many stories to tell. Like the young man who said all he knew was that he was blind but could then see I am saying I have been 'dead' but now live. Like the eaglet that had been trapped in a chicken run to the point of accepting it was a chicken, and later set free, my mindset has been renewed and restored. My incarceration was more internal than outward. For many years I emulated chicken-living to the point of almost forgetting completely who I really am. The good news is that I have finally been loosed to join my own folk; other eagles and now I am soaring up in the sky. I believe that you will hear me well even if you have your own challenge or trap. I used to be in there, so I will be careful to walk you through my story without confusing you. I do not want to hide the fact that where I live and soar is not really comfortable for those who are accustomed to living in groups and conforming to status quo regardless. I know at the end, we will smile together as you celebrate my deliverance too. Be blessed!

Chapter 1

He heard my cry

o o o o o o o o o o o o o o o o o o o o o o o o o o o o o o o o

He was there all the time
He was there all the time
Waiting patiently to touch me
He was there all the time!

God was there all the time for me! I cannot stop shouting with joy! In my heart I am like one standing on a high mountain, lifting up my voice, telling all passers-by and those who are stuck by crossroads not knowing which way to take that there is hope. Some of these people even see no point in carrying on with life. I am here to shed light and give hope to those people who are desperate because all around them seems to be very dark. Even if you have never really been at the point I am talking about, I believe you have a slight picture of the situation. In my spirit I am standing up, shouting, and telling everybody that there is a way through. Jesus said to him, "I am the Way, the Truth, and the Life. No one comes to the Father except through me" (John 14: 6). When you feel trapped and you see no way out, remember it is not the end; help is very close.

I have been at crossroads many times and some of those times were so severe that I wanted to die. I wanted to just vanish from here and get to Heaven although it was not yet my time. I wanted to take my own life and 'assist' my Father, God, the Life Giver who calls us home when it is time. What I wanted to do was the way of cowards. Whenever the pressure was high I seemed to forget the words of Life and Truth for a while. But, whenever I redirected my focus things changed. Above all, I survived because God was there all the time and He stopped all my deadly attempts. He did that because I was crying for help all the way through. I did not stop calling His name. I continued calling His name even when the situation around me looked like God was not there at all.

God saw all my tears. He did not just look, but He felt my pain. He understands what those who weep feel because He also wept: "Jesus wept" (John 11:35). He reacts when His own suffer and call upon His name for help:

Call upon me in the day of trouble;
I will deliver you, and you will honour me."
(Psalm 50: 15 NKJV)

The Lord said,
"I have indeed seen the misery of my people in Egypt.
I have heard them crying out because of their slave drivers,
And I am concerned about their suffering.
(Exodus 3: 7 NIV)

The kind of tears I used to shed are gone. Now I shed a different kind; tears of joy. Today I continually shout with joy because I am delivered, from the shackles of the enemy. I am not talking about shackles that bind a non-believer. When those shackles ensnared me I was already a Born Again Child of God. This may be difficult for some people to understand, but I am a witness; there are all sorts of shackles. The devil is very cunning. He is not scared of invading the Lord's flock. He performs his luring stunts from a distance and tampers with the mindset of his target. He roams about roaring like a lion seeking for one to devour:

Be self-controlled and alert.
Your enemy the devil prowls around like
A roaring lion looking for someone to devour
(I Peter 5: 8 NIV).

Satan uses every opportunity he gets. I was not even aware that with my decision I was giving Satan a foothold in my life. Let me warn you beloved, all the enemy needs is a toehold. Actually he needs anything as small as a pin head. You give him that; and my, he uses it to the maximum level. He is experienced in his game. He is excellent at gold spray-painting worthless material in order to lure those who do not double check what they are offered. The secret rests in testing every offer before deciding to receive.

Satan managed to use his cunning ways to shut me in for many years. Yes! This is true, he held me hostage. Again, beloved, I say this to infuse in you; when I got into my trap I was already a Born Again Child of God. I did not see it happen, but I realised the moment the snares closed in. Today, I can identify with Samson, the Nazirite who had been set apart by God before even his conception (Judges 13). He had a powerful anointing, but he did not realise that his anointing made him Satan's target. Satan wanted to strip him off his God-given strength which enabled him to do what other people could not do. Samson got used to his strength to the point of taking it for granted. Beloved, never take lightly what God has put in you. It is not found in anyone else. I like the words "Remember, you are the only person on earth Who can use your ability (Zig Ziglar). This is strong and very deep. Think about it a bit more.

Samson did not safe-guard what God had imparted in him, and therefore played about exposing it in wrong places. If you have ever watched the Disney film, *Lion King* you will understand better. The young lion, Simba was destined for greatness. He was meant to be king after his father. Like all believers destined for greatness such as Samson, Dinah, Jacob's daughter[1], as well as you and me, Simba, was given clear instructions about where to play and where not to play. Again, like some of us, including Samson and Dinah, Simba ignored the instructions and landed in the dangerous territory of the hyenas. When Simba was desperate and did not know what to do, his father rescued him. Oh, I like Fathers! I mean real fathers who emulate our heavenly Father and are there for their children. I have a small word of advice for men: Never call yourself a father if you are not there to protect, provide for and promote those to whom you regard yourself as father. ***Please ponder on this!***

Similar to Simba, the young lion, when Samson was held hostage by the Philistines he cried to God for help. God, the Father responds promptly when his children cry for help. Samson made a foolish decision, but he did not just give in to his plight. He remembered who he was. He cried out to God and God heard his cry (Judges 13 to 16):

> *Then Samson called to the LORD, saying,*
> *"O Lord GOD, remember me, I pray!*
> *Strengthen me; I pray, just this once,*
> *O God, that I may with one blow take*
> *vengeance on the Philistines for my two*
> *eyes!"*
> *And Samson took hold of the two middle*
> *pillars which supported the temple, and he*
> *braced himself against them, one on his*
> *right and the other on his left. Then Samson*
> *said, "Let me die with the Philistines!" And*
> *he pushed with all his might and the temple*

3

fell on the lords and all the people who
were in it.
So the dead that he killed at his death
were more than he had killed in his life
(Judges 16: 28-30 NKJV)

When I was in my trap I had recurring thoughts of suicide. There was inner turmoil in my life. Most people around me thought that my life was normal, but I was suffering because what was inside me was not in agreement with who I was expected to be and therefore, trying so hard to become. I strived to act normally in my abnormal situation. The eagle that God had created in me was trying to fit into a chicken's lifestyle. After I got into the trap my life changed completely. If you had known me as a girl and saw me grow into a young woman, you would definitely tell God had something in me that was going to shake the kingdom of Satan, and Satan did not like that. He wanted to completely silence me.

The way out of any kind of hostage is to call and cry for help. Help is only a call away. Calling the Father is the key to that big door leading out of the hostage dungeon to fresh air. I like singing about the miracle working power that is experienced when one calls the name of God. The following are some of the songs I like and some of them are taken directly from verses of scripture:

The name of the Lord is a strong tower;
the righteous run to it and are safe
(Proverbs 18: 10 NKJV)

In the name of Jesus
I have victory
In the name of Jesus
I have victory
****

When I call upon the name of Jesus
No one can stand before
Jesus, Jesus, Jesus, Jesus!
I have victory

When I was still entrapped, calling upon the Lord sustained me. Many times I would ask my mother to pray with me and all she gave me was scripture such as "*many are the afflictions of the righteous, but the Lord delivers him out of them all*" *(Psalm 34: 19 NKJV)*. This verse became some kind of pain killer pill which you take whenever you feel pain. Pain killer pills are good, but there is need to identify the real source of the pain and deal with it. I thought the verse was losing its meaning, because there were afflictions about which I had cried year after year, and nothing seemed to happen. I knew God lives and answers prayer, because I had seen and still saw Him answer prayer, but I felt baffled because there was this one special area of my life in which my afflictions were evident and not getting better at all. I was losing hope.

I felt frustrated because the devil was making a laughing stalk of me, especially among non believers who knew what was going on in my life. Actually, in that one area many non believers were doing much better than me. I laboured to cover up the nasty image from the public eye. I became what Bishop T.D. Jakes refers to as 'cover girls' in his book *Cover Girls*. I believed strongly in my heart, that God has answers to all sorts of problems, but seeing no change was frustrating to me.

I held onto my faith in God and believed that just like the children of Israel who had been crying, and for some time it seemed as if God did not even care, but the day came when He moved. Amen! It was not easy to keep on believing even when I saw nothing happening, but I carried on anyway. There are other parts of scripture that I associated myself with and experienced peace knowing that my change was coming such as these:

I sought the Lord and He heard me;
And He delivered me from all my fear
(Psalm 34: 4 NKJV)

The righteous cry out,
And the Lord hears,
And delivers them out of all their troubles
(Psalm 34: 17 NKJV)

And they drew near to the gates of death.
Then they cried to the Lord in their trouble
And He saved them out of their distresses.
He sent His word and healed,
And He delivered them from their destructions
(Psalm 107: 18b-20 NKJV)

Hungry and thirsty, their soul fainted in them
Then they cried to the Lord in their trouble
And He delivered them out of their distresses.
And He led them forth by the right way,
That they might go to a city for a dwelling place

(Psalm 107: 5-7 NKJV)

They fell down and there was none to help.
Then they cried to the Lord in their trouble,
And He saved them out of their distresses
He brought them out of darkness
And the shadow of death
And broke their chains in pieces
(Psalm 107: 12b-14 NKJV)

And they are at their wits' end.
Then they cry out to the Lord in their trouble
And He brings them out of their distresses.
He calms the storms, so that its waves are still.
(Psalm 107: 27b-29 NKJV)

But now, thus says the Lord, who created you,
O Jacob and He who formed you O Israel:
"Fear not, for I have redeemed you.
I have called you by your name: you are Mine.
When you pass through the rivers,
they shall not overflow you.
When you walk through the fire,
you shall not be burned,
Nor shall the flame scorch you.
For I am God the Lord your God,
The Holy one of Israel, your Saviour …
(Isaiah 43: 1b- 3a NKJV)

Here, what God promises Jacob is for all of us believers, who believe we are His. I like to take personally everything God says to His children. Whenever I come across a promise in the Word, I receive it. This declaration by God is a guarantee that whatever I go through, God goes through it with me. In the above mentioned narratives (Psalms 107), the Psalmist does not say that God asked the people in trouble why they were in trouble or how they got there. All we are told is that when the distressed people cried, God rescued them. What I am saying now is that I am delivered by God who was there all the time.

If what I have said so far is not very clear and raises questions which I have left hanging all the while, you will soon get your answers as we walk through this, together and without any hurry. Let us just take our time because my story may be an enigma even to people who think they have always known me. May be a good starting point is to tell you about some Biblical characters whom I regard as my friends because I have had similar experiences with them. Remember, the aim of my telling you this is to help you avoid some of the painful experiences I have had, wherever possible and also acquire the better things I have received from God. Now let us pay a quick visit to my friends from the Bible. These friends were captives in their various small worlds.

Chapter 2

He came to set the captives free

o o o o o o o o o o o o o o o o o o o o o o o o o o o o o o o o

So if the Son sets you free,
You will be free indeed
(John 8: 36 NKJV)

The thief comes only to steal and kill and destroy;
I have come that they may have life,
And have it to the full
(John 10:10 NKJV)

The above Word of God says Christ came so that people may have abundant life. Satan is aware that if Christians take this truth fully, he will be in trouble, and then he plays his old trick of twisting the truth like he did to Eve in the Garden of Eden. The above scriptures pronounce that the mission of Jesus was to set free all captives. The Bible has many such people, but I will demonstrate with a few people who were presumed to be normal but still lived abnormal lives. The devil is a liar, and has preached many sermons right inside churches, saying suffering is a portion for God's children. No way! I heard this kind of sermon over and over again to a point where I believed it.

The sermon that believers have to suffer on earth and then have their joy in heaven only is a clear lie that mixes up some of the scriptures that talk about suffering. Our suffering does not have any intonation of desperation and it is coupled with overcoming as our Lord Himself says and it has a strong element of boldness as the Apostle Paul says to the Corinthians. Let us see both scriptures here:

These things I have spoken to you,
that in Me you may have peace.
In the world you will have tribulation;
but be of good cheer,
I have overcome the world
(John 16: 33 NKJV)

Great is my boldness of speech toward you,
great is my boasting on your behalf.
I am filled with comfort.
I am exceedingly joyful in all our tribulation.
(2 Corinthians 7:4 NKJV)

Emphasizing suffering as a way of life for the believer makes believers live like a baby that sucks a pacifier when the mother's real fresh breast-milk is actually there. Babies who suck pacifiers suffer from colic wind and more. I want to make a bold decree against spiritual pacifiers: Away with fake stuff! Our heritage, God's Living Word states clearly that we will enjoy the 'good of the land'. Beloved, do not be deceived. The eternal joy that awaits us in heaven does not mean that we have to forfeit our 'grapes, milk and honey' here on earth. The Living Word states that we were meant to enjoy the good of the land, so let us enjoy our blessings in this land of the living. Some of the blessings in life are meant for enjoying here on earth and in heaven they just cannot apply!

The Bible says the Lord will not withhold anything good from us:

For the LORD God is a sun and shield;
the LORD bestows favour and honour;
no good thing does he withhold
from those whose walk is blameless.
(Psalm 84: 11b NIV)

According to the Word we are blessed when we come in and we are blessed when we come out. What is to be blessed? I know being blessed is not determined by the manifestations only. We are still blessed even before we see the manifestations, but there has to be a point in time when the signs of our blessings show up. There was a phase when as Jacob was running away from his brother Esau after being blessed by his father Isaac. He had to sleep in the open and use a stone for a pillow, which does not correlate to a blessing, but there came a phase in his life when the blessing in his life had manifestations. Looking at him one would not ask whether he was blessed or not. All abnormalities that are contrary to being blessed are authored by the enemy. Joy in heaven is a sure case for those who will end there, but children of the King of Kings start enjoying some of their benefits in this very land of the living. There is no need to live a life of captives when you have already been set free.

The verse about captives cited at the beginning of this chapter is not directed only at people whose sins have not been forgiven, as we normally take it, but it means exactly what the words say: He came to set free **All the oppressed.** The **oppressed** covers a wide range of conditions, and we do not need to start putting brackets, leaving out some of the oppressed people. Jesus came for all those who fall under the category, **oppressed**. Now I shout with joy because not very long ago, I used to be **oppressed**, but praise God I am free now! I have dwelt in bondage without even knowing it, because everyone seemed to think all was well with me. Some of those who had known me before I was held hostage had so many questions that stayed unanswered. And now I want to reassure them that God is good all the time. God is on the throne and He will not allow the evil one to have the final word *if* you turn to Him and are willing to do as He commands. If you call Him during your distress, He will surely come for you, but He will give you some instructions to follow. Now how do I explain the situation of a believer held hostage right inside the good dwelling place of being a believer? I will take a quick ride to the Bible and illustrate with a few of the people I call my friends because I have had similarities with them.

Surviving blind man of Jericho

I would like to take you back to Bible times and take a walk with you in the streets of Jericho. Walking down the road we get closer to a man who looks just like anyone else. As you get closer to him you may see an ordinary man with nothing worth talking about, but I tell you if you ask those who have been close to Bartimaeus you would get the truth. Once you have heard his story you would realise you just walked past a 'walking miracle'. That man used to sit down in darkness because his eyes could not see at all; therefore this is no ordinary man. He had an encounter with the Son of God and then got his eyesight. His story is related in the Bible:

> *Then they came to Jericho. As Jesus and his disciples,*
> *together with a large crowd, were leaving the city, a blind man,*
> *Bartimaeus (that is, the Son of Timaeus), was sitting*
> *by the roadside begging.*
> *When he heard that it was Jesus of Nazareth, he began to shout,*
> *"Jesus, Son of David, have mercy on me!"*

*Many rebuked him and told him to be quiet, but he
shouted all the more,
"Son of David, have mercy on me!"
Jesus stopped and said, "Call him." So they called to
the blind man, "Cheer up! On your feet! He's calling
you." Throwing his cloak aside, he jumped to his feet
and came to Jesus.
"What do you want me to do for you?" Jesus asked him.
The blind man said, "Rabbi, I want to see."
"Go," said Jesus, "your faith has healed you."
Immediately he received his sight and followed Jesus
along the road.
(Mark 10: 46-52 NIV)*

You may then wonder where my case intersects with that of Bartimaeus. I do not blame you because, I, myself was not aware, that I was in the same situation as the blind man. Bartimaeus was alive. He ate and did everything which people did, but he had one problem. He could not see. People around him might have spoken of many things they saw. Imagine him at table, ready to have dinner with his family. He could smell the nice food before even tasting it. Before they said grace to eat, one of the family members could even make a remark about the food; "wow that looks good!" When hearing that and combining it with with the good smell Bartimaeus would know that he was about to eat a good meal. You know good cooks make sure their food tastes good and they also garnish it to make it appealing and appetising. Whereas all the other family members would enjoy the smell, of the food and how well garnished it was, Bartimaeus would miss out on the latter because he could not see. When they finally ate the food, his taste buds would help him enjoy the good taste of the food. He could then make a remark as well; "That was delicious!" or "How scrumptious!" Sadly enough, that is as far as Bartimaeus could go.

In the morning when people want to decide what to wear, they look outside to check how the weather is. Bartimaeus could not check the weather this way; actually he did not have to decide what to wear according to the weather. Whether it was cold, sunny, windy, you name it, he wore the same clothes. He always had his blanket that he used to cover himself. The blanket helped Bartimaeus to function in his abnormal situation. The blanket was a 'make do' for him. In my own abnormal and limited condition I had my own 'blankets' too that helped me stay in there, just hanging in there.

God has blessed us human beings with all assorted colours to enjoy such as Black, green, yellow, red, white, pink, blue, lemon, cream-white and more. We decide the colours of our clothes, our cars and even houses. The colours are just for beauty. A painted and unpainted house would serve the same purpose, but the beauty of the colour is for the people to admire and just enjoy. Around the houses, there are gardens. In these gardens there are vegetables, meant for food, but there are also flowers meant to beautify the environment. Some flowers have strong sweet scents. Bartimaeus could not participate in any talk about the beauty of houses, flowers or people's clothes. He was left out. At least he could smell the sweet scent of flowers such as roses. He could smell people's perfumes, but that was as far as it went and no more.

Like Bartimaeus, I have lived with a condition that I got used to. I learnt to function within the abnormal situation and had my own way of manoeuvring and hanging in there. I knew the earlier mentioned verse "The thief does not come except to steal, and to kill and to destroy. I have come that they may have life, and that they may have it more abundantly" (John 10:10), but to tell the truth, I hated referring to that verse because I knew very well that even though my sins were forgiven I would lie if I would say I had abundant life in the true sense of the phrase. I had issues, I had to sit on, and hide inside my 'Bartimaeus blanket'. I had to make a show for the people around me.

I believe that when Bartimaeus heard people talking about something beautiful around that he could smell, he also joined in smiling about it as a sign of appreciation. If they talked about something they saw and felt he joined because he could only touch and feel it. If someone cracked a joke and accompanied it with funny faces like some of us do sometimes, and then everyone around laughed, Bartimaeus joined in the laughter because he heard the joke and the sad truth is that he missed out on what others saw. His eyes could not see.

I have said a lot about Bartimaeus, may be I should leave him alone now. Actually he may not even be the best person to use in illustrating my point, because all the people of Jericho knew about his problem. They knew he was blind, and probably some did not even know his name was Bartimaeus, but just called him 'the blind man'. I believe some of the people who helped Bartimaeus to get by in life did so because they knew he had a problem. As for me very few people knew I had a problem.

Ugly situation by gate called 'Beautiful'

I now want to tell you about another person who could use all his five senses: How perfect! How normal that was! You know, the ability to use all our five senses does not mean that all is well with us. You may use all senses well, but still have a limitation somewhere, somehow. This other person who was in an almost similar situation to Bartimaeus was the lame man who sat begging for alms by the gate called Beautiful. The Bible does not actually give this man's name, so people might have easily called him 'the lame man by the gate called Beautiful'. Mark this; the gate was significant and had a name, Beautiful, but this man's name is not given. He was in a very difficult situation. His ankles were weak. He could not walk. He sat by the gate begging for alms from people who came to pray in the temple. He might have found it hard living this way, but eventually he got used to it. The people who went in and out of the gate were also used to his condition. Those who had sympathetic hearts gave him coins of money. The whole story is in the Bible:

> *Now Peter and John went together to the*
> *temple*
> *At the hour of prayer, the ninth hour.*
> *And a certain man lame from his mother's*
> *womb was carried, whom they laid daily at*
> *the gate of the temple which is called*
> *Beautiful, to ask alms of those who entered*
> *the temple; who seeing Peter and John*
> *about to go into the temple, asked for alms.*
> *And fixing his eyes on, with John, Peter*
> *said, "Look at us." So he gave them his*
> *attention, expecting to receive something*
> *from them. Then Peter said, "Silver and gold*
> *I do not have, but what I have I give you:*
> *In the name of Jesus Christ of Nazareth, rise*
> *up and walk"*
> *(Acts 3: 1- 6 NKJV)*

I will not quote the whole story, but that man got healed. He instantly started walking and leaping with joy. All those who saw him after that knew very well that something extraordinary had happened to him. I mention this man because his behaviour of leaping and praising the Lord was not a norm among the other people there. This man had experienced a miracle and could not hold it to himself. Like the man, when you see me being so robust again, singing and praising God, sometimes in a 'crazy' way, understand the reason. God has put strength in my weak 'ankles'. Where I was weak, He has made me strong. That is also why I composed one of my songs called *Delight in the Lord*:

> *I can't keep it to myself*
> *I can't lock it within*
> *What the Lord has done*
> *Is inexpressible*

What God has done is great beyond measure
What God has done is inexpressible…

If you find this lengthy and cumbersome, bear with me because you might need this for yourself. Before losing track of my testimony I want to draw your attention to a different kind of a person, who was not a man, but a woman, which makes her get a bit closer to my own case.

A woman with issue of blood

I am greatly fascinated by our similarities. This is not only about her being a woman. This woman was 'normal'. Like me, she did everything that other women do. She lived among people, and when Jesus Christ came into her area, she joined the crowds that went to see Him. Like her, I also moved with the crowds towards Jesus. I moved with the crowds and at times would not even be noticed because I was right inside the crowds. The most intriguing thing about this woman is that she had a very serious problem, which the crowds did not know about. If you saw the woman before and after her encounter with Jesus, you probably would not see anything special about her. She appeared the same way.

This woman had a problem which people were not aware of, except for those few she consulted, trying to get help. Sad to say, none of the people she consulted were able to provide her with the help she needed. I believe they ended up giving her tips on how to live with the condition, which I believe she had labelled as 'her condition'. I have said these words so many times too: 'my-this, my-that …' I have confessed negative conditions and problems were mine. I thank God that now I am not going back that road of ignorance, claiming possession of what God has not given to me. The devil is such a liar and it is time we expose him so that all those who still dwell in ignorance of the truth may be freed by the truth.

The problem of this woman was a shameful thing to talk about. In some cultures, you do not talk about issues labelled as shameful. In some cases people end up living with the undesirable conditions until death comes to rescue them. It is really a sad truth that even inside The Church such cultures have influence, which results in the Bible being altered and interpreted to align with the cultures of the people. So this woman kept her condition to herself and only the few who happened to know about it.

Similar to the woman I have spent a large part of my lifetime, avoiding reality. I have been an expert in living a lie. It does not mean that I deliberately decided I wanted to live a lie. I was not even aware I lived a lie. I can relate to this woman because I have been there. This woman haemorrhaged for twelve years. That is a long time! If you live with an odd condition for that long, somehow it becomes part of your identity. Whether people know it or not you find yourself adopting the problem as your personal possession. Before this woman came out of the miserable condition she went through a few things I want to highlight now. She lived a double standard life. She was a miserable woman inside and had to privately deal with bleeding, and on the outside she was normal like everyone else. I have given the world a smile because that was the right thing to do. I have wept for days on end, and came out with a smile for the world. Sad to say, there were times when the outward smile and inner weeping occurred simultaneously. How pathetic! God is good all the time and He does not allow people to live in such horrible situations forever.

When Jesus was walking about and teaching, the woman was there listening with the rest of the crowds. Sadly, many people live in misery yet Jesus is in their vicinity. Jesus is right beside them, but they have unresolved issues. This woman could have listened to the good teaching of Jesus Christ and returned to her house with her condition, but in her heart, she had an idea. I wonder how many times we have ideas and we simply abandon them because we fear those around us. Forget about the crowds around you. Think of the sleepless nights and all those miserable moments you go through alone, and then make a decision to listen to that inner voice giving you a new idea.

In her heart, the woman had the idea that if she could just touch the hem of the garment of Jesus Christ, she could be healed of her condition. I believe she was not even next to him at the time the idea hit her. What I know however is that she ended up in close contact with Jesus[2]. She had to squeeze herself through the crowds, pressing through towards Jesus. At that moment putting other people first had come to an end. She gave priority to herself because of the reality at hand. If she missed that opportunity she might never had got it again. Jesus' itinerary was neither known by the people nor by his disciples. More amazingly, it was not known to Him as well because He was doing the will of the Father, and went as the Father led. So the woman had to seize the moment, and you know the story well:

> *And a woman was there who*
> *Had been subject to bleeding for twelve years,*
> *but no one could heal her.*
> *She came up behind him and touched the edge of his cloak,*
> *and immediately her bleeding stopped.*
> *"Who touched me?" Jesus asked.*
> *When they all denied it, Peter said,*
> *"Master, the people are crowding and pressing against you."*
> *But Jesus said, "Someone touched me;*
> *I know that power has gone out from me."*

Then the woman, seeing that she could not go unnoticed,
came trembling and fell at his feet.
In the presence of all the people,
she told why she had touched him
and how she had been instantly healed.
Then he said to her, "Daughter, your faith has healed you.
Go in peace."
(Luke 8: 43 – 48 NKJV)

The woman was healed instantly and the bleeding stopped. The woman is the one who noted the instant change within her body. The crowds could neither see, nor sense it. That is why His disciples did not understand how Jesus could ask the question He asked: "Who touched me?" I learn something very significant about this woman. She took initiative. God does not decide to bless certain people and leave out others. He has done His part of loving the whole world. The love which includes every good deed is readily available for whosoever wants it. However, you do not get it simply sitting down and doing nothing about an area of concern. Sometimes you have to move; you have to do something towards receiving it. This could be anything such as moving your lips, tongue, or even crying out like Bartimaeus did. Sometimes it could mean moving the hands out as the lame man did when asking for alms. As this woman did, it meant her having to move her legs; placing one foot after the other, as well as using her mouth to say "excuse me please, may I pass through." This woman had to negotiate for space to get to Jesus through the crowds.

Receiving requires some kind of ***action or doing***! Do not buy the lie that God will bring it to you *someday*. Ask Zaccheus how he got Jesus to come into his house. He had to run ahead of everyone else, and then climb a sycamore-fig tree (Luke 19: 1 – 9). God is such a good God and rewards those who reach to Him without laying down requirements which are difficult for people. Anyone who is alive can reach out or draw the attention of God in any possible way. Please use your imagination to list possible ways of reaching to Him and start using any of those. The results will be amazing!

Before I stop this 'medley relay', I want us to look at a man found in the Old Testament. I believe I share some qualities with him. Sometimes the victim of an undesirable condition is not even aware that help is available, but when the opportunity knocks at the door it is important to open and receive the offer. Such was the case with the man we are looking at now. He was an honourable man who had a dishonourable condition.

A skin disease in honourable places

In Syria there was a man called Namaan. He was commander of the army of the king of Syria. He was a great and honourable man in the eyes of his master, because through him Syria had experienced victory. Although he was a mighty man, he was a leper (2 Kings 5: 1). To some people, comparing myself with such a man may sound a bit ridiculous. In the past I would have played the game of false humility, but now I say things as they are, so I will not fake this. I may not be an army commander or be close to rulers, but when you talk of positions accorded some kind of high status to a certain degree, without being explicit I believe I have had my own portion of that. I want to say that because I know there are many people who have looked up to me in a positive way, as a role model of some sort. Others have aspired to be where I was. Such positions may not be much to those who have it all, but to those who looked at me the way I have just described, I think it is important that I venture into Namaan's story. The Bible says "by him the Lord had given victory to Syria", so I want to declare as well that whatsoever achievements, great or small that I have had everywhere I have been are not my own, but the Lord Has done it through me.

In my small country the Lord has put my name in certain places which are not worth mentioning to the great achievers of the world and even some of my country, but I have had some significance and influence on some people, but similar to Namaan I had a serious problem, which I will refer to as 'leprosy' for the sake of Namaan. I have already mentioned my 'having issues' earlier, but I bring in Namaan's case because of the process he underwent to receive his healing. Namaan was not identified by his leprosy. Probably some people were not even aware that he had this condition. His wife knew about the leprosy, but could not do anything about it. She probably believed he had to live with it. He also believed nothing could be done about it. I believe he had accepted he would live like that the rest of his life.

The good news is that in Namaan's house there was a captive girl who waited upon Namaan's wife and knew something could be done about Namaan's condition. She told him about Elisha, the prophet of God. Namaan had to face reality and do something about his leprosy. He accepted the advice the girl gave him. He went to his master and asked to go to Israel to receive his healing. "Then the king of Syria said, 'Go now, and I will send a letter to the king of Israel.' So he departed (2 Kings 5: 5). I want to stop here because you can get the full story in the Bible (2 Kings 5: 1-27).

Elisha, the prophet gave Namaan some instructions which he had to follow in order to get his healing. Like most of the instructions leading towards a miraculous event, Elisha's instruction was not rational. It infuriated Namaan.

Elisha told Namaan to "Go and wash in the Jordan seven times, and your flesh shall be restored to you and you shall be clean" (2 Kings 5: 10). The whole encounter was ridiculous and undermining to Namaan's acclaimed status:

1. Elisha did not address him personally, but sent his servant;
2. Elisha instructed him to go and wash in a river smaller than the rivers where Namaan came from;
3. Elisha instructed him not to just wash, but to **dip** in the water **seven times**, which made him feel like he was going to look stupid in the **process**.

Although many people would not, Namaan followed the instruction from the Prophet Elisha, and the dividends were amazing and indeed *the instruction you follow determines the future you create3*

Like all these Biblical characters, I have been through certain situations as well, and I had gotten to a point where I believed nothing could be done about the conditions, so ended up devising ways of operating within the abnormality I was in. This testimony is here to make you all aware that God is great. He is the same God who performed miracles in Biblical times. As Jesus said before going to Heaven, if we believe in Him we can do miracles even greater than the ones he performed whilst still here on earth. This testimony is meant to leave no stone unturned and in the process help other brothers and sisters avoid the trap I got myself into, which almost cost my life many times within two decades.

I am now whole and fully restored; a woman of God, a servant and a steward of the mysteries of God (I Corinthians 4: 1). As I go all over the world proclaiming the Good News, I do so openly, lifting up His name, telling and showing the world what believing in God can do. I believe every word the Bible says, and I sing about that all the time in a number of my songs. I live by the Word. I apply the Blood of Jesus in every situation challenging me and the Name of Jesus is my key in life. I live by Faith.   Again, I want to clarify from the onset that I have done nothing except to believe in the Lord Jesus Christ as the Lord and Saviour of the world. I am part of the world. Having heard about the Good News in God sending His only begotten Son to save the world (John 3: 16) I realised I am included in 'the world', and went for the gift. I metaphorically present my testimony in the form of an eagle basing it on a story of an eagle that believed it was a chicken when it was actually born an eagle. I also relate to the principles of an eagle which I find my journey to have incorporated. Like the eagle that went astray and landed in a wrong place, God started something beautiful in my life, but somewhere down the line I did not take precautions to guard safely what God had etched in me. I behaved like some young people I will talk about later such as Dinah, Jacob's daughter and Samson, the Nazirite.

Great things do not always come wrapped in shiny big packages, they come in small uninterestingly wrapped up parcels. I believe that some of the packages are not only small, but almost invisible. In helping you understand the making up of this eagle that landed itself in a chicken run I really have to take things back to the beginning. The beginning here will be what God Himself would call the beginning, where He has His noble plans to prosper people and plans to give them a future: not just a future, but a very good future. Please come with me to the early 60s and get the facts straight!

Chapter 3

The Destiny Child's Beginning

○ ○

For I know the thoughts that I think towards you,
Says the Lord,
Thoughts of peace and not of evil,
To give you a future and a hope
(Jeremiah 29: 11 NKJV)

When God wants to use you He does not look where you come from, or who your parents are. If He did that, He would not have used people like Rahab, the prostitute; David, the illegitimate boy and murder schemer; Moses, the murderer; Saul (later called Apostle Paul), the slayer of believers; Matthew, the tax collector and Zaccheus, the cheating tax collector. Actually the list is very long and includes people like the Samaritan woman who had five husbands, who were not even her own. That woman became one of the first evangelists, and went out to her neighbourhood telling people to come and see the man who told her all about her sinful life. It is a wonder some believers even start arguing about the possibility of God using a woman, to draw people to Him. Anyway the issue at hand here is that God can use anyone who is willing to be used by Him. I like the song that puts this truth so clearly:

Just ordinary people
God uses ordinary people
He uses people just like you and me
Who are willing to do as He commands
God uses people who will give Him all
No matter how small your all may seem to you
Because little becomes much when you place it in the Master's hand

Just like that little lad who gave Jesus all he had
All the multitudes were fed with the fish and loaves of bread
What you have may not seem much, but when you place it in the care
Of the Master's loving hand then you will understand
How your life will; never be the same!

I believe every word that God says in His Word, the Holy Bible. I claim as my own all the promises He lays in there, because the main factor is whether a person believes or not. I therefore believe that God has a plan for my life. This is a good plan to prosper me and not to destroy me as the above verse states.

God's plan for my life

God has a good plan for all of us people if we allow Him to implement it by not coming up with excuses. This is not for a special few as we have heard so many times and eventually bought in the lie. For instance, when God called Jeremiah, the latter had excuses saying that he could not speak because he was only a youth, but God corrected him:

Before I formed you in the womb I knew you;
Before you were born I sanctified you;
I ordained you a prophet to the nations;
Then I said "Ah, Lord God!
Behold, I cannot speak, for I am only a youth.
(Jeremiah 1: 5-6).

Jeremiah did not think he was a suitable candidate to be used by God, but the Creator knew what He wanted. I have learnt in life that God has a good plan for every person alive, but He does not force it through into the lives of people. He allows the people to make choices. The choice is ours, we can choose to allow God to do His work in our lives by saying 'yes' to Him or simply reject Him, in which case I believe we are at a loss. I believe in my own case things started in my family. When I was born my case was very hopeless. Everyone in the family did not think that my mother's pregnancy was going to get to fruition.

My father came from a non-Christian background. My mother on the one hand was from a Christian background and her father was a preacher of the Good News. My mother has told me so many times that my grandfather (daddy's father) was very fond of her as his daughter-in-law. I believe this is because through my mother my grandfather saw the possibility of his family name staying on. Swazi people regard children as an essential element of marriage. It was therefore with great excitement and expectancy that my mother pulled through the nine months of her first pregnancy. She knew this would make her 'valuable' and more acceptable in her new family of Swazi Royals, the Dlamini clan.

When my mother's time had come, she gave birth to a beautiful girl, Nomathemba. She was such an adored bundle, upon whom all the hopes of the couple were placed. Both my parents, James and Rose were excited to see the fruit of their love. My father would have appreciated having a son for a first child as Swazi people place value in male 'heirs'⁴. Nomathemba's name is from the phrase *themba* (hope). My parents had hope for many things that a girl-child comes with, as well as hope for a baby boy in future. Nomathemba was my mother's pride, but this was too good to last, and that special baby died before even the age of one. My parents tried for another child quickly after that loss. My mother conceived and the pregnancy developed well. When her time came she had a still born. That was a great blow. All hope was 'almost' lost.

My mother fell pregnant again a third time around. This time my parents' spirits were no longer high as when they started. What worsened the situation is that my mother became very ill. Doctors said the pregnancy was going to be short lived but a nurse at the clinic where my mother went for her antenatal examinations said although chances of the pregnancy developing to birth were very slim, she was going to do her best to help preserve it by giving my mother a series of over twenty-seven injections. My mother had to go to the clinic regularly and this caused her severe pain. She took it all graciously, because she was desperate. She wanted to have the baby, not just for herself, but her in-laws.

The pregnancy period was a rough time for my mother and the whole Dlamini family because that was the year my grandfather died. This was not a usual death in a family like my father's, a typical traditional family. My grandfather, Thebeni Dlamini was a grandson of one of the former Swazi kings, King Mbandzeni. The traditional religion of Swazi people is ancestral worship. My grandfather had subscribed to this religion all his life, but something unusual happened before he passed on.

Hope in a hopeless situation

When my grandfather was ill, a Zion Church preacher paid him visits. He used to come and talk to my grandfather and pray for him. The preacher, Maloba Maseko explained to my grandfather, the story of Jesus Christ and how a person can make a personal decision to accept Him as Saviour. My grandfather accepted the Good News. After making this decision God started revealing things to him. He knew he was going to die soon and he told my grandmother how she should lead the family after he had gone to heaven[5]. It is Swazi custom to make feasts in honour of ancestors, and my grandfather gave an order to my grandmother that after his death the custom of ancestral worship should stop. He said everyone in his family should know that there is one God, the God whom the preacher, Maloba Maseko had told him about.

My grandfather asked his nephew, Mphostoli (Apostle) Nzuthu Ginindza who was a young preacher from a different church (Gwamile Apostolic Faith Church) to be the overseer over his family matters because he had an understanding of God. As his illness took the better of him, my grandfather surprised all those who came to visit him to pray and sometimes cry because of his deteriorating health, by encouraging them, telling them not to cry because he was going to heaven, his new home. He ordered everyone to sing the hymn, *Nxa ebizwa amagama* (When the roll is called up yonder). It became apparent to grandmother and all in the house that my grandfather was leaving them. She started crying. My mother has told me this story umpteen times how my grandfather smiled and told them with a faint voice of what he saw:

"Hey stop crying. Look, look what I see is so beautiful. I can see little children wearing white clothes. It is not really children. It looks like children. These are beautiful beings. They are singing. It is so lovely…"

My mother tells me that although my grandfather's voice was faint and hoarse with illness, it had some kind phenomenal energy when he spoke about what he saw. When I heard the story as a young person I used to wonder how my grandfather saw those heavenly beings and heard their lovely singing when the people in the room did not see or hear anything. Now I understand how such things happen because I have lived to have my own special supernatural encounters with God. This is a true and spiritual experience. I regard my grandfather's experience to be similar to that of the prophet Elisha. When the king of Syria made war against Israel, God's people, the situation looked hopeless, but Elisha saw a multitude of horses and chariots. "The mountain was full of horses and chariots of fire all around Elisha" (2 Kings 6: 17). Elisha's servant did not see all this until the prophet, Elisha asked God to open his eyes (2 Kings 6: 8-17).

As they were singing, my grandfather slid on to the other side. He died in style, wearing a smile on his face! What a way to be ushered home. As a widow my grandmother wore a white mourning gown as the custom was among the Zionists, as opposed to the normal black ones those who mourning widows used and still use to this day[6].

Belief in God is a legacy that my grandfather left for his family. You may wonder why he had a smile on his face. He knew all was well. As a Swazi man, dying and leaving no grandchild could have been a real problem resulting in his dying with a sad face. He had experienced disappointment as he saw his first born, Thomas deciding not to marry at all after he was let down by a young woman he loved and seeing his second son and his wife lose two children. Those two loses did not stop my grandfather to believe in children coming into his family. The instruction he left for everyone in his lineage to follow Jesus is very strong. I see him to be similar to the prophet Elijah who told his servant to run because rain was coming (I Kings 18: 43-44). Elijah said that because after sending his servant seven times to check toward the sea if rain was coming, the servant reported that he had seen a small cloud in the sky, only the size of a fist. In that small cloud Elijah saw the possibility of heavy rain coming. "Meanwhile, the sky grew black with clouds, the wind rose, a heavy rain came on and Ahab rode off to Jezreel" (I Kings 18: 45). My grandfather saw grandchildren coming. Although the first two had died, he believed in more to come and left the order that did not really make sense at the time. His hope; his 'small cloud' was the bump in his daughter-in-law's stomach. My mother was five months pregnant when my grandfather died.

My mother persevered taking the injections prescribed by her nurse. When her time came she had to go and deliver her baby in the capital city, which was only a town then, at the Mbabane Government hospital. The day was a Saturday, February 11 that special year! My mother gave birth to a healthy big baby. The baby was a girl. She was given so many names because of the special position she held in the family: *Sibongile*, meaning "we are grateful for this baby"; *Lomjovo* from *jova* (inject), the idea being that the baby survived because of the injections; *Lomgcibelo* (the one born on Saturday); *Lomagugu* (precious and dear one), *Nabozitho zibeletha abantwana* (the one with legs big enough to carry babies), and Cherry, which my parents told me meant 'something precious and dear' in a language I do not even remember now. My mother gave me this name because that is how I was to her. However, the name Cherry did not stay long.

Some destiny babies fight death battles

My mother's cooperation with the nurse by taking the painful injections in order to preserve the life of her unborn baby did not make the devil fold his arms and accept defeat after the baby was born. My grandfather's faith manifested by his proclamation of a future generation when there was no grandchild yet, is the kind of faith that provokes God to perform miraculous deeds. When God has a plan for a person's life, Satan tries to sabotage the plan, so he was more determined to steal my life even after birth. This kind of a scheme to kill children of destiny is an old one which we read about in the Bible where we see Satan attempting to kill numerous infants for whom God had a special life assignment He had ordained them to carry out later in their life.

The evil one's scheme can be traced back to the time of God's fulfilment of His promise to Abraham, the Father of Faith. Abraham's grandson, Jacob is the one through whom the first signs of many children started showing. God came to Israel's son Joseph in a dream. The dream was a revelation of greatness on the young boy. Jacob's whole family did not understand Joseph and thought he was too forward. Through Joseph's brothers Satan thought he was going to incapacitate God's plan for Joseph's life. When Joseph's brothers wanted to kill him, God intervened through Reuben and as the story states, they sold him to Ishmaelites.

Joseph went through a lot of difficulties, but in all those situations God's Favour was upon him. He worked in Potiphar's house where Potiphar's wife had intense lust for him. She framed Joseph and he ended in prison. Joseph's significant difference made him excel in prison as he had excelled in Potiphar's house. Joseph's excellence led to his promotion from the position of a prisoner to a top governor residing in a palace in Egypt.

Years later as the Israelites multiplied they became a threat to the Egyptians, who in turn, oppressed them. The Israelites cried out to God. He heard them and He worked behind the scenes, planning their emancipation from the slavery in Egypt. God was going to use one of the Israelites to lead them out of their bondage and the devil sensed this and wanted to impede God's plan through Pharaoh who made an order for all male infants to be killed. God's plan prevailed because Moses' mother did something 'crazy' and placed her baby boy in a basket and hid him by the reeds in the river Nile. The princess from the palace found the baby and took him into the palace where Moses got all the necessary knowledge God wanted him to get in order to implement His plan of leading the Israelites out of Egypt.

There is an ongoing pattern in the battle between God and His enemy, the devil who tries to destroy those who are in line with God's will, but every move of destructions ends up shaming the devil and giving more glory to God. Again, when God wanted to carry out His great plan of saving the whole world through His only Son Jesus Christ, the devil tried to counteract Him at the time of Jesus' birth. Herod the king wanted to kill Baby Jesus. He spoke treacherously to the wise men from the east, asking them to tell him once they had found where Jesus was going to be born so that he could also honour the baby king. When the wise men did not show up Herod made an order for all male infants to be killed. God had already preserved Jesus by telling Joseph and Mary to hasten and take the baby to Egypt secretly. God always sends His angels to tell His stewards what to do to carry out His plans. He did it even in the 20th Century and He still does it in the 21st Century.

I am not really sure what God promised my grandfather, or how he felt in his heart about his decision of accepting Jesus into his life, but from what my mother and my grandmother told me as I have related above, I believe my grandfather realised his salvation was not just for him, but a legacy to be passed on. He had a futuristic view of things when he made the order that in his household everything should be done God's way, the Christian way. To me it sounds like he ordered all his children to accept Jesus Christ into their lives too, but we know God does not force people, it is a matter of choice and what a brilliant and smart decision to those who opt to go the "God way".

Whatever God promised my grandfather was going to be carried out through one of his own children or grandchildren. As usual, Satan would not let the plan just happen uncontested, so he tried to stop it. He had already tried and had probably thought he had been successful when he took away my father's 'significant' children (in his culture); the first born and his first male, but I think in my spirit I can hear God saying "Satan, wait a minute, I have news for you: my plan will work even through what may appear to be insignificant". In my father's Swazi culture a third born is not very important, let alone one that is a girl.

Satan never gave up and he attempted to take my life countless times. One instance that my mother has told me of repeatedly, and often with tears brewing in her eyes as she talked is the incident whereby I almost drowned in one of the Great Usuthu River tributaries. She had gone to fetch water and did not see me following her. As she was turning to go she saw me gasping for what looked like my last breath as I was drowning. She says she threw away the water bucket not knowing how much of me was left before I died. Through God's grace she managed to rescue me. She says she cried and was shaking throughout that day imagining the catastrophe that almost befell her that day. Satan was trying to terminate God's plan for my life. He was trying to stop what I am doing right now and even more: what I am still going to do! Both God and Satan look ahead of times. We may not be aware of possibilities from small beginnings, but Satan is aware, and he does not waste time. He uses the slightest opportunity he gets to carry out his deadly plans.

There are other incidents that my mother has told me about where I almost died, but there is one I personally remember well which happened when I was about nine years old. We were swimming with other children in the pool part of one of the tributaries of the same Great Usuthu River. As we were all enjoying the cool water on a hot summer day, one of the boys who were also swimming came for me and pulled me down under water. At that age I already could swim very well and could stay under water for some time, but that was only if I was doing it myself. I remember like it was only yesterday how I struggled for air as he held me down under water. I struggled to free myself and I had already given in to death in my heart when somehow Samson let go. I do not know whether he was doing it as a joke or what, but what I know is that many young children have died without any explanation in that same pool. My mother did not want me to go there, and I do not remember whether I had been allowed that day or I had sneaked away without permission. What I remember clearly is that as soon as I got some oxygen and realised I was still alive, I came out of the water, ran home with my dress in my hand, crying aloud all the way through.

When I got home I related my ordeal to my mother expecting her to sympathise with me and say some comforting words. It did not take long for her to give me my 'reward and medicine' as she used to call it. You know when my mother caned you she did not hurry: she took her time to do it. She did it with both hands and mouth. As she hit you she also gave you a verbal lashing which accompanied each stroke:

> *Hey you, you are messing with me?*
> *You see I have no children,*
> *What do you want to show me? Hey?*
> *You want to show me a mess?*
> *You are so mischievous!*
> *Take this! You hear me?*
> *Here is your medicine! Hey!*
> *Here's what's yours!*
> *You mischievous one!*
> *(Translated from SiSwati)*

My mother would go on and on, alternating words and lashes until she was satisfied that the 'medicine' was in all my veins. As soon as she was through I had to tell her I was sorry and would never do it again. Anyway this is not about how my mother corrected me with a stick, but it is all about the instances Satan wanted to steal away my life. As for my mother's stick, it worked well in me because I was really scared of being beaten and so throughout my childhood I successfully avoided being beaten as much as possible.

Sometimes it is not easy to be good on one's own accord. I tried to obey my mother, but some things seemed just irresistible. That river; that river…! The next attempt to steal my life was by the river again. Along the edge of the river there were some big *umncozi* (blueberry) trees. When the fruit was ripe they were plump and shiny, probably because the trees were well nourished all year round. This is probably why I understand clearly the scripture at the beginning of the book of Psalms:

> *He shall be like a tree planted by the river of water,*
> *That brings forth its fruit in its season,*
> *Whose leaf also shall not wither;*
> *And whatever he does shall prosper…*
> *(Psalm 1: 1- 3 NKJV)*

This verse is about the blessed person in Psalm 1, but right now I am talking about the evergreen blueberry trees by our river. I also know blueberry trees inland. In winter they have no leaves, but the river ones have leaves all year round. The fruit from the riverside trees is juicier than the inland one! Satan tried to use the shiny and plump blueberries by the river to lure me to my possible death. The plump and very ripe ones were at the very top of the tree on the small branches of the tree. I climbed up the tree and started enjoying the blueberries. Each time I looked at a cluster above me 'it beckoned me.' I had no problem climbing because each mouthful I had made me go for the better ones above my head.

All was well as I enjoyed the berries and I was enticed to go for the better ones at the very tip of the tree, but the top and weak branch could no longer endure my weight, so you can imagine what happened. As the branch broke, I lost grip of any part of the tree. Swoosh, I went! That was not a swimming area. The river had some rocks with sharp edges right in the water. I went headlong and everything else happened very fast. Oh, beloved friend, God is good all the time. When His finger is on you because He has an assignment waiting for you He never lets go. There are times when He literally sends those invisible beings, the angels to take charge over you:

> *For it is written*
> *He shall give His angels charge over you,*
> *And in their hands they shall bear you up,*
> *Lest you dash your foot against a stone*
> *(Matthew 4: 6) and (Psalm 91: 11-12)*

When Satan quoted these words he was tempting Jesus to abuse what God has readily available for us, His children for use in times of need, not something we deliberately get ourselves into. I was a child, only wanting to enjoy the berries. On the other hand Satan, the opportunist wanted to kill me, but God protected me.

As I have just said, I went headfirst and there were sharp edged rocks which could easily cut through and crack my skull, but the assigned angels did their work. I do not know how the sharp edge missed my skull, but it managed to shave off, a part of my hair to skin deep. I had no pain from the rock-hair-cut and the splash into the water at that instant. Physically all was well. I could have easily kept that incident a secret but the incomplete hair-cut was there to tell the tale that something had happened. I wished someone could cut all my hair before my parents could see the odd appearance. No one was there to do that, so you know what followed. After interrogations, 'little white lies,' confessions and negotiations nothing worked and I got my 'medicine.' The 'medicine' was fine, but the big issue is that now I can loudly and boldly say 'Satan, boo! You lost again!' God was there and preserved me.

The blueberry and rock-hair-cut year was the same year my grandmother decided I had to be transferred to the Mission school affiliated to the church she went to. That would make it easier for me to participate easier even in the Sunday school there. Although the devil attempted he could not stop the good work that God had started the day my grandfather gave his life to God and said the rest of the family should follow suit and put their trust in God even after his death.

A new life and a new name

During my childhood days, in Swaziland we used to have two official names a home and a school name. The western or Christian name was the school one. My school name therefore was Cherry. I was called by this name for three years of schooling before my grandmother transferred me to the mission school in her church.

At that time and even now some Swazi people use 'Cherry' as a slang term for girlfriend. It is a common thing to hear '*yi Cherry yami leyo*' meaning 'that's my girlfriend.' My mother did not give me the name to mean a 'girlfriend,' but 'something precious.' On the other hand, my grandmother who had never been to school hated the name for its 'harlotry' intonation as she said it sounded as a 'loose' person's name. She wanted something that, to her, sounded suitable for Christian living as her husband had left her with the assignment of maintaining Christian living in the family.

I really do not know exactly what was going through my grandmother's mind, but she gave me the name Betty, much to my mother's disapproval. Both of my parents actually liked Cherry and did not like Betty at all, but my grandmother, as head of the family had spoken and no child of hers could oppose that. The name, Betty stayed on to this day. It displaced all my other names. To my grandmother a name change was significant in Christian living. Her own Christian name was Ruth. Changing of a name may not be a requirement when people become born again, but biblically, there are numerous people whose names changes after their encounter with God such as Abram and Sarai changing to Abraham and Sarah respectively. In the New Testament, also, Saul's name was changed to Paul. That is not the subject of my focus right now, but as a matter of fact I got a new name. Although I did not really like this name as I grew up, I love it with passion now because it was given to me by one of my best women that I regard as a Women of Honour!

I started school in a community primary school close to our home and my new one, Encabaneni Mission Primary School was many miles away. Not very far from home there were other big and more acclaimed primary schools where most of the children in the neighbourhood went, but my grandmother had identified something which other people in our area had not seen. Although education in the other schools in the area was good my grandmother wanted more than education for me. In me she saw so many possibilities. She did not waste time and before I turned eight she had introduced me to walking the long distance to church with her. Sometimes we got a bus to church and sometimes we walked all the way through. In spite of the long walk, Sunday was my best day. By the time I went to school at Encabaneni I was accustomed to walking a long distance, but walking that long distance for six days was quite a strenuous exercise for a young girl of that age.

It did not take long for me to identify a group of children who lived not very far from my own area. In the mornings we ran most of the time than walk in order to get to school on time and avoid beatings on the hand. Sometimes when we got the bus we would be a few minutes late because it arrived there after 8:00 am the starting time. On those occasions we then got our hand beatings and I hated that so much, so walking became the only way to go! After school we walked rather than run. We only ran when racing to pick the best fruit along the way home. We used to enjoy the wide range of fruits available for free such as guavas, passion fruit and a variety of berries.

Whenever we saw clusters of ripe fruits we raced towards the trees. I was new in the area. One afternoon as we saw the ripe fruits from a distance we started running. It was a hot afternoon and as a new girl in the area I did not see the shiny barbed wire we had to bend under before getting to the fruit tree. I ran fast in front of everyone else and went straight into the barbed wire. One sharp thorn of the barbed wire pierced right into the part of my face between the eyes. I felt the sharp pain and was confused and pulled back tearing away the flesh there. Blood started oozing like I had been stabbed. The other children were scared. They tried to stop the bleeding but failed. I only got help when we came to a house where the woman there gave me First Aid, washing up the wound and bandaging me. She marvelled how my eyes were not touched. I thank God for these eyes! That day Satan wanted me to lose one or both of my eyes. Again, I should 'Boo Ha hah!' him for his losing the battle!

Beloved, you may be wondering why I am telling you about all this personal stuff that may even sound very petty. As a matter of fact these incidents may not even sound as horrific as some other incidents you may have heard of or experienced before, such as in newspapers, radio or television. We can derive my reason for 'crying so loud' from the Bible. Now back to biblical times I believe Hannah was not the only childless woman during her time. Probably many other women were provoked by their co-wives such Peninah did to Hannah. However, the real matter is what the provoked women did about it and what came out of the situations. As you have heard from the other Biblical stories I have referenced earlier, at the beginning of my testimony –they were all familiar problems. I believe Bartimaeus was not the only blind man in his area at the time; the woman with the issue of blood had a problem many women are familiar with. I can go on and on, and you will agree with me, every day we encounter people who are still swimming in the 'suffering pool' infested with those issues, but what I am bringing up here is what has a bearing with the larger picture of my testimony.

At the beginning I have referred to the song *He was there all the time* and I believe that in my case, indeed He was there all the time from even before I was born. I believe what my grandfather left as only a bump in my mother's body was a Woman called for a great and significant assignment:

> *The Spirit of the Lord is upon me*
> *Because the Lord has anointed me*
> *To preach good tidings to the poor*
> *He has sent me to heal the broken hearted*
> *To proclaim liberty to the captives*
> *And the opening of the prison*
> *To those who are bound*
> *(Isaiah 61: 1)*

Chapter 4

Effective Parents

o o o o o o o o o o o o o o o o o o o o o o o o o o o o o o

'God presents great things in small packages'. This truth is evident throughout the Bible. Moses, the man who was destined to lead God's nation, Israel from bondage in Egypt to Canaan came into this world as a small 'bundle'. He came at a very 'wrong' time and 'wrong' gender at the time; a baby boy. Hebrew boys had death waiting for them. The Hebrew women whose baby boys were killed loved their sons very much, but they felt helpless - not Moses' mother! She had something in her hand. She was skilled at basket weaving. In her, I see similarities with the uncommon woman, popularly known as the Proverbs Thirty-One Woman in Christian spheres:

She girds herself with strength
And strengthens her arms
She perceives her merchandise is good
And her lamp does not go out by night
She stretches out her hands to the distaff
And her hand holds the spindle
(Proverbs 31: 17- 19)

Making a crazy decision

I can mentally visualise Moses' mother going beyond having sleepless nights wondering how to deal with the possibility of losing her son. I can see her focusing on how she could safeguard her son. I imagine her taking what was a big problem and pondering over it to birth an idea instead of just worrying and mulling over it. I don't know how many ideas came into her mind but the winning idea was attached to what she had within her. She realised that her solution rested on the abilities she had and other available human and natural resources. Obviously, she was a basket weaver! I can see her with my mental eye busy focusing on the basket she was making. I can even imagine her lips tightening and having some kind of frown as she examines the product she is about to finish weaving.

Let us imagine the determination of Moses' mother as she put some tar to avoid water penetrating through the basket; see how she lines its inside with some soft cushioned material, and now the basket is ready for baby Moses to be placed inside! I feel persuaded to write more about Moses' mother preparing the inside of the basket, but I will leave that to your imagination so that you may go beyond my own limits and see in the Spirit what a woman determined to preserve an endangered life can do. The life of her baby boy was at stake!

Moses' mother succeeded! She made it! She left her basket with her baby boy inside by the reeds of a big river; the longest river in the big African continent. Personally, I come from an area located near the biggest river in my country, Swaziland, the second smallest country in Africa. The Great Usuthu River has crocodiles. I grew up hearing numerous stories of people who died because crocodiles bit and had a meal of them. I know something about crocodiles. They like the edges of the river, by growths such as reeds. Looking at them from outside the river, crocodiles in water are disguised. A crocodile may look like a little floating bark of a tree or dead log. Under the water there is a huge reptile with big sharp teeth ready to tear to pieces any person who wades into the water. This brief background information about big rivers is only a glimpse into the danger baby Moses was exposed to. His mother had faith that the impossible could be possible. She believed that her baby was going to survive. She did what she could and left the rest to the Master, God.

You know when God has whispered some words of hope into your spirit, stop asking questions which may bring doubt; just do what He says to do. Do not even discuss it with other people who were not there when God whispered to you. I believe if Moses' mother was to start working out; I mean really reasoning, figuring out how baby Moses was going to survive in that basket and how he would be hidden as a young or even teenage boy when his age mates were all dead - she was going to 'go crazy'. So, all she did was obey the inner voice prompting her to save her baby at that dangerous time in the lives of Hebrew people, especially boys. She followed the inner instruction and left her baby by the crocodile-infested river, Nile. She assigned her daughter, Miriam to mind the basket. I see Moses' mother as one of the pioneers of the kind of woman described in Proverbs 31:

> *She also rises whilst it is yet night*
> *And provides food for her household*
> *And a portion for her maidservants*
> *(Proverbs 31: 5)*

Some versions of the Bible elaborate the last part of the verse to show that this woman gives her daughters and maidservants their daily duties. Moses' mother gave her daughter Miriam her duty to carry out. Miriam's eyes had to be on the basket. It excites me just to think how God uses women to dig and lay foundations of skyscrapers! Wow! Where are the women of God?

> *Where are you sisters?*
> *Can you agree with this bard:*
> *A seed of Cwatha James of Thebeni;*
> *A seed of Mbandzeni;*
> *A seed of Somhlolo, the mysterious who saw secrets from the Heavens7;*
> *Where are you women's Regiment, Lutsango, the Hedge?*
> *I mean you trusted ones*
> *Where are you 'tender-hearted' warriors?*
> *Where are you silk worms that produce silk not fit for commoners but*
> *For Kings and Queens?*
> *Where are you nurturers of life…?*

I do not want to spoil my testimony and get carried away by the volcano raging within me, celebrating womanhood at an era when it is common to mourn and regard women as the disadvantaged ones. Away with mourning at a time of celebration! All I see when I see women is a group of movers and shakers! Women, stop yearning for what you are not. Use what you have to create what you do not have. The same God who gave Moses' mother an assignment she could do is giving you an assignment appropriate to you. Do not think ahead of God; do your part and He will do the rest! I am thinking of Keith Green's song right now, about God giving His people including Moses and Noah instructions to carry out tasks for Him. The song emphasises the importance of obedience and knowing that God will *Take care of the rest...*

God is very serious about liberating His people. He is as serious about liberating the believers today as He was serious about liberating Israel. He is still looking for women to use as He was looking for them in the past. During Moses time God needed a woman to fit into this big, big puzzle. All the woman had to do was carry a baby for nine months like all other women, but when the other women surrendered their babies to be killed, the woman God needed had to:

1. *Refuse to surrender her baby;*
2. *Hide her baby for three months;*
3. *Weave a basket for hiding the baby;*
4. *Leave the baby in the basket in a danger zone of the river;*
5. *Assign her daughter to keep an eye on the 'basket'...*

Just imagine how good God is! He did not require the woman to do what she could not do. You may know the story well:

> *Now a man of the house of Levi married a Levite woman,
> and she became pregnant and gave birth to a son.
> When she saw that he was a fine child, she hid him
> for three months. But when she could hide him no
> longer, she got a papyrus basket for him and coated it
> with tar and pitch. Then she placed the child in it and
> put it among the reeds along the bank of the Nile. His
> sister stood at a distance to see what would happen to him.*
>
> *Then Pharaoh's daughter went down to the Nile to
> bathe, and her attendants were walking along the
> river bank. She saw the basket among the reeds and
> sent her slave girl to get it. She opened it and saw the
> baby. He was crying, and she felt sorry for him. "This
> is one of the Hebrew babies," she said.*
>
> *Then his sister asked Pharaoh's daughter, "Shall I go
> and get one of the Hebrew women to nurse the baby
> for you?"*
>
> *"Yes, go," she answered. And the girl went and got
> the baby's mother. Pharaoh's daughter said to her,
> "Take this baby and nurse him for me, and I will pay
> you." So the woman took the baby and nursed him.
> When the child grew older, she took him to Pharaoh's
> daughter and he became her son. She named him
> Moses, saying, "I drew him out of the water."*
> *(Exodus 2: 1 – 10 NIV)*

After Moses' mother had obeyed and had done her part, God took over and did the rest. Beloved, now I get excited when God gives me a 'crazy' instruction. It is not always exciting but I encode myself to be excited and I wait with great expectancy wondering what He would do next. I like watching movies, so my walking with God is sometimes like watching the movie of my own life; wondering what would happen next. It is so exciting because even now as I write I have no idea what my Father will do next with me; one thing I know however, is that whatever it is, will be good for me.

The Bible does not even tell us if Moses ever spent a single night by the Nile. We do not need to know. What we need to know is that God intervened. He removed the baby to the best place in that country, the *palace*! Beloved, what I see God do here excites me, but this is not about Moses. It is my testimony! In a similar way that God proved Himself to Moses' family He did to mine.

God, mother, and grandmother cooperation

I strongly believe that the kind of faith that my grandfather had attracted God to his family and preserved me. God entrusted me into the hands of two women: my mother and grandmother. He assigned them to bring me up by His way. My mother's assignment is almost obvious; she is the one who was directly to look after me as all mothers do, but my grandmother felt she equally had a God-given assignment to carry out. I thank God she did! I do not know what she saw or heard from God, but I tell you that Woman of God, *Gogo* Ruth Gule, Mrs Dlamini is a History maker! Hallelujah! She was determined and did what God said regardless of what any person said.

First and foremost, being a widow, my grandmother had to carry on the new belief her husband had accepted before going to heaven. My grandfather did not live to be the one implementing the necessary changes as a sign of assuming Christian living, but he left the stern order that in his household there should be no more ancestral worship! That is a strong one to deal with. My grandfather's nephew Mphostoli who was a Christian had to somehow fight his way through getting into the Dlamini family businesses. Sometimes my father and his brothers became rebellious and refused to follow what their mother and cousin said. They felt like they were misled to throw away their SiSwati heritage of ancestral worship. My grandmother insisted: "The head of this family said we should follow this Christian way. Whosoever wants to deviate from that should kill me first then do as they please!"

Listen, beloved, God blessed my grandmother with long life. When she went home in 2001, she actually wanted to go. Whenever she said she wanted to go we all laughed telling her we still wanted her here. I do not know how old she was when she went home, but strongly believe from historical comparisons she was in her nineties. She saw one of her daughters and all her three sons pass on before her and did not like it, but God kept her. None of her children reached fifty two years except for my only aunt Esther, my grandmother's last born, who is more of a big sister than an aunt to me now. God rewarded my grandmother's obedience with long life as promised in His word.

My grandmother also got a very peculiar reward of a daughter-in-law who has been proclaimed by the community to be more than even many sons. This attribute has been proclaimed by both believers and non believers within the area I come from. She negotiated and paved her way to the heart of my strong willed grandmother. It was not easy for my mother, but glory to God by the time her mother-in-law went home they were the best friends; praying and fasting together once a week. This is about God receiving the glory due to Him! As a result of the faith these two special women have imparted into my life, I call them the Eunice and Lois in my life taking it from Timothy's mother and grandmother:

> *When I call to remembrance the genuine faith that is in you,*
> *Which dwelt first in your grandmother Lois*
> *And your mother Eunice,*
> *And I am persuaded is in you also*
> *(2 Timothy 1: 5).*

I do not exactly know what Timothy's grandmother, Lois and his mother, Eunice really did to influence his life. Seeing their names in the Bible sometimes makes me feel they were extraordinary women who did extraordinary things. When I actually pause to look a little deeper into the life of Timothy as a young man, I realise he had the stigma of being brought up by women only, his grandma and mother. The Bible does not tell us much about his father, except that he was a Greek, so I regard these two women as being the only ones who raised Timothy up. Even if Timothy's father was alive and there as the young man was growing, he may have been absent father as far as Timothy's faith life was concerned.

When I think deeper about Eunice and Lois' task of raising a boy on their own, I realise they were women like all other women, but they valued the task before them. They did their best to inculcate into the life of the young man, what they had found of value in their own lives. They had faith in God, so they passed that faith on to the young man. From Paul's account that Timothy is who he is as we see him Biblically because of the strong scriptural base these two women in his life had given him, I deduce that they diligently did their assignment, and I also believe they asked their God to assist them so that they could do it efficiently.

The book of Proverbs has many verses that emphasise the importance of bringing up a child in God's way, and it states lucidly what this special assignment entails:

> *Train a child in the way he should go,*
> *And when he is old he will not depart from it.*
> *(Proverbs 22: 6 NKJV)*

> *Foolishness is bound up in the heart of a child;*
> *The rod of correction will drive it far from him*
> *(Proverbs 22: 15 NKJV).*

> *Hear, my son, and be wise;*
> *And guide your heart in the way,*
> *(Proverbs 22: 19 NKJV)*

Paul writes to Timothy and stresses that he should not depart from his mother and grandmother's teaching, but instead he has to live an exemplary life:

> *Let no one despise your youth,*
> *But be an example to the believers in word,*
> *In conduct, in love, in spirit, in faith, in purity...*
> *(1 Timothy 4: 12)*

Love for Sunday school

Many hundreds of years after Timothy's era, I have lived to practically experience what he experienced as he grew up. Some special women including my grandmother, her counterparts, *Gogo*8 Zondi-Ngwenya and other Sunday school teachers instilled the same faith in me. *Gogo* Zondi-Ngwenya had a special way of even using facial expressions to show how bad it would be for us, her Sunday school class to be jeered upon by people because of our behaviour. I loved Sunday school and for me it was more fun than regular school. My grandmother instilled in me the culture of seeking God diligently. I learnt for my Sunday school teachers that I could have a personal relationship with God. They helped us memorise numerous scriptural verses which I have treasured all my life such as these:

> *My son, if you receive my words,*
> *And treasure my commands within you...*
> *Then you will understand the fear of the Lord,*
> *And find the knowledge of God.*

For the Lord gives wisdom;
From His mouth come knowledge and understanding;
(Proverbs 2: 1, 5-6 NKJV)

The fear of the Lord is the beginning of knowledge,
But fools despise wisdom and instruction.
(Proverbs 1: 7 NKJV)

My son if sinners entice you, do not consent.
(Proverbs 1: 10 NKJV)

Be strong and courageous, because you will lead these people to inherit the land
I swore to their forefathers to give them. Be strong and very courageous. Be
careful to obey all the law my servant Moses gave you; do not turn from it to the
right or to the left, that you may be successful wherever you go. Do not let this
Book of the Law depart from your mouth; meditate on it day and night, so that
you may be careful to do everything written in it. Then you will be prosperous
and successful. Have I not commanded you? Be strong and courageous. Do not
be terrified; do not be discouraged, for the LORD your God will be with you
wherever you go."
(Joshua 1: 6 – 9 NIV)

This book of the law shall not depart from your mouth,
But you shall meditate in it day and night,
That you may observe to do according to all that is written in it.
For then you will make your way prosperous,
And then you will have good success
(Joshua 1: 8 NKJV).

Fear not, for I am with you;
Be not dismayed, for I am your God.
I will strengthen you,
Yes, I will help you,
I will uphold you with my righteous hand
(Isaiah 4: 10 NIV).

Similar to Timothy, both my mother and grandmother impacted on my life
in different ways. My grandmother instilled in me the importance of giving
my life fully to God. She could not even read, but from memorized scriptures
she made me love God's word. When Miss Joan Scutt, the missionary in our
church brought bibles to sell at subsidised prices, my grandmother was one
of the first to buy a bible. She bought it for me. I was the first child in that

Sunday school class of 9 to 10 year olds to have my own bible. She said I was her eyes, to read the bible for her. I did, and enjoyed it. Every evening I would read the bible before we prayed. She was very good at memorising the special bible verses she liked. In my mind I can still hear her voice reciting these and asking me to double check if she was saying them right:

He who has the Son has life;
He who does not have the Son does not have life
(Translated from SiSwati -I John 5:12)

Yet to all who received Him
To those who believed in His name,
He gave the right to become children of God
(Translated from SiSwati -John 1: 12)

In Sunday school there were many exciting activities ranging from dramatising stories from the bible, singing in groups or even solo, drawing pictures based on stories from the Bible or reciting verses and fishing people. We were taught to be fishers of people. Whenever you brought another child who did not come to Sunday school you were said to have fished that person and you were rewarded!

There were record books with our names and this idea gave me a slight idea of God and His record books in heaven. Every Sunday the teachers took the attendance register. There was a 'star' for attendance. There were also stars for participating in the various activities. At the end of the year there was a big party and every child present left with goodies such as sweets, toys and bigger prizes for those who had the highest number of stars. Due to my love for Sunday school I participated in almost all the activities. I gathered most of my stars from acting and memorising long passages of scripture. For the last two years before I went to boarding school at the age of twelve, I got the overall prize for all age groups including two age groups above my own.

At the time, apart from the fun I got from Sunday school, prizes motivated me to love my Bible. The songs we sang also instilled love for God and the Bible. As a result of this love at the age of twelve I did a Bible Correspondence Course called Light of Life with a College in Roodeport South Africa. At the time I somehow felt the good works of people could earn them entry into heaven, but that mindset was continuously corrected by the emphasis on the love and grace of God for sinners. The whole experience was good, and I have learnt that God's love is amazing and His mercies endure forever. It is all so amazing how God has so much love that to Him people who have been in the

Lord all their lives and those who do not live long after accepting Jesus will enjoy the same joy of being in Heaven.

Looking back now, I realise that the foundation that my grandmother, mother and others laid before me has sustained me over the years on all the hills and valleys on which I have set foot. No one can uproot me from God now. The amazing thing is that the passion for God and His word that I had as a child is now rekindled, revived and just blazing more than ever before. For this reason, I want to emphasize now that mothers and grandmothers have to come out of the cupboards where the devil keeps hiding them. They have to move from the backseat of the bus and take their active role of moulding the nations whilst still tender and mouldable. Teachers in schools can do their part of giving children knowledge and friends can also do their part of influencing other friends, but if all the parents: fathers, mothers, as well as grandparents can do their parts, with God's help the world may take a better shape.

A piece from Mama's bag

My mother always cautioned and told me that as a girl she did not do well before her parents who were Christians. She fell off school when she was in Standard 7 due to pregnancy. She continually told me how she was not the same as her siblings who were in good positions: politics, education, health, media and so on. She told me that professionally she was the least because of her disobedience and she therefore, impressed in me the importance of obeying parents. When I was young she did not go to church but she read the Bible to me, putting emphasis in the book of Proverbs, especially the sections on obedience to parents as well as disciplining children God's way. Before, and sometimes after getting a stick on my buttocks my mother would make reference to the scripture where God orders parents to use a stick as a device of correcting their children:

> *He who spares his rod hates his son,*
> *But he who loves him disciplines him promptly*
> *(Proverbs 13: 24 NKJV).*

My mother read me children's stories from English books, so she showed me the pictures and told the stories in *SiSwati*. Most of the stories were very interesting and always had a lesson attached to them. In a way similar to Daniel, who purposed in his heart not to defile himself "with the portion of the king's delicacies…" (Daniel 1: 8a), I purposed in my heart not to be a disgrace to my parents. My mother always told me about all the women who excelled academically in the country, and made me believe that I could do it too. Whenever, a girl in the community had fallen pregnant and dropped out of school, my mother would talk strongly about it to me. Sometimes, she spoke to me harshly as if I had intensions of sleeping with boys and falling pregnant too. In my heart I detested disobedience. I always wanted to achieve, but the achievement was basically about impressing my parents and doing them proud. Achieving great things for my own fulfilment came very late to me. My determination to always excel was not at all difficult to attain because God had made me to learn things a bit faster than the rest of my classmates all those years. I found myself taking the first position in all my lessons, all my years of primary education.

Chapter 5

More Hands Laying a Foundation

o o o o o o o o o o o o o o o o o o o o o o o o o o o o o o o o o

When I was in Standard 5, the final year of primary education, I was struck by an unusual illness. My body ached all over and I would not even let anyone touch me. At first we thought I had rheumatism, but the nurses at our local clinic did not understand what was wrong with me because whatever remedy that normally worked in such a condition seemed not to work in me. I missed out at school and that was an important year, Standard 5, so something had to be done; swiftly! Whenever nurses and doctors did not understand a person's illness, normally Swazi people would say that it was '*kugula kwesintfu*' (an illness caused by people), which could only be cured by traditional healers. At that time, traditional healers were called witchdoctors. There is a lot of controversy about that but I am not even focused on it now, so I will leave it. Now I know there are people who understand herbs and are not affiliated with witchcraft at all, but at the time all traditional healing specialists including herbalists were referred to as witchdoctors.

My father was not ready to lose his first child and as a sign of obsession with being a father he had monitored my growth rate by making marks on the wall all the time to check how tall I was. That was something which never happened to my siblings after me. My father was determined to preserve my life by taking me to a 'witchdoctor'. By that time I had already accepted Christ as my Saviour, so I would not hear of it. I was a child and could not even resist my parents in anyway, let alone that I was then down with illness. The only thing I knew to do was pray. Beloved, as a child I cried to God. I prayed to God. I pleaded and even said I did not mind dying and going to heaven than being sent to a 'witchdoctor' and losing touch with my God. I was scared of hell and thought if I would be taken to a witchdoctor heaven's gates would be closed. People were already recommending traditional healers to my father and he wanted to take me to a certain Mafindi Sibandze.

God heard and answered my prayer. I was not sent to Mafindi, the acclaimed traditional healer my father had in mind. Somebody recommended a certain Dr William Dlamini who was a medical doctor with a unique understanding of herbs and peculiar illnesses. I was healed. That was a big thing to me. It was a great experience to be back in school after missing out a significant number of days. When I returned to school the days I had missed out seemed to be nothing because I excelled even more, behaving like a fish that had been on the sand and somehow gets into water again.

Protection by change of location

After I got healed from the strange illness, God intervened in my life using the head teacher of my primary school, Mr Khanyile, who invited my parents to school so that he could talk to them. He had overheard some women who were complaining that all prizes were taken by this girl whose parents did not even come to church and their children were getting left over prizes. This whole thing of prizes may look petty, but Mr Khanyile advised my parents to take me to a boarding school if they valued my life. He did not disclose names but emphasised that my illness was a deliberate act by someone. My parents took the advice. My application was made and the whole family including my father's eldest brother who was a teacher himself agreed that I had to go to a Christian High School.

God's ways are high and mighty. Today I do not want to figure out whether someone had really applied some witchcraft on me or not but what I am definitely sure of is that God had high plans for my life. He had chosen Mankayane High School as a training place for the high calling He has always had for my life. My school was not an ordinary school. We were spiritually fed with God's word in an amazing way, but by that I do not mean that every one of those students 'ate what I ate.' Some of the students left that school being worse than they had been in primary school. What I know is that the seed my grandmother and mother had sown was nurtured. The school motto was *Deus Primus*, which means 'God First'. Our emblem was an anchor, emphasising that God is the anchor of the school. It was stylistically written in a SiSwati or isiZulu as *Anka*! All Mankayane High School (MHS) students proudly displayed the *Anka* insignia whenever we went for interschool competitions regardless of whether they embraced the idea of God being the anchor of their lives or not.

At MHS we had a daily morning assembly where there was serious, proper reading of the Word and preaching, unlike the general morning assemblies found in school these days. As said earlier, I had already given my life to

Christ in primary school, but I remember accepting Christ into my life again and again as feelings of guilt attacked me in some areas, which may look trivial to many people today. We had small singing groups and various clicks of friendships. Each time we 'gossiped' about someone in our small circles of friends I felt like I had backslidden and needed to give my life to Jesus again. There was a lot of ignorance and naivety but I thank God for all those experiences. I liked being part of a group and was strongly attached to my friends. In most cases the 'accepting of Christ' and 'backsliding' was done as a group. I thank God because He is a God of hearts. He saw how passionate I was. He spared me from numerous dangerous activities which young people of my time indulged in. The same God who came in a dream to Joseph, the father of Jesus did it for me through my primary school head teacher:

When they had gone, an angel of the Lord
appeared to Joseph in a dream.
"Get up," he said, "take the child and his mother
and escape to Egypt.
Stay there until I tell you,
for Herod is going to search for the child to kill him."
So he got up, took the child and his mother
during the night and left for Egypt,
Where he stayed until the death of Herod
(Matthew 2: 13-15 NIV).

God knew there was a 'monster devouring' young people of my age in the schools. He did not spare me just to complete school, have a profession and have a comfortable life. He had more for me. He saw me as a vessel He wanted to use like He did to His prophets like Jeremiah as stated earlier. He knew that the best training ground was a school dedicated and fully focussed on Him such as Mankayane High School. By this I do not imply that God cannot use other people schooled in other settings other than Christian. At MHS, God had faithful servants who fully regarded their lives as not their own but as being there at God's service. Most of the Men and Women of God there taught us how to live this Christian life, which was referred to as 'The Way" in the book of the Acts of The Apostles, but I will single out three of them because of the significance and imprint they had on my life. Those are the missionary from Transkei, South Africa, Mr Loid Magewu, Matron, Lois Mndzebele who played the mother role at the girls' hostel and Mr Luke Dlamini, who was the school's chief chef.

Leading and teaching by example

Mr Magewu was a tall man and admired by most of us students because of his calm nature. I adored him like my father. He walked like there were eggs on the pathway and he was careful not to step on them. The same tact applied to the way he made his utterances. The whole student body highly respected Mr Magewu. He respected people of all ages in a special way I have not yet seen up to this day. To a great extent students perceived him as a 'Jesus man'. I do not remember him raving at anyone; he talked. Even the most delinquent of students dreaded having to face such a man because coming before him because of wrong doing was dreaded more than even punishment sometimes.

I do not know how Mr Magewu was before he gave his life to the Lord, but what is important is that he led a very exemplary life. To us students, his light shone in a very unique way. I have countless memories of the school but this is a testimony and right now, I am focusing on the bricks some men and women of God laid in building the foundation of my life. Many other people have laid a brick or two into my life, but there is something special about Mr Magewu which I want to highlight here.

This man of God taught the Bible with great clarity. When it was his turn to lead and teach-preach the Word during morning assembly sometimes he did not read from various scriptures as most teachers did. He liked to preach-teach on one book of the Bible at a time. The ones I remember very well are the ones that greatly imparted on my life; the Book of Nehemiah and the Book of Esther. I will not go back to all that he taught, but in the book of Nehemiah his teaching clearly painted the picture of the evil men, Tobias and Sanballat. He demonstrated how Nehemiah was focused on his work and refused to be moved by the foul acts of Tobias and Sanballat. Mr Magewu vigorously massaged it into my life that as a believer I have an assignment which in order to bring to completion I need to build with one hand and with the other hand have my arsenal ready for use as each situation demands. This is very deep and I will not get into it now.

Teaching on the Book of Esther, Mr Magewu clearly demonstrated the contrast between Mordecai the Jew and Haman, the evil man who was close to the king. The most outstanding teaching and demonstration was the one about the dramatic part where the opportunist Haman had used his position to plan the destruction of the Jews. One night King Xerxes cold not sleep and was led to open the important books of records where he found that Mordecai had previously done act of kindness to him and had saved his life, but was never rewarded. Ironically, Mordecai the man the king wanted to honour was the main reason why Haman had planned the destruction of the

Jews. After discovering the oversight King Xerxes summoned his most trusted man, Haman to give him advice on how to honour someone that deserved the greatest honour possible.

> *When Haman entered, the king asked him,*
> *"What should be done for the man the king delights*
> *to honor?"*
> *Now Haman thought to himself, "Who is there*
> *that the king would rather honor than me?" So he*
> *answered the king, "For the man the king delights to*
> *honor, have them bring a royal robe the king has*
> *worn and a horse the king has ridden, one with a*
> *royal crest placed on its head. Then let the robe and*
> *horse be entrusted to one of the king's most noble*
> *princes. Let them robe the man the king delights to*
> *honor, and lead him on the horse through the city*
> *streets, proclaiming before him,*
> *'This is what is done for the man the king delights to*
> *honor!' "*
> *"Go at once," the king commanded Haman. "Get the*
> *robe and the horse and do just as you have suggested*
> *for Mordecai the Jew, who sits at the king's gate.*
> *Do not neglect anything you have recommended."*
> *So Haman got the robe and the horse. He robed*
> *Mordecai, and led him on horseback through the city*
> *streets, proclaiming before him,*
> *"This is what is done for the man the king delights to*
> *honor!"*
> *(Esther 6: 6-11)*

Mr Magewu used to dramatise the story as he preached and since then I have never ever heard anyone preach on the book of Esther with such great dexterity and clarity. Haman's end, where he had to hang on the gallows he had constructed for Mordecai was quite intriguing! In addition to all the wonderful biblical teaching that Mr Magewu gave us, he had an amazing way of motivating us young people. His voice was not anywhere close to the contemporary motivational speakers who sometimes shout to make their point. His was soft and very dignified. It was effective without the aid of shouting and kicking. He liked to make reference to Dr J.E.K. Aggrey, popularly known as 'Aggrey of Africa.' Mr Magewu used to call him *uAggrey weAfrica!* He told us the story which he said Dr Aggrey utilized to motivate his African people at a time when they were despised and dehumanised during the highest point of imperialism. That was the story of an eaglet.

The lost little eaglet

There was once a farmer that found a little eaglet in the forest. Having pity on the little stray bird, which had no mother to bring up, the farmer decided to bring up the eaglet with his farm chickens which he kept in a chicken run. As the bird grew up with the chickens it started behaving like a chicken. The little bird had nothing else to do but behave as a chicken because that was all bird behaviour it had been exposed to. I was an eagle in every fibre of its strong body but it had been socialized with and as the chickens. Five years later, a naturalist came to visit the farmer, and noticed the eagle. He told the farmer that it was an eagle, not a chicken. The farmer agreed it was an eagle. However, he said since it was trained to be a chicken it was therefore no longer an eagle, but a chicken.

To avoid arguments the farmer and naturalist agreed to test the bird. The naturalist decided to help the bird by holding it up and speaking to it. He said, "eagle, eagle, you are not a chicken; you are a bird of the skies. Now stretch forth your wings and fly." The eagle looked sideways and seeing the chickens eating from the ground it went to join them. The naturalist tried several times but each time the eagle would come tumbling down like a chicken. After attempting to help the bird fly so many times with no success at all, the farmer remembered one of the principles of an eagle: the eagle is the only bird, and only living animal that can look right into the sun without any problem. Actually, it does not just look into the sun, but by looking into the sun, when the eagle's eye connects with the sun something is stirred within its body that makes it to soar higher and higher into the sky. After remembering this principle, the naturalist then started taking the eagle to an elevated place at sunrise. He tried to make the eagle look into the sun but it just did not look up. It behaved like the chickens which are accustomed to looking down, scraping for little twigs and bits to eat. The naturalist helped the eagle look at the sun and spoke the usual words, "eagle, eagle, you are not a chicken; you are a bird of the skies, so spread those wings and fly away!" As he spoke it happened that the eagle's eyes locked in with the rising sun. Something happened within the body of that sky bird that no man could interfere with. Its eagle nature became alive, and the wings started spreading bit by bit and began to flip-flap, flip-flap, flip-flap, and away it flew never to come back to the chicken run. It was indeed an eagle and so flew away never to be in the chicken run ever again.

Mr Magewu repeated Dr Aggrey's words, "My people of Africa, we were created in the image of God, but men have made us think that we are chickens, and we still think we are, but we are eagles. Stretch forth your wings and fly! Don't be content with the food of chickens." He explained the implication of the story to us students, which was basically to make us aware that we were meant for greater things than what we sometimes believe of ourselves. I really liked the story because it made me believe that within me are greater possibilities and potential that I may not even be aware of. At the time I had no idea that the story was to have such a huge bearing on my life which will emerge as I proceed with my testimony.

Matron at the girls' hostel

Matron Mndzebele was popularly known as *Make9* Mndzebele. She was a retired teacher, who probably took early retirement so that she could work as a matron at the girls' hostel. She was a mother figure indeed, and in some cases did more than some mothers could do for their children. In addition to minding us, adolescent girls in the hostel, *Make* Mndzebele fed us spiritually. She liked the chorus, *Peace Perfect Peace* and made us sing it as our anthem when we were lined up for prayer in the long hallway of the old hostel. We sang it in both English and Zulu, and as we sang she would start preaching and eventually pray. Most of the girls gave her a problem and enjoyed seeing her sometimes yell at them as need be, but for me she was the mother that also imparted on my life as I spent all those five years away from my parents (excluding vacation time).

Her favourite scriptural verse was, "There is a way that seems right to a man, but in the end it leads to death" (Proverbs 14: 12). She massaged that verse into my life in a way that makes it impossible to ever forget it! It is more meaningful now that I have lived to see the practicality of this verse in my own life and that of other people. The last but not least person I want to reflect on is Mr Luke Dlamini, the cook.

Food for the body and spirit

As ANKA students we liked Mr Dlamini because he was the best cook whose food was tasty even if it was a 'beans' day. We hated beans the most those days yet they were served on most days than the other dishes we enjoyed. He played his piano accordion very well and accompanied His music with his guttural voice. He was also scheduled to preach at Sunday evening services. Sunday evening was the best service and that was when all the various choirs from solo, duet, trio to the main one sang. The opportunity to sing was open to those who wanted to, so the service normally took longer than the rest of them.

One Sunday evening, on 22nd February 1976, which is the birthday of former American President George Washington, it was Mr Dlamini's turn to preach. He started with his testimony, stating how he used to be very bad and dangerous. He related how he was brought up in a Christian background, but like the prodigal son left his home and country. He headed for Windhoek, the capital city of present day Namibia. He joined thugs and used guns and other dangerous weapons. He went on to tell us that one special day he gave his life to Jesus Christ. He described the dangerous life he lived before he became a Christian. As far as I was concerned people who had been robbers and had used guns like Mr Dlamini *deserved* real big punishment on the other side.

The more Mr Dlamini preached was the more I compared the two of us and I soon noted that I was a *goodie-goodie* girl who had never done anything horrible at all. I felt 'better and holier' than Mr Dlamini. However, the longer he preached I realised that bad as he had been he was heading for heaven. I was not very sure about myself at that time because it was at one of those periods I felt like I had backslidden. Together with my clique of friends we had boyfriends with whom we exchanged love letters. As for me I was scared to death to even talk to mine. Having a boyfriend was a big sin in that mission school. The fact that I could not even talk to my boyfriend Oxford, but only enjoyed reading his letters and enjoyed writing to him did not matter. I was sure I was heading for hell, period.

I hated the thought of Mr Dlamini being in heaven one day in spite of all those 'big' sins and me in hell with my 'petty' sins. There and then, I made up my mind and decided to correct the 'unfairness'. The only way out of this unfair end was to accept Christ into my life anew and never play the on and off game that was common in my school. I had done it many times before, but I realised the problem was that on all those numerous occasions we had been accepting Christ into our lives as groups of friends. One of us would have the conviction and we would all say 'Oh yes let us accept Him'. That gesture gave us some kind of comfort which made it easy to live a group life where we ended up easily having the puppy love affairs like I had with 'my' Oxford. At the time, my understanding of salvation was a little obscured than I fully understand it now. There were strong elements of legalism.

As I listened I realised I was not happy with my life which was centred on my friends. I decided to make my own decision without the company and approval of anyone. Those days we had to lift up our hands or sometimes stand up as the preacher made an invitation for those who wanted Christ in their lives. When I stood up to be prayed for, I remember one of my friends sitting next to me tried to hold my hand and said, 'yes my cousin let's accept Christ'. Something raged within me, and I snatched my hand. I realised that if I continued playing the 'group salvation' thing I would get nowhere. Later some of the boys in my class made fun of me saying, 'we know these girls; they accept Christ for a week, backslide and do it again.' I thank God for those boys' comments because they birthed within me some kind of drive that said 'watch and see!' I never looked back, and my relationship with God was not a group thing, though I drew close to a group of sisters who were a few years ahead of me. Being with those sisters even when they had private bibles studies and fasting times introduced me to the ministry of casting demons.

Demons invading a mission school

As a child I had heard about witchcraft and stories about demonic experiences people had, but I had never encountered any of the things I heard in stories. My first encounter of demons at work was at our girls' hostel. One of the girls fell ill and no medicine they gave her at the school clinic helped. TT became very weak and did not even eat. She stayed in bed and did not go to class. Staying in bed for a day or two was a norm for illnesses and people recovered and went back to class however TT's case was unique because she started showing strange behaviour. She would speak in strange voices. Sometimes she would speak in a squeaky voice things like:

"Look at you people; you think this is TT. That one is not even here. We have captured her. She is in the far Northern part of the country!"

The voices would go on and on and then laugh. It was then that it became apparent TT was demon possessed. We came together as Christians and rebuked the evil spirits. As for my part, I had never been part of anything like that before, but I believed that the Jesus I had in my life had the power to cast out demons through me and those who had the same faith. As we prayed for TT other students peeked through to see what was going on. We ordered them to leave. They did. As we cast out the demons it was apparent that they were resistant, but on the second day we had fasted and they had to pack and go! We sang songs in Siswati/Zulu which among many whose theme messages were about stepping on the demons in the name of Jesus and the power of the name of Jesus Christ. The demons could not stand against the name of Jesus. They squeaked through TT's very mouth. After that as we called her name she responded and cried. She was so weak and hungry. She ate after having not eaten for a number of days.

My second involvement with casting out demons was in the same girls' hostel and this time ES, a young Form 1 girl had a demonic attack. Similar to TT, ES said strange things in a voice that did not sound like her own. It was not even a voice, but voices. They said they had come to take ES away. Our matron allowed our small group of girls, some of whom were older than me, to go to ES's dormitory and pray for her. As we prayed a lot more girls sneaked into our group and started singing too. At that time something strange happened; although ES had been weak and in bed for some time, she sprang up and started charging. She attacked some of the girls and scratched the faces of the girls who had come to watch. She also started calling them by names,

"Hey you so and so, what do you think you are doing? We know you and we won't listen to you!"

One of the girls who actually made a mockery of Christianity was hurt on the eyes. The head girl ordered the rest of the girls to leave. Some of the teachers who were involved in evangelism and had experience in casting out demons came to the girls' hostel to pray for ES. Our Lord is ever victorious and the demons cried out and said they were leaving. We thought the demons had all left, but they had not because when one of the male members of the praying team asked ES to look him in the eyes, the girl would not look him in the eyes and that was a sign the demons were still there. As we sang and cast in the name of Jesus, the demon cried,

"Okay, okay, I am leaving now! Leave me alone. You are burning me."

We prayed more and called the name of Jesus and when we stopped singing ES shouted even louder saying "leave me alone. I am going now." She started writhing on the floor like a snake. She slithered on the floor on her stomach, heading for the door. We continued singing and by the time she got to the door she stopped and we heard her crying in her normal voice. When we called her name she responded shyly and cried. We praised God because He had won. The demons left. I had no idea that I was to be involved in casting out demons even later than that. It is important to know that when we call upon the name of Jesus nothing can stand before us!

All my high school years I grew more and more passionate about serving God. It was back then that I realised there is an evangelist part of me. Whenever I sang in small groups there would be a time when the group would hum the melody and I would start preaching and inviting those outside Christ to come to Him. Whenever that happened I had some strange boldness which I never had outside that scenario. During school vacations I had a strong urge to reach out to the other children in my home area. I realised I had something they did not have and wanted to share it with them. The love to spread the Good News has never plummeted instead it has grown to some kind of intense force that I cannot keep within.

Answered Prayer

As I grew in the Lord, whilst still in high school I started praying for my whole family to be born again. At the time in the whole family my grandmother and I were the only born again Christians. My mother prayed everyday and read her bible, but she did not go to church. That confused me about her status with the Lord. What I realised is that the whole family believed in Christ, but had not made any personal commitment to Him. God answered my prayer because when I was in my final year of school my mother committed her life fully to Jesus. She even started going to church. Her not going to church all along had been an issue of concern to me, and sometimes confused me when she made reference to scripture yet, she could not come out publicly as a child of God. So, when she made this great turn around in her life, I saw the faithfulness of God in my own Christian living. By answering this prayer, God was laying an even stronger foundation of faith in my life that would help me carry on in my Christian walk and believe even when things look bleak, knowing that if you believe, God answers your prayer.

Seeing my mother go to church every Sunday increased my faith in God. My father used to drink and smoke at the time. I hated the smoke from cigarettes, but as a child I had no choice, but put up with it. As the eldest child I remember, sometimes my father would send me to the grocery store to buy him a packet of cigarettes, even on a dark winter late evening. I was scared of walking in the dark. I don't remember whether I prayed about his smoking but I hated it and I rejoiced very much the day my mother told us that our father had stopped smoking. People say it is easier to stop drinking than smoking, but amazingly, God helped my father to stop smoking. He was not born again but he just stopped. I wished he had stopped smoking because of salvation but, he was not. Those were the early days of my amazing walk with my heavenly Father, God. I had no idea where He was going to take me. No one in my family had an idea what was to come out of my love for God. My siblings and cousins knew I had something they did not have, and as the eldest I never stopped witnessing to them. At different times they accepted Christ one by one, but I will not say much about them here.

Chapter 6

More rooted in the Word

o o o o o o o o o o o o o o o o o o o o o o o o o o o o o

By the time I was in my final year of school my commitment to God had rocketed. Although that was a mission school, the Christian faith was not everyone's cup of tea. Some of the students had been brought by parents who wanted them to get the Godly atmosphere that prevailed there. As time went on I saw myself drifting away from some of the friends I had been attached to from Form 1, our first year in high school and I got closer to new friends. One of my new friends was Dudu Dlamini who was new in the school. She loved God and singing and on top of that she had a very beautiful voice. We soon started singing together as a duet. Our songs included some of Pastor Andréa Crouch's songs. That was so marvellous!

I loved singing so much that I asked one of the boys from my home area that could make a tin and gut guitar to make me one. He did and I hid it in my luggage and took it to boarding school, because I knew if my mother had seen it she would not let me take it there. No other student had done that before, so the girls who saw it thought I was crazy. Other Christian girls joined me and Dudu and soon I introduced drum beating into our singing. I beat a homemade drum. That was good but some people felt like I was bringing something quite strange into the Christian environment. I liked bringing something new into whatever I did. I remember like yesterday how we sang Crouch's song "I don't know why Jesus loved me... Oh but I'm glad!" I beat the drum for the first time ever in our big Mankayane Mount Harmon Church. The singing was unique and it sure brought something different and very infectious in a way I had never experienced.

Leaving school at the end of 1978 and waiting for results during the first school term of 1979 was going to be such a lonely time, but God spared me all that lonesome time because first time in the history of the school they hired four of us girls to be temporary teachers. This was for the time whilst waiting for the O' Level results, which delayed anyway because the exam was marked in Cambridge, England. Coming back to Mankayane High School as a teacher was fun. Students called us by our first names and they called me Miss Betty, as opposed to Miss Dlamini. Being at MHS as a teacher made it possible for me to continue singing in church with my friend Dudu who was then in Form 5, the final year of school.

Evangelism at work

Going to the staff room at break time was a bit strange for us four girls after we had been students in the same place. We soon got used to it, but for me going to the staff room for tea break stopped when one day I felt so strongly led to witness about Christ one on one to one of my Form 1 students. I invited him to come with me and sit under a tree outside at the back of the staff room. The boy came and after I had spoken he accepted Christ there and then. After I had prayed with him I encouraged him to share his good news with another friend or bring the friend to me on the following day. Oh my Lord God had just started something real big there! What followed is one of the things that really bothered me for many years later when I experienced my wilderness years.

On the following day at break time, before I knew it, there were two boys waiting for Miss Betty. I smiled and took them to 'our spot.' I discovered that my faithful convert had already told his friend about Jesus Christ, so I was there to lead the other boy in prayer as he accepts Jesus into his life. I will not relate what happened on the next day and the next, but the amazing fact is that for the whole term, everyday except for one day if I remember well, more and more students came to our meeting. The thing grew so big that more boys and girls did not go for their short break, and those who did would come running to that meeting. Students including Form 5 students came there, and the number had gone to over 50. The other teachers would peep through the window wondering what 'craze' had gotten into Miss Dlamini. Today I can agree with the statement that everything starts small and grows with time. God's finger was upon me. No one could stop the raging volcano from within. I was also not really aware of the immensity of this thing, but what my grandmother had planted could never be uprooted.

It was the very same year, 1979 that my pastor, Mr Simelane started giving me the opportunity to preach in our evening service at church, once in a while. The very first time I stood in that church with both men and women, young and old, my knees wanted to betray me a little, but remembering that what I was up to do there was like testifying about Christ and saying what I knew about Him gave me the strength I needed and preaching that first sermon gave me more confidence in my God! I had no idea God was preparing me for more vast white fields waiting for harvesters!

The enemy fights anything good. He does not like to see us have a good standing with our Father, so the day I was to preach in the evening service he set a trap that was to instil great guilt in me. I had been in a situation where I did not stand for my faith, but felt like Peter when he enjoyed warming himself in a fire with non believers resulting in his denying Jesus. The enemy shouted in my ear telling me that I was not good enough to go and stand on that pulpit because I had not been bold enough to stand up and out for Christ. If I had a way I would have withdrawn, but there was no way and as the evening drew close the condemning voice became louder.

As the evening approached I was really shaken in my spirit with the enemy shouting at me saying I was guilty, but in the midst of that I remembered salvation is really about: forgiveness. I mentally visualized Peter and saw him crying bitterly before Jesus because of his denial. I cried out to God too and my situation became the message for that night. What I remember now is that I stood up and read the Word exactly in the part where Peter denied Jesus. I related how we could deny Jesus in various ways and how I also felt I had just denied Jesus. That was a genuine message. What came out of that was something I will never forget. No one told the congregation to pray and no one closed the service. The same Jesus who received repentant Peter received me with a smile together with the rest of the believers who felt they needed forgiveness in one way or another.

Freedom

Sometime in March 1979, the Cambridge O' level results came out and I had passed. The Swaziland Scholarship Selection Board encouraged people to go into fields where there was a shortage in the country. I was offered to go and do a course in nursing at the Institute of Health Sciences which was just opening that year, but I strongly hated nursing. I ended up accepting the offer to go to William Pitcher College for a Secondary Teacher's Certificate course, which started in May. There was a need for Maths teachers in the country and if you had credited it they recommended your taking it as your special subject. I specialized in Maths and English. The idea of living on my own, away from my parents, and away from school, the two strict environments was exciting. I imagined what I would do with all my time outside lectures.

Before long, during the very first if not second week some beautiful young women came to me and asked me to join a beauty pageant and go to modelling place in town. I had never thought myself as eligible for those kinds of things but they convinced me and I got excited. They also told me that the college had ball room dance lessons in the hall every Sunday night. I naturally like dancing and all they sounded good to me. I was carried away!

The Good Shepherd

Before I had committed myself to all those 'exciting' events, one of my lecturers, Mr Myeni called me and my newly found friend, Zodwa with whom I shared a room and was in the same Educational Psychology class. We excitedly went into Mr Myeni's office, not knowing what was awaiting us. God is an amazing and good Shepherd who 'never sleeps nor slumbers... and who will not let your foot slip.' He looks after His own sheep. Sometimes they tread on dangerous zones unaware and He comes and picks them up before any fox breaks their tender and delicate bones.

> *Even though I walk*
> *through the valley of the shadow of death,*
> *I will fear no evil,*
> *for you are with me;*
> *your rod and your staff,*
> *they comfort me.*
> *(Psalm 23:4 NIV)*

God sent His faithful servant, Mr Myeni to stand in position to save all new students whom the enemy had already targeted. His God-given assignment was to witness to new students and therefore identify new believers who could easily disappear without anyone knowing them if not welcomed soon, as was often the case. Many students who had been Christians in high school, especially those from mission schools, sometimes found it hard to profess their faith in Christ once they had stayed quiet too long, and sometimes found themselves having made associations with wrong people. After talking to us Mr Myeni discovered that both of us were believers and he gave us small tracts entitled '*the assignment*' which focus on reminding each reader, especially believers that each person has a God-given assignment which needs to be done before they hit the deadline, death.

Mr Myeni read through one of the tracts with us and at the end all in tears we prayed and I committed myself to taking on my assignment and doing what God wants me to do here on earth. Right there and then I knew Mr Myeni was taking the baton from my Christian parents in high school. He told us about the regular services in the Lecture Theatre which coincided with the so-called ball room dance sessions I was geared to go for. I had to make a choice between ball room dance and the services. God used Mr Myeni to wipe away all the naivety that had clouded me and I saw very clearly what I almost got myself into.

More Evangelism

Within the first term of college I was already one of the *Dabulamazwe* (Those who cut across nations) Outreach Group that went evangelising every weekend. To me that experience was out of this world. Mr Myeni ignited a passion that was to stay for life. Being part of the Damulamazwe Outreach Group meant we had to forfeit the best meal of the week with the Sunday fried chicken. The joy of taking the Good News to parts of the country where no church building had ever existed and where in some cases people had literally never heard anyone preach about Jesus Christ was unparalleled. No fried chicken could make me miss out from that. I was one of two youngest members of the crew, but felt equally grown.

New Skill

The year 1979 came with many good things and it was then that I learnt how to play a guitar. Vusi Dlamini, a former high school classmate whom I regarded as my brother, lent me his guitar. I borrowed it because I had a deep urge to sing in the accompaniment of some musical instrument. During school and college vacation some Bible College Students were on outreach around my home area. They were very good and I loved the music they played in the new church that had been just planted in my home area. I observed closely how well and with ease they played a guitar.

I asked them to teach me how to play a guitar and one of them agreed to teach me the basics by drawing guitar chords in a small notebook. He taught me how to fine tune a guitar as well as the ways of playing which were the International and what they called Spanish. I understood the drawings well and I worked hard to practice on my own after they had gone back to New Haven Bible College. They had written some songs I knew such as "*This is the day that the Lord has made…*" and had written what chords to play as I sang. They had made provision for quite a number of keys too, to enable me to transition from one key to the next. It was such a dream-come-true when I listened to my playing and realised there was coordination. Well, veteran guitarists may say it was simple strumming, but to me that was heaven come down. I started composing songs and the flow of new songs from within me was incredible.

On the first weekend after I had properly learnt to play and sing, there was a national conference in our church at Encabaneni mission. I took my guitar with me and wrote on a small piece of paper asking for an opportunity to sing. I sang alone there, and that was a divine experience because it marked my stepping into where I had never stepped before. Back at college, I started singing in accompaniment of a guitar. One of the members of the Dabulamazwe Outreach Group, Sister Christine, gave me a tape recorder to use when composing songs. That was a present and a half. More songs flowed out of me. One of my songs, "My soul will never die" was later sung around the country but only a few people knew who the composer was.

Before I knew it, I had to return Vusi's guitar. What a blow! I could not live without a guitar. I emotionally plummeted in a way that disturbed even my parents. I turned into some kind a zombie because whenever I had free time I had been used to playing that guitar and each time I did I had a new song or just sing an already existing one. My mother could not afford a guitar, but seeing what was happening to me, she sacrificed some essential family needs in order to buy me one. Together with my mother we went to Dee Bee Stores in Manzini and got my medium sized steel stringed guitar. That day I was the happiest girl! With my new guitar I came back to life! Praise the Lord!

Back at back William Pitcher College now with my new guitar, I sang with my friends and we started a trio and sang in the services at the Lecture Theatre. That was life to me! The Maths room was close to the Music room and often at break time Lot, one of my Maths classmates who could play a piano went to play in the music room. I would stand there watching him. Before long I could play and sing a few songs. I loved playing and singing *The Lord's Prayer* and *Psalm 23* songs very well. Those experiences really keyed me up! The new experience was the beginning of a real long journey for me.

My first year at William Pitcher College was a time of growth in a way I had never experienced in high school where everyone was either a Christian or had to act as one. At college people lived the life they liked. No one had to be impressed. I really enjoyed living that kind of free life. At the end of the year some of the strong members of the Dabulamazwe Outreach Group had graduated and had to go to their various places of work. As the New Year 1980 started, I realised life was different without them.

When I was at home during schools and college vacations my father took pride in calling me and making a show off my singing when he was drinking with his friends. He would call me,

"Bongiwe![10] Come and show them what you can do!"

My father would tell his friends he had a Margaret Singana, referring to one of the popular South African singers of his time. I did not like singing for my father's friends, but because he had asked me I did it. Sometimes he asked me to imitate some singers and told me to sing specific songs. I obeyed and he was happy. Somehow this makes me realise how embarrassing it was for the king when Queen Vashti refused to be shown to the people. Obedience to authority goes a long way and in my case I believe the results of my obedience to my father coupled with my prayer for him and the prayers of my mother and my grandmother for him somehow influenced his making a decision to accept the Lord as Saviour!

Chapter 7

Associations determine your future

○ ○

Blessed is the man
who does not walk in the counsel of the wicked
or stand in the way of sinners
or sit in the seat of mockers

But his delight is in the law of the LORD,
and on his law he meditates day and night.

He is like a tree planted by streams of water,
which yields its fruit in season
and whose leaf does not wither.
Whatever he does prospers.
(Psalm1:1-30)

Everything starts with a seed. Every seed that is deposited into good soil germinates and grows. In my father's fields during the ploughing and planting season they had a variety of seeds to sow into that well fertilized soil. I remember seeds of corn, sweet cane, beans, peanuts, pumpkin and a lot more. A few weeks after planting, the fields assumed a beautiful lush green look. From afar we could see the corn crop growing beautifully, but walking close to the new growths it was clear that there was a lot more than the desired plants. We had to start weeding because some other unintended seeds had planted themselves there. In the field of my life the enemy used a beautiful and 'nice' woman to sow a seed that led to what I regard as the greatest mistake of my life. I am a friendly person and the enemy knew that, so he used it as an entry point. All I did was to be friendly.

One of the things I had heard about college life was that most people got their life partners there and I decided not to follow that trend. I was so adamant about this to a point that whenever some of the 'brothers' in the Lord came close to me in a way that indicated their having interest in me I backed off. Those who made an open move and spoke to me about having a relationship leading to marriage lost me as a sister right away. We had heard many stories of Christians who had been married only to experience bitterness immediately after marriage, so we started making little pacts with my friends and agreed not to fall prey to men who would hide under sheep skin and show their true identity after marriage. However serious the agreements had been they did not last long because soon one of us was in 'love' and was soon to be married after we graduate.

My friend's decision did not intimidate me and it actually made me even more determined to stay focused and choose a husband when I was already working. I do not have any idea where we got the idea that what really mattered was when we got married. At the time we did not even consider all that I now regard as important issues to consider before you say "I do." We were only determined to prove a point that we were better than the 'weaker' sisters who had fallen. I now realise that the enemy used our attitude against us. On my own part I did not even see it coming because I was **fast asleep in my naive mentality**, but it soon came. As a genuine person who always say what I mean I stupidly believed other people do the same. Somehow in my mind I felt like the deceitful people would come dangling some kind of spiritual label on their necklines or wearing some badge written 'danger, danger! Run for dear life!' It was this mindset that blindly drew me to my own trap of almost two decades.

The danger of being too sociable

When I was in my second year of teacher training, in addition to being part of the Dabulamazwe Outreach, I became the secretary general of the Students Christian Fellowship in my college. I am naturally outgoing and my Christian life enhanced this further. Many of the Christians of that time did not associate with non Christians. Sometimes this was taken to the extreme of not even talking to them. I thought that was wrong, and being naturally friendly, I befriended most people who got close to me. Like naive Dinah, Jacob's daughter I gave time to people whom I now know did not deserve that kind of quality time from me. Dinah went outside her boundaries and got her destruction. She went to see women of the land and not the men, but through her going to see the women she was raped:

Now Dinah,
the daughter Leah had borne to Jacob,
Went out to visit the women of the land
When Shechem son of Hamor the Hivite,
the ruler of that area, saw her,
he took her and violated her.
(Genesis 34:1 – 2 NIV)

As a cultured girl Dinah was aware that she was not supposed to visit the men of the land, so she visited the women. It is not very clear how she landed herself in the snare of the sexual assault. I believe there were signs of the looming danger but Dinah was too comfortable in the company of the women to realise what was happening to her. Her experience also reminds me of the experience of Simon Peter, who did not do anything 'wrong' per se, but simply warmed himself in the company of the people who were in the courtyard at the time Jesus was taken to task by His accusers. It was the time when Peter had to be with Him the more:

But when they had kindled a fire
in the middle of the courtyard
and had sat down together,
Peter sat down with them.
(Luke 22: 55)

We all know the story how Peter ended up denying Jesus Christ three times. He did not plan it. He would not do that, especially after his bold declaration that he would never leave Jesus. What he did was find some comfort in the company of people outside Jesus Christ's circle of associates. Simon Peter did what is contrary to the man the Psalmist calls blessed:

Blessed is the man
who does not walk in the counsel of the wicked
or stand in the way of sinners
or sit in the seat of mockers.
(Psalm 1: 1)

Simon gave room for some seed to be sown into his heart. The more time he spent sitting there in the counsel of those men who had not been in the meetings of Jesus Christ; people who did not have the passion Peter had was the more his Spirit man got blunt. He lost his sensitivity to the Kingdom principles Jesus had taught them all the time they were with Him. He lost his connection to Jesus and 'boldly' denied that he was one of the disciples of Jesus. To those who knew me in 1980 this may sound like I am too harsh on myself, but today, now that I can see so clearly as I reflect on everything, I know that I gave time to a wrong woman whom I will call Trusty here. This is actually the direct translation of her Zulu name in English.

Trusty became very friendly to me and always complemented me. I liked it and eventually found myself always talking to her. Next, each time she made a complement she also mentioned a young man she called her 'brother' because they were from the same region of the country. Sometimes, as Trusty made complements, she would tell me that her brother was the one who had noted whatever was complemented in me. The complements were about my singing in the lecture theatre, how I dressed, hair, you name it. I soon discovered that 'the brother' also came to the Lecture Theatre services. As I got closer to Trusty she started telling me her 'brother' really loved me, and wanted to marry me. I somehow liked what I heard from Trusty, but her 'brother' had never personally told me he loved me. The seed Trusty had sown in my heart grew. I began to observe the 'brother' and soon realised she was right, he liked me indeed. I was bothered by the fact that he did not say anything himself.

I was brought up in a society where marriage is viewed as the vocation for every woman. This was emphasised such that from the time I was in school one of the most popular questions we asked in Christian youth discussions was: "How will I see my life partner?" We wanted to do things well and at the 'right' time, so when I heard this man loved me something within me was stirred. My main concern, however was to know God's will. I started praying to God to reveal His will about this man whom I already liked very much. As said earlier, there were other believers who had shown interest in me and had clearly stated the intention of marriage. The other brothers had come to me when my vows to wait were keenly operating. One of them who had similar passion with me for the things of God was somewhere on my on-hold shelve for consideration later. With Trusty's brother whom I would like to call 'the brother' things were different. He had a predecessor, a sister who spoke the 'right' words. What I kept hearing Trusty say to me blunted all my spiritual antennas.

Trusty was such a sweet and smooth talker that I did not even bother to think about the fact that she was not born again. I had never even seen her at our church meetings in the Lecture Theatre. I kept telling myself that God was going to reveal Himself more about Trusty's brother. It was not clear to me what I exactly meant by God revealing Himself, but I drew closer to Trusty and liked to hear her talk about her brother. We lived in the same hostel building with her, so in the evenings she used to come and tell me what her 'brother' had said about me each day. Each time she told me something new, my liking for him grew.

The truth is naive as I was, I did not want anything that was not from God in my life, so I prayed 'for guidance' and wanted to know if this thing I felt for the man was from God. At the beginning of August I prayed asking God to clarify this thing to me. In my prayer I said if this man was my future husband, God should let him tell me he loved me before the end of the year. I was **anxious** to know what the future held for me. Through Trusty I already knew this man liked me and was going to approach me soon anyway, but in my anxiety, his approaching me was going to be God's way of saying 'go ahead girl.' That is something worth thinking deeply about, right there. Indeed the brother approached me before the end of the year. I did not know much about him, and I am not really sure he knew much about me either apart from my singing and acting on stage plays or observing me move about. Five months later I gave my positive consent. That meant the beginning of wedding plans.

Soon, news spread around the college that I was 'in love.' Several people who knew Trusty's brother and who had watched soccer matches where he played came to me and advised me to think deeply before I make any serious commitment to him. One brave young man told me blatantly that I had made the worst mistake of my life. I thought he was jealous. I stopped talking to that young man. I had heard that 'the brother' had had a radical change in his life from someone who used to drink, smoke and more, and that made me love him more as someone in whose life the Lord had done a good job. I felt like all those who warned me were merely denying the good work the Lord had done in the good man's life. I thought that a man with a real past and signs of repentance was even better than the people like me who had been in Christian backgrounds from childhood. Each time I got a negative report about my man I interpreted it to be a confirmation that he was the man meant for me without giving any thought to what was said. I dare not write all the naivety, but it happened anyway.

One of the Christian sisters, who was engaged and about to marry came to my room one evening. She asked me if I could still love this man if he could backslide and go back into sin. I do not remember what my answer was. What I know is that I was too much in 'love' to even pause and give attention to the sister's words. I was a very committed Christian girl. Did God just leave me to go ahead without flashing any red lights to warn of what was ahead? God, our Father is Love and He does not let us go without any caution. He kept whispering to me in a still voice but I was too busy rushing to my 'blissful' life to even pay attention.

Another young man from my class even suggested that before I get married I should at least go to watch my man in the football pit where he was one of the strongest players. He told me that by being there and watching a match to the end I would discover something worth knowing. With my kind of commitments: my Christian responsibilities and studies I had no time for football. Looking back at the whole thing now, I find it absurd not to even have interest in knowing more about the obsessions of one's 'better-half-to-be'. One more sister from the Student Christian Fellowship told me I was heading for my doom and I got very angry with her. I thought the sister was jealous. Soon I was ready to start work as a qualified teacher and my former school, Mankayane High School recruited me before I started making any applications. As I started teaching marriage plans were in my top priority list.

Chapter 8

More Spiritual Experiences

○ ○

Coming back to Mankayane High School was not as challenging for me as we had been warned at teacher training college about our occupation as new teachers. Firstly, that was a Christian environment, which is home for me. Secondly, I had been there since the age of twelve. My friend, Zodwa with whom I had shared a room at college during my first year had also been recruited by my former school. We shared a house again, but this time we were young ladies. There was also a third recruit, Simon, the man who had been the chairman of the Christian Students Fellowship when I was the secretary. Within the very first week we fitted into the system like hand in glove. We were all at home!

One thing I noticed right away was that the short break meetings I had established in 1979 had died during the years I was away, but the general Christian aura still prevailed! Life was fantastic at school in the classrooms, in the staff-room as well as after school where we shared a three bed-roomed house with yet another teacher Sarah who was a graduate teacher also a former product of the school. It did not take long for the three of us young ladies to become family. We just clicked. We giggled, prayed, sang and did a lot together. For neighbours, we had a lovely couple, Vincent and Liza Makhubu. The Makhubus loved God in a unique way which was associated with younger and unmarried believers. They were very much into reaching out and getting more of God in the form of conferences and whatever was available outside the local church.

It was with the Makhubus that I first encountered the acclaimed Man of God, Evangelist Reinhard Bonnke. We went to his crusades in Fairview, Manzini and that is where I experienced my baptism in the Holy Spirit and speaking in a spirit language. I had heard some sisters pray in tongues when I was in my first year of High School, but that was discouraged in my school. It was also in Evangelist Bonnke's tent meetings that I saw and heard clearly about the ways God was going to use me in ministry. This was to be confirmed a year later at an international church conference in South Africa where I got the opportunity of going on stage to share and demonstrate my song composing skills with the conference participants. A year later I heard the Ladysmith Black Mambazo[11] group singing over the radio the same song I had composed and shared at the conference. I was thrilled!

Together with the Makhubus we attended all accessible *Christ For All Nations* major events at the time, and travelled to places within the Transvaal Province of South Africa such as Whitfield, Pretoria, Mabopane and more. My passion for evangelism grew stronger everyday as we had fellowship with the Makhubus. When the school employed another young lady to work as the school bursar we had to move to a much bigger and four bed-roomed house and share that house as a group of four ladies. Thabsile had just graduated from The Swaziland College of Technology (SCOT) and she was equally on fire for God.

We left the Makhubu block to live uphill in a much bigger and posh house. We worshipped God in that house; basically it was a 'crazy' house. Thabsile had been to Reinhard Bonnke's crusades too and the four of us were more than enough to form a congregation. We pushed aside the living and dining room furniture often as we wanted to worship the Lord in various forms, sometimes dancing like nobody was watching as King David! That was sublime! Soon my friend Zodwa left the school because she was getting married. She was replaced by my sister-friend, Dora who had gone to school there too. She was a temporary teacher waiting for her results like I did for three months before going to William Picher Teachers' College.

Prayer Group Interdenominational Ministry

Thabsile introduced us to her friends from SCOT. As we shared about our experiences in our training colleges I realised that Thabsile and her close friends in Mbabane had experienced something similar to our *Dabulamazwe* outreaches in Manzini. We networked with some of our colleagues from when we still at college and in no time we founded an outreach ministry whose central pillar was prayer. We wanted to have monthly prayer meetings whereby there would be an outreach in each selected venue and then prayer in the evening.

There were five of us on the very first day we committed ourselves to keeping the flame of God ablaze. The Lord led us from strength to strength as the group multiplied to cover almost all four regions of the country. That night as we prayed together to establish the Prayer Group Interdenominational Ministries we had no idea that what was being birthed was to go beyond the little circle of friends and associates we knew then. We established the group because we had realised that after students graduate from the institutions of higher learning and they are in the outer world on they own there was a tendency for some of the most vibrant and dynamic believers to simply disappear and never be heard of again. We wanted to be a group rooted in prayer where even the various challenges we faced could be presented to God in the monthly meetings we were going to hold. This also meant that any member who was isolated in a work place where there was no fellowship similar to what we had whilst at college or university could still keep the fire ablaze through the monthly meetings and also bring an outreach to the 'dry' place.

As a point of taking off we decided to have meetings in our own towns where we were located, and next, we were going to take them to our home areas and then spread out as the Holy Spirit led us. We had meetings in the three towns where apparently most members lived. When we took the meeting to our home areas the idea was to go to the place on Friday night, have a service wherever we were accommodated and then have an outreach on the following Saturday. Saturday night was to be our prayer time and then we would worship in any local church that had accepted us. God's hand was upon us and wherever we went doors opened. Many traditional churches accepted us and received from the Lord. The group grew rapidly.

When my turn to host a month end meeting I decided to have it in my home area because my work place was a mission school anyway. I was thrilled because I had prayed for my father's salvation and felt that was an opportunity for him to get the Good News from evangelists who had come into the area through his daughter. We camped in a local primary school. I had talked about the event with my father and he agreed. We worked strategically to have the mature members of the group to be the ones to go to my father's house. At the end my father spoke and told them that he really appreciated what we young people were doing. He said he loved God too. When the invitation to take the step of inviting Christ as a personal Saviour was made, my father did not even bother. He was all smiles showing that he was exempted from those who had to accept Jesus Christ. A part of me was disappointed because I had high hopes for my father's salvation that weekend. At the time I believed that if you pray for someone's salvation and they do not respond positively it reflects a problem in your own prayer life.

I continued praying for my father's salvation. Although I did not see signs of a possibility for his salvation, I had a very strong feeling that made me believe he was going to receive Jesus Christ as Lord and Saviour someday.

I did not want to be in heaven eternally without my father. When the father of one of the group members gave his life to Jesus on one of those outreach ministrations we held I just wished the same could happen to my father. The passion of my life was to do God's business and see people come to Christ. This passion was so strong to a point that most of my weekends were occupied by our outreach ministrations.

In my local church, our pastor, Mr Simelane continued giving me as well as others the opportunity to minister. That was a great time of my life. I do not regard those days as a past that I need to forget. They were the foundation of my life and they are the years which made me see who I was meant to be in God's kingdom. Sometimes I had a very strong urge to stop teaching and work for God fulltime, but I remember very well although I had not had that much experience in walking with God, that I did not have to stop teaching because I was going to do His work within my teaching job as I ministered to students.

One thing I remember and appreciate about the Prayer Group Interdenominational Ministry is that we were loyal to our pastors. As part of my active involvement in my church, The African Evangelical Church (AEC) which had been formerly called South Africa General Mission (SAGM) I went to youth camps and conferences. The strong urge to be loyal to my authorities stemmed from what I learnt as a young Christian in church youth camp meetings. Out of numerous camp meetings I attended I especially remember the one where a woman of God, Madam Sibandze taught from Deuteronomy 28. She explained lucidly how the blessing and curse operate. She explained that the enigma could be unlocked using the little key word *if:*

*If you fully obey the Lord your God and carefully follow all his commands I give you today, the Lord your God will set you high above all the nations on earth. All these blessings will come upon you and accompany you if you obey the Lord your God: You will be blessed in the city and blessed in the country
The fruit of your womb will be blessed, and the crops of your land and the young of your livestock—the calves of your herds and the lambs of your flocks. Your basket and your kneading trough will be blessed. You will be blessed when you come in and blessed when you go out.*

The Lord will grant that the enemies who
rise up against you will be defeated before
you. They will come at you from one
direction but flee from you in seven. The
Lord will send a blessing on your barns and
on everything you put your hand to. The
Lord your God will bless you in the land he
is giving you. The Lord will establish you as
his holy people, as he promised you on
oath, if you keep the commands of the Lord
your God and walk in his ways. Then all the
peoples on earth will see that you are called
by the name of the Lord, and they will fear
you. The Lord will grant you abundant
prosperity—in the fruit of your womb, the
young of your livestock and the crops of
your ground—in the land he swore to your
forefathers to give you. The Lord will open
the heavens, the storehouse of his bounty,
to send rain on your land in season and to
bless all the work of your hands. You will
lend to many nations but will borrow from
none The Lord will make you the head, not
the tail. If you pay attention to the
commands of the Lord your God that I give
you this day and carefully follow them, you
will always be at the top, never at the
bottom. Do not turn aside from any of the
commands I give you today, to the right or
to the left, following other gods and serving
them.
(Deut 28: 1-14)

In that youth camp meeting I heard and understood well that God had laid before me both blessings and curses and all depended upon my obedience to His commands. I made up my mind to fully obey the Lord's commands as the text orders. I was determined to get those promised blessings. I also started confessing as Madam Sibandze had instructed. I believed that whatever I touched would be blessed. Indeed the blessings started flowing and I lived to see the manifestation of that word. I was and still am blessed coming in and coming out!

Dr Betty Sibongile Dlamini

Inception of a lucrative business

As I have said earlier, about the blessed person who meditates on God's words, the blessing is upon us even before we see any manifestations. As the manifestations started, I was not even aware of it. God immersed me into a business I did not plan. It started as only a hobby and grew into a business that became lucrative at a very high speed. I had been taught about tithing and doing it was not as great a struggle as I hear people say. I believe that is caused by the fact that people's struggles vary from person to person. I soon realised that the more I tithed was the more money I had. Actually, the more I gave generally, was the more I received. The business God gave me stemmed from my love for 'nice' things.

I loved clothes from a very early age in life. My mind was very fast in imagining fashionable clothes and I believed I could design and sew any kind of dress or outfit I wanted. I always asked my mother to buy me cloth to sew, but she said she had no money to waste. I only quenched my yearning for designing clothes by using the empty calico maize-meal bags we got whenever they were available. I made dollies, dollies' clothes and my own play clothes, especially skirts. Nobody took serious notice of what I did. I think the first time my mother took note of my budding talent was when I got my first salary as a temporary teacher and only bought fabrics. I sewed various styles of clothes resembling what I had seen in catalogues.

I practiced more sewing when I got to William Pitcher College. Whenever we were given our allowance I used to buy fabrics and then make my own stylistic clothes. Those were my learning days because there were instances when as I tried to design an outfit I would make a mistake. From each mistake I would end up creating a new design. I used the college sewing machines in the Home Economics Department. I was not affiliated to that department, but after discovering that they had sewing machines for the students studying home economics I negotiated and the lecturer in charge allowed me.

After graduating from William Pitcher College, every month end when I got my salary I bought fabrics. I asked Mrs Bilger, one of the missionary teachers, to let me use her sewing machine and with great pleasure she allowed me to use it because she liked what I did. In 1981, the same year I started work, my sister who comes after me went to boarding school and I gave her some of my special outfits I had made whilst still at college. Many of the girls in my sister's dormitory liked the outfits and they placed orders. The order was so huge I felt embarrassed to borrow Mrs Bilger's sewing machine. I decided to buy my own. It had never clicked in my mind that I would need a machine of my own so soon.

I cannot forget the excitement I had the day I brought home my first sewing machine which was a Singer brand. That was a great development in my life because I could use my machine at any time convenient to me. I decided not to buy clothes at all, except for tailored suits and jackets, but even that changed later. At that time all girls were boarders at Mankayane High School and soon rumour spread that 'Miss Betty' made all her clothes. Girls from wealthy families asked me to sew clothes for them and when I was reluctant they offered to give me large sums of money. I agreed. Soon my free time, especially evenings, became valuable and I could not use it for chatting as the trend was among us young teachers. My time became money.

In Mbabane I discovered a shop which had remnant materials that were not available from the ordinary fabrics shops unless one travelled to big cities in South Africa, such as the Oriental Plazas in Durban and Johannesburg. When the girls ordered something exactly like mine, sometimes I could not get that same fabric and some of the girls offered to pay me large sums of money if I sold them the very clothes I had already worn. I always agreed because I knew I could make for myself anything I liked at any time. I later developed the habit of buying fabrics in large quantities. That way I found myself handling what appeared to be big money to me at the time.

With the extra income I managed to help make improvements in my parents' house, such as new curtains, the dining room suite, bedroom furniture and the kitchen scheme. I literally tasted having God bless whatever I touched with my hand. I afforded going on holiday to places in South Africa, which was quite a luxury during my days. Spending time by the sunny beach in Durban was fabulous. The extra income from my sewing business made me afford even to attend the annual international conference that rotated between Swaziland, KwaZulu and the Transkei, which was in Nseleni (KwaZulu) that year, 1982. I managed to sponsor my friend, Dudu who was still at college to come along so that we could sing together in that conference.

Glorious Prospects

The Nseleni conference was more like a vacation to me. We young people had great fun by the beach when it was excursion time. As I was playing my guitar and we were singing with Dudu we got connected to other singers from South Africa. They were very good in music and I was tempted to put my guitar aside and let the likes of brother, Jerry Nobela play for us. We sang a lot of Pastor Andréa Crouch's songs. Before the end of the conference there was a session when the conference participants were taught how to compose songs. Before the facilitators started teaching us they asked if there were any people who had already experimented with composing. I was one of the few who already had, so they asked us to share our songs with all conference participants as a way of encouraging aspirant composers and making them realise composing can be done by people like them and not any special people far away and abroad as people may sometimes think.

I was the only young person who came up to present what I had already composed before coming to the conference. I was asked to also share ideas how I did it. Holding a microphone and addressing the hundreds of heads was quite an experience! As the conference drew to a close we were over the moon with Dudu seeing that our dream was indeed coming true. We wanted to minister in outreaches by singing for the Lord. The encouragement we got was immeasurable! Looking back at that time, I can confidently say that was the time my DNA and belief system were interlocked and no wonder the explosion of blessings!

When I was back in Swaziland I excitedly told my fiancée about my conference experiences and some future prospects I had anticipated from that. Within the year and a half of teaching experience since I left college I had been busy occupied with the Lord's activities and I communicated with my spouse-to-be through writing. I do not want you to think it was just us who had this kind of remote relationship, but at the time in 'religious' spheres it was not a good thing for lovers to be seen together. At the time I did not want to be a misfit and I was quite pleased I never had any time with the man I was to marry. Although it was regarded as a good thing not to be seen together, I feel like mine was an extreme case. We wrote each other and sometimes talked over the phone. I excitedly shared my conference experience. After that he borrowed my guitar. That was the time I literally said 'good bye' to playing my guitar. Actually it took over 20 years before I played a guitar again after major radical changes in my life.

Women's classes: God's way or culture?

I was very excited about getting married and one of the ladies at church advised me to start attending women's classes so that I get familiar with what the role of women in marriage really is. I went for those classes. The common message in those classes was that women had to be submissive to their husbands. The kind of submissiveness taught was different from what I have grown to learn as I study God's word. The teachings instilled a mentality of inferiority into the women. The meaning of being submissive as I got it in those classes was that of a picture in which the woman would accept everything the man says without questioning. I was very eager to do the right thing, so I started thinking like a married woman as I had been taught in those classes.

Another important point the classes emphasized was prayer. As a matter of fact the women who went to the classes were called Women of Prayer. I learnt that prayer was the best way of dealing with challenges women face in their marriages. I really liked that because even as a girl and young woman I had already seen God move and answer my prayers amazingly! I believe teaching about the importance of prayer was good, but the dangerous aspect of the teaching was that it took everything to extremes and loaded upon prayer even issues that could be solved by two people sitting down to talk about their life. What I have grown to learn, which I did not know at the time is that the teachings in the women's meetings were mixing Godly ways and aspects of culture that contradict the meaning of marriage according to God's standards. The biblical truths were bent a little bit to suit Swazi culture in a way similar to what Satan did in Eden when he approached Eve:

> *He said to the woman, "Did God really say,*
> *'You must not eat from any tree in the garden'?"*
> *(Genesis 3:1b NIV)*

When the serpent asked this question he mixed the truth and lies. It is true God had said they should not eat, but He did not say not to eat from 'any' tree in the garden. God had a specific tree from which He prohibited them to eat. Similarly, the women's classes were intended to build up families, but they were lopsided and focused on what was not always true. Some of the un-godliest of teachings came out of those teachings such as telling women to leave their bedrooms when their spouses brought in girlfriends. The Bible states clearly that the marriage bed has to be treated holy! Some people take this to mean the literal bed and think that it is okay for a man to go all over the place having multiple sexual relations with women as long as he has not brought them home. What a concoction!

From attending those meetings I decided I was going to be the best wife ever. I decided to follow those teachings. I started behaving like a married woman and decided not to question anything my fiancé would say even if I strongly felt against it. More than anything I was concerned about having approval from society. I also took things out of proportion and believed that the verse, "a good name is more desirable than great riches; to be esteemed is better than silver or gold" (Proverbs 22: 1) meant people's approval was very important.

I carried on with my wedding plans having that mentality overriding me. Soon, I got engaged on the same weekend my *lobolo* (bride price) was paid. The Prayer Group members came to the event. That Saturday night a mini-bus full of prayer warriors came and parked in front of my father's house.

They were willing to support me by attending my engagement ceremony that Sunday morning. Some of the men slept in the bus and the young women slept anywhere there was space including the floor of the dining and living room, kitchen and girls' bedroom. I thought the engagement service was great because we felt the presence of the Lord. By the end of Sunday my ring finger was shiny and to me that ring was equally binding as a marriage one. I knew an engagement was not a marriage per se, but in my heart there was no room for breaking up that relationship.

The elders of my church wanted to meet my fiancée and talk to him before we married as was practice in the church. They also wanted to meet some members of his church family. He did not meet those requirements. I tried hard to convince my leaders that it was impossible for my fiancé to bring people from his family and church, but the pastor responsible for marriage and counselling in my church insisted that they were not going to send me off before meeting my fiancée, a member of his church and family. When it became apparent that none of that was going to happen I begged my leaders to bend the rules because of our 'difficult' situation. The marriage officer only met my fiancée, and that was a very brief meeting because he had to return to the Southern part of the country in the afternoon of the same day of meeting. The protocol of my church was altered. I was not one to break anything good and important in my church, but I was 'too much in love' to see all that.

During the last three months before the wedding there were instances where this remote relationship had to change as we had to meet and talk about things pertaining to the **wedding** day. I was more obsessed with the wedding day than the marriage as a whole. We did not talk about our lifelong plans and values of our marriage. I personally took for granted that my marriage was going to automatically work well because I was a born again child of God. It was on one of the wedding plan meetings that I got my warning. From what I saw I had great inner conflict, but I quickly resolved it by telling myself I was already engaged and 'people' already knew of the coming wedding, so I had to pray about things and there was going to be a change. As preparations were in progress I told myself I had no choice but to brace up for marriage. I interpreted the warnings to be love tests which 'I' had to conquer. The red 'traffic' light was right there in front of me, but I crossed the line anyway. What a mistake! I went on ahead believing that through prayer I was going to change the things I was uncomfortable with in our relationship.

Another young man from my home area came to ask me if I was sure I knew what I was doing by getting into that marriage. He told me to wait and make sure I knew the man I was marrying before I did. I waxed my ears, judging the young man as jealous. It did not take long for the brother's words to make sense. While discussing something pertaining to the wedding, we had differing points of view and as I tried to clarify my side the reaction I got really terrified me. Right there at Nhlangano Park, I saw a side of my fiancé I did not know. I was appalled, but the 'softy' in me coupled together with the 'good wife' goal made me to keep quiet thinking that was the best to do. That was not good at all. I was being foolish and gambling with my life. At the time I did not know that God wants His people to be free to be who He made them to be. Right there, I gave away my birthright, my God given right to be who He has made me to be. I allowed my fiancée to completely shut me out. I allowed him to let his opinion rule regardless of what it really meant for us. I was not aware that I was removing myself from a free life in God, straight into my entrapment!

Although I did not realise at the time, now I can see clearly through the people that had warned me all along that God was giving me an opportunity to pause and check the car I was ready to drive on a highway. I carried on with the wedding plans. We left out **communication,** which is a principle I now regard as the chief pillar of relationships. There was no communication from the onset and I did not realise that without it there *is no marriage.* I had no idea that what I was overlooking and permitting was going to 'bite me' almost to death for almost two solid decades. As I the wedding day drew closer I believed my marriage was going to be a light in the world. I wanted to have a perfect marriage where I would submit to my husband and I strongly *believed* he was going to be a loving husband who will lead the family even in Godly matters. All my life was centred on God, so I thought our lifestyle as a couple would follow suit. Whenever my fiancé did not come out clearly about his stand regarding some of the issues which were very important to me such as my involvement in the ministry I assumed that he was in agreement.

Before saying I do make no assumptions!

The phase of life before marriage is very important, but I did not realise that. I assumed that everything was going to be fine. I had seen prayer work for me and I thought I was going to pray to God to change the things I had already identified not to be good for our relationship. I was ignorant in many areas, but did not know that. I was in love and excited that finally I was going to live with the person I loved. It did not come to my mind that there was a need for people planning to marry to have acquiescent persuasions and philosophies. I knew what my persuasions in life were and assumed that my fiancé had the same. I did not know exactly what his long term dreams were because we had never taken the time to talk about that. I had just told him what I was passionate about and assumed his lack of comments meant he was in agreement.

People have varying definitions of concepts such as abuse and fidelity. As a matter of fact there are people who think that 'abuse' does not exist. They have definitions which justify physical and emotional abuse as ways of correcting other people or training them. Sitting down to talk about all these issues is important because shoving them away under the carpet or somewhere private does not help. They eventually surface themselves and when they do it is not always easy to deal with them because it is normally after things are completely unbearable. It never occurred to me that all these things had to be dealt with before one walked down that aisle to say those sacred words 'I do!'

I assumed everything was going to be fine because I had a dream just about the time of my 'crowning' my fiancé, telling him yes, I was going to marry him. I regarded the dream to be foretelling my glorious future. The morning after the dream I had feelings I regard to be similar to those of the dreamers of biblical times such as the Baker, the Butler, Pharaoh and King Nebuchadnezzar to name some of them. They clearly felt that their dreams had meaning and I similarly felt my dream had some significance bearing on my future.

The Special Dream

In my dream I was walking uphill and the place had shrubs, some of which were thorny. There was tall dry grass and all sorts of tangled vegetation found in winter. As I was walking, suddenly I came to a clearing where there was a big mansion. Its walls were crystal clear with gold frames in some parts such as windows and doors. I stood outside stunned and did not want to enter because the place was extraordinary and exuding radiance. I heard a voice, which told me to enter, saying that the place was where I had said I was going, so I had to enter. I staggered in like a drunkard would do.

When I stepped inside the floor was carpeted with a rich deep maroon carpeted that looked and felt like fur. My feet 'sank' as I walked like a toddler learning to walk. The interior had only three colours; crystal clear, deep maroon and gold. It was prodigious; phenomenal beyond anything I had ever seen before. The voice told me to enjoy because that was the home I had wanted to have. As I was still in there I somehow felt like the place was translated to another state and I felt like I was in heaven. I did not want to leave, but as you know in dreams, that was when I woke up.

When I woke up I had a strong feeling that the dream had to do with my future. I thought it had to do with my marriage life and I was inwardly convinced the dream meant that I was going to have a phenomenal life with my spouse when married. I told my mother about the dream and did not tell her my own interpretation for it. She said she felt like the dream was about something good that I was going to experience in future. I embraced that and hastily interpreted it to mean God affirming my interpretation: that the marriage I was entering into was going to be glorious. You know the term 'future' is such an ambiguous and flowing one: the next moment is the future; the next ten minutes is the future; the next month, day, decade, century are all under the 'future' category. One thing I rested assured of was that God had good plans for me as the book of Jeremiah states:

For I know the plans I have for you," declares the LORD,
"Plans to prosper you and not to harm you,
Plans to give you hope and a future
(Jeremiah 29: 11 NIV)

I believe some dreams are from God and are there to convey certain messages to us people of God. I also strongly believe that my 1981 dream was one of the dreams that God Himself engineered to tell me something. He is the same God who gave Joseph dreams about his future. I am also quite aware that when Joseph was in the pit there was no correlation between his situation then and his God-given dreams. Neither was there any correlation between Joseph's dreams and his life as a man-servant in Potiphar's house or as a prisoner! We know what eventually happened to Joseph, so let us leave his case alone and come back to mine. After that amazing dream, which I now realise was meant to awaken me and make me ponder on things, I did not really wait. I did not check, interrogate or scrutinise; I plunged into the marriage like I used to do in the swimming parts of the Great Usuthu River!

Marriage or just a wedding day

Being fully armed with my God-given fashion designing and sewing skills, I went to South African cities to search for the best fabrics I could ever get and afford to make my own wedding gown. I had never made one before, but I had great confidence I could do it after closely scrutinising some of the gorgeous wedding gowns I liked in some bridal boutiques I visited. I bought books, magazines and was fascinated to learn all these things about weddings. I put together a lot of new ideas I had never seen in any single wedding before. My mother was concerned that wedding regalia were not something to be tampered with by an over-ambitious girl. My aunties also agreed with my mother, but none of their *hush-hushing* could stop me.

The outcome of that determination shut everyone's mouths as they saw the bridal set ranging from the wedding gown and all its accessories; dresses of eight bridesmaids and two flower-girls. I bought my silver crown and head gears for the girls. I had never planned nor thought of having a bridal business, but that attempt was the birth of what in a few years later was to end up being a huge and very busy business in two parts of Manzini, the central city of Swaziland, Betty's Bridal Boutique and Betty's Own Creations, a warehouse where all the manufacturing was done.

On Saturday, the 14th May 1983 I got married, and indeed it was a 'great' wedding day with all the choirs and all the 'right' wedding outfits. I really want to pause a little here. This is a serious issue. By writing this testimony I believe I am not just hanging my linen on the line for the world to see and have yet another issue or object of scrutiny. No. I have this big **assignment** to help warn you if you are still single and you are blinded of some issues. Marriage is not something to rush into **without considering a number of things.** I am passionate about relationships, especially marriage. That is something no person can disengage from me. I love seeing people in love, and therefore want to see the marriage institution flourish. Marriage was designed by God Himself, so I really do not want to see it sneered upon as if it is impossible. Marriage is a reality. It is dynamic and never static. It needs to be continually fed with its essential 'oxygen' of communication and other relationship 'nutrients'.

Many people of God have written about the subject of marriage. Others even preach about it. My pastor, Pastor Matthew Ashimolowo, the founder of Kingsway International Christian Church (KICC) in London has preached thoroughly about marriage in his teachings *Don't Date Devils* which come in both book and tapes series. The teaching is phenomenal! His tape series 'True Love Waits' is also dynamic and shows that marriage is more than a wedding ceremony! When I first listened to the tapes and then listened to him preach at one Singles' Summit, I was in tears all the way through, saying 'if only someone told me all these things when I was still nineteen years old I could have saved myself and my children a lot of pain'. The decision I made determined the hills and valleys I have walked. Each decision an individual makes expands to affect a large part of their life like the two arms of an angle. The longer they get the clearer the significance of each bearing becomes! Waiting and pondering pays dividends!

May be what I have just said now sounds like I am mourning; please hear me well; it is true I used to cry a lot, but that is history! Now, I can exclaim like Joseph who was sold by his brothers that what the devil meant for destruction, God has turned around into a blessing. Joseph's brothers thought they were destroying him, but they were actually pushing him toward his destiny. The dreamer in him could not be easily stopped by the change of location. That is why some years down the line Joseph walked from prison into the palace, and changed from those prison rags into regal robes. I have had my portion of tears, but God the Almighty who is my Father has opened my eyes. I have realised that all the lies that the enemy pumped into my ears through culture and religion, that pain is a believer's portion are not true. Now I know God never meant pain to be a believer's portion. That was a lie I believed for many years and it held me hostage, but it has dawned and I have said 'enough is enough –no more!'

Many people believe the enemy's lies and embrace their suffering as a God given experience for Christians here on earth. The evil one enjoys seeing believers take spiritual pain pills which work for a few hours. He is annoyed when he hears people say 'enough is enough' and hates to see them go for a spiritual diagnosis to identify the real cause of their pain because he knows that this will lead to the end of the pain. I feel compelled not to just tell you my story, but extend to state that the decisions I made without elaborating on repercussions, have affected my life immensely. Some of those decisions caused me endless nights of shedding gallons and gallons of tears, but that is all history now. I just jumped the gun to that part from the onset so that as you plod on with me here, you may connect the story telling and my main mission to tell it!

Beloved, hear me very well here, because I did not just get married, cried and then said 'No more!' God, my Father has seen me through a couple of things. I mean a couple of situations. Now when I sing Pastor Andréa Crouch's song, "Through it all", I know what I am talking about. I am writing this so that you as a reader may also sing the song with understanding if you happen to sing it. I do not wish to see more people; both young and old go the road this 'girl' talking to you now went through.

Some of the danger zones I have treaded on could be avoided. God has a good plan for each person's life which could happen without the involvement of pain and affliction. However, pertaining to pain and suffering, there are some exceptional cases such as Job's, where Satan asked God's permission to test Job after they had a conversation about him. The discussion of pain is not the main purpose of this testimony, so, I do not want to explain the kind of pain I have experienced. Also, going into depths and explaining the pain would take its own toll, which is not the focus of this testimony. I am not giving glory to Satan, but on the contrary I am stepping him lower and lower; reminding him that he is under my feet and can be under the feet of whosoever assumes their position as a child of God, the Creator of the universe!

Well, for the progress of my testimony, yes, I got married, or so I thought. In order to determine if I got married we need to explore God's word and then identify clearly what marriage is. Marriage is not what many people think it is. It is not just the wedding day and neither is it simply about two people; male and female living in the same house, having physical intimacy and bearing children. It is more than that. The whole truth about marriage was spelt out from its very inception when God made the first woman:

And the Lord God said,
It is not good that the man should be alone;
I will make him a help meet for him.
(Genesis2: 18 KJV)

The Amplified Version elucidates more:

Now the Lord God said,
It is not good (sufficient, satisfactory) that the man
should be alone;
I will make him a helper meet (suitable, adapted, and
complementary) for him.
(Genesis2:18 AV)

God instituted marriage mainly for companionship or simpler put, friendship between the man and woman. In marriage, God was making a miniature version of the relationship He Himself wanted to have with humans when He created them. Some of us overtly known to have been married at some point in time have never experienced anything close to companionship. Personally, I have never had any friendship with the man known to have been my husband. We were strangers and sometimes we were like foes that had very differing and opposing priorities in life. When I say sometimes we were like foes I do not mean to paint a bad image of 'us'. We were a wonderful 'couple'. I need to clarify something a little bit to help you get this and also help you in your own choices of relationships at various levels.

When I was young using tractors for ploughing was not very common. It was used by commercial farmers more than those who farmed for personal consumption. I used to see one of my uncles yoking oxen together to pull the plough. There were two other men in my home area that had both cattle and donkeys. These two men would sometimes use a span of oxen and sometimes a span of donkeys, but I do not remember them teaming up donkeys and oxen in the same span. I think this is because donkeys and oxen are different in so many ways. Their physical strength, interests, physical make-up and a lot more is different. In the Bible there are a number of references against yoking together what is different:

Do not plant two kinds of seed in your vineyard
If you do, not only the crops you plant

But also the fruit of the vineyard will be defiled
Do not plough with an ox and a donkey yoked together
Do not wear clothes of wool and linen woven together
(Deuteronomy 22: 9-11)

Do not be yoked with non believers
(2 Corinthians 6: 14a)

In the case of marriage things go more than just yoking Christians together in marriage. There are choices that God has allowed us to make in life such as the lifestyle we live and a lot more areas in which Christians can be of differing views. If you put a cat and a pig together you just create trouble because one of them is an extra clean animal and the other enjoys eating and playing in a filthy place and even eating stinky food. Ducks like water but chickens never go swimming. Marrying a duck and a chicken requires more than compromise; it is like literally mixing oil and water which never mix anyway! My point here is that being a Christian is not the one and only qualifying factor when choosing a marriage partner.

I had just jumped into the marriage wagon when I realised that 'our' values as a couple were in great conflict. Some of these issues go beyond even background and upbringing. They rest on who one is as an individual. The question to answer is 'when making you, what special things did He fix in there which are not found in other people?' I know very well that people are not the same. A Godly marriage will not force you to live a lifestyle less than that what God called you to live. Any relationship that subtracts you or makes you less than what God made you to be is not a good thing for you. Also, any marriage that demands you to stretch beyond what God made you to be is a deadly relationship and I will not even call it marriage.

It is very important to know who you are in God. From the time I was young there was evidence in my life that God had called me for His own purpose like what He says to Isaiah:

Listen, O coastlands, to Me,
and take heed, you peoples from afar!
The LORD has called Me from the womb;
From the matrix of My mother
He has made mention of My name.
²And He has made My mouth like a sharp sword;
In the shadow of His hand He has hidden Me,
And made Me a polished shaft;
In His quiver He has hidden Me."

³ *"And He said to me,*
'You are My servant, O Israel,
In whom I will be glorified.'
(Isaiah 49: 1-3 NKJV)

Before you marry, it is important to know who you are as God made you to be and also who the person you are marrying is. I regard marriage also as a plant that grows when a seed or seedling and soil gets together. If you plant a small indoor plant in an open field, it dies because it cannot take all the harsh weather out there. On the other hand, if you plant a cedar tree seedling on a pot for indoor plants that is disaster because the plant becomes too big for the pot and then eventually dies. That is what happens when two people get into marriage just because they like each other without sitting down to talk and explore who they really are and what their persuasions in life are.

According to God's concept of marriage the two people become one, not only through sexual physical intimacy, but in their total life. When one hurts the other is affected. When one stumbles, the other makes an effort to lift him or her up. It is not always an easy ride, but it works because the two pull together:

Two are better than one,
because they have a good return for their work:
If one falls down,
his friend can help him up.
But pity the man who falls
and has no one to help him up!
(Ecclesiastes 4:9 NIV)

For us children of God, Father has set standards that are to be followed. Here, I am not teaching about marriage per se, but my point is that I got 'married'. Now the big question is what happened next, after I said 'I do'.

Chapter 9

Tampering with the DNA

o o o o o o o o o o o o o o o o o o o o o o o o o o o o o o o

Strife is the evidence that two Belief Systems have collided!
(Dr Murdock: Wisdom Key 958)

On Sunday, 15th May the wedding ceremony continued at the in-laws' place. That was still a big event, but slightly different from the Saturday one which had taken place at Encabaneni High School Hall. In my culture, the bride distributes gifts to her in-laws and her husband. During my days the gifts included anything ranging from valuable house-wares and mink two-in-one reversible blankets, but now people have grown to include more furniture such as bedroom suits, La-Z-Boy recliners and more. After all the gift giving and feasting was over, cars from town had to go back. It was when the last car and the big bus hired by my father to carry people from Khalangilile, my home area had left that it dawned clearly to me I had just made a major turning point in my life.

The excitement that stemmed from all the music, choirs, speeches, fancy clothes, decorations, food and everything that goes with a wedding celebration had already gone and almost forgotten. I was very nervous. We did not go anywhere for our honeymoon. Right away I had to prove my worth by displaying the expected skills of a newly wedded woman. I served my in-laws for those few days I spent with them before schools reopened. Soon, on the following week we had to leave my in-laws' place and go to the work place. I will not even start to describe the shock I got when I got to the drought stricken place with no water, no electricity and no telephone facility because that may interfere with my testimony as if that was the main issue. The condition of the place is not at all an important issue to me because even the Sahara Desert can be my paradise if love abides there.

As I settled in my new home, I realised that the life I had just got into was like east and west from the life I had always believed God was taking me to. One special memory that came back to me in a flash was the day I had got good news from ZTG, my mother's cousin during the time I was busy engaged with wedding preparations. That day she had told me that I could pursue my degree through the Primary Curriculum Unit (PCU), where she worked. They offered a part time sandwiched degree programme which did not interfere with one's teaching because the larger part of the work was done during school vacations. Knowing that I was to get married soon, ZTG was prepared to help us by negotiating with some school head teachers in Manzini so that I could access the PCU easily. About three schools had vacancies that suited us. I was excited.

Getting such an opportunity was very important to me because, through it I saw part of my dreams being realised. Going to William Pitcher College was clearly not my end. I had heard so many times as a child that I was meant for something much bigger. The words of almost all my primary school teachers and some of my high school teachers really troubled me. The leading voice that always echoed in my mind whenever I thought about my future occupation was that of Miss Lydia Nhlengetfwa, whom I overheard talking to my mother,

"This child is unique. She is set to do great things on earth..."

Miss Nhlengetfwa had been talking to my mother, telling her that my grandmother was right to suggest I transfer from the Khalangilile Lower Primary School, where I started, to Encabaneni Mission School. Actually, at Khalangilile, Miss Nhlengetfwa made me do a two year program in one year. There used to be First Year Sub A and Sub B. In that group I was the only child that moved to the next level without staying in Sub B. Some of the women in the community who had seen me acting in skits as a young child started calling me by my character roles. This had followed me from Primary school to even William Pitcher College where I had multiple names such as Sidi or The Nurse. At William Pitcher College, the college Principal who saw me act the role of a nurse called me 'Nurse' and that has been my name to him up to now. Hearing all the positive words from the adults in my life over and over again made me believe in a higher and more significant occupation in life. So, the opportunity ZTG was according me at PCU was going to be a gateway to the greater thing I believed lay ahead for me.

I was still on cloud nine when I broke the good news to my fiancé. With sparkling eyes of joy I looked at his eyes expecting a response... Oops! Bang! I dropped down to mother earth when the steady voice calmly told me no one was going to work in town, but we would work in the rural country side. He said it would help us to live in the country and save money so that we come back to the city later when we would be financially established. I was disappointed, but my *feelings* for my man made me talk to myself and say, 'no problem girl, the man is right.'

As I settled in my new home all the memories and thoughts from my earlier days in life started playing. I had been to a similar kind of extreme rural area once when we went on evangelism with the Dabulamazwe Outreach group from William Pitcher College. That weekend I first tasted hard water I could not drink any of it and only quenched my thirst with drinks from the grocery store close by. At the time I had no idea that I was to put up with that kind of life for six full years of my life.

I do not want to emphasize the challenging state of the new work place because challenges are there everywhere, and all they need is to be tackled appropriately. The main question I want to suggest we ask ourselves over and over again is who each one of us really is. All along as a child and young woman there had never been a single moment when I had any conflict within myself regarding who I was. I had been just flowing smoothly from one stage of life to the next, but in the year 1983 I was awoken to start questioning a few things because I found myself in a position where I felt trapped. There was conflict between the person I had always believed myself to be; the person I had always been and the new person I found myself being obliged to become.

What do you do if you have been passionate about singing, I mean singing when cooking, taking a bath or shower or just getting by doing your house chores and all of a sudden you realise that you are not allowed to sing in what is supposed to be your own house? What do you do if all of a sudden you realise that you have no one to talk to in your house except for students at school or strangers you encounter along the way? When the early heat waves hit me I thought it was probably some kind of natural shock that occurs as a person moves from one stage of life to the next. For some time I thought it was a marriage shock thing, but I remembered that married women do sing in their houses. My mother used to sing all the time and even now she still sings and hums her own self-composed songs as she sits knitting on her Empisal Knitting Machine. Remembering all this made me realise that what I was experiencing was some kind of force that was tampering with the very essence of who Betty Sibongile Dlamini was made by God to be, I mean her God designed DNA!

Relating all the above nuggets about my abilities, aspirations, dreams and all that come along with it is a way of showing what happens when a fish gets removed from water to be among lizards or what happens when an eagle gets lost and find itself in a chicken run. Sometimes when this kind of change occurs death happens instantly as in the case of a fish. It just cannot survive among lizards in dry land and crevices of rocks. In other instances adaptation takes place such as the case of the lost eaglet living among chickens. People who see it surviving there may be deceived to believe it is a chicken, but as a matter of fact an eagle will never be a chicken!

DNA adjustments throttle

I regard what I am sharing with you now as the main reason for this whole testimony. As I have already insinuated above that I got married having not really discussed the important issues which need to be discussed before people get to the alter in marriage such as their life persuasions and philosophies, I will now bring into view what the repercussions of the negligence of something so important may be. This may not be the case with everyone, but taking precautions will always help. I cannot stress enough the importance of ***knowing*** exactly what it means to say 'I do' ***before you actually say 'I do'.*** Sad to say, many people say 'I do' first and then struggle to understand what they really meant by those utterances.

I believed that the essential ingredient in marriage is 'love' for each other, but now I cautiously use the term 'love' because it has been abused a lot. People use it a lot when all they mean is 'like.' They use it to mean 'lust' and a lot more. Attraction is not love. I was attracted to someone who was attracted to me and he was a good person, but our persuasions and life philosophies were worlds apart to a point that I know very well that up to today the good man does not even know the real Betty and I also do not know that good man at all. Having been taught a lot about the importance of a woman being submissive in marriage, I was ready to give up my life thinking that was submission. By my life I do not mean just the personal development issues such as education and material wealth accumulation. That department, especially the financial one was excellent, but my real *personhood*, the *Betty being* as seen by God was throttled almost to death.

As I have already related above about my salvation and passion for Christ as a young person, there are numerous practices that became part of my life to the extent that taking them away from me literally meant tampering with my heart. Without those there would be no Betty. Well, there could be some being that looked like me, but really that would be a zombie. Some of these practices include having fellowship with other believers, ministering through singing, evangelising, preaching, sharing the Word in small church groups, tithing, giving offerings, acting and just living a vivacious lifestyle!

Loss of fellowship

There were no churches close to the school, so for the very early days we got a ride from one Christian family that had a van. Those were very welcoming days for me. The church was not like what I was used to, but the fact that Christ was preached made me feel at home. I fitted into that community and looked forward to being part as I had always been elsewhere before. We started off well and had evening prayers which soon proved to be too good to last. Within a short time going to church also died the death of a bubble! I found my situation to be at conflict with the kind of life I had chosen to live from the time I was young. I had decided to live according to God's commands in his Word, but then I found myself at sixes and sevens as I saw it was not happening!

The Bible encourages fellowship among brethren and my grandmother had taken that very seriously to the point that apart from attending church every Sunday, the Thursday women's meetings and the Saturday Proverbs 31 Diligent Women's group, she made us have family fellowship every night. As a young person, daily family prayer was part of my upbringing and removing that from me is similar to depriving me of essential meals such as breakfast or dinner. I felt very miserable and alone. In my heart I was the same person except that I was becoming malnourished because fellowship with other believers is very enriching to our spirit being. In my miserable and solitary life I ended up praying alone in the bathroom or in the bedroom when I happened to be alone in the house. This situation tampered with my mind to a great extent because I was taught and believed that church starts at home and also that a family that prays together stays together!

The culture of praying together was planted into my life at home; it sprouted at Mankayane High School both at the hostel and school; it was nurtured at William Pitcher Teacher Training College and further nurtured at Mankayane High School when I worked as a qualified teacher. The more I grew was the deeper my roots went as far as communal Christian living was concerned, so when I lost this kind of fellowship I became like a plant that has been uprooted from the moist soil in which it has always thrived. The sudden change of affairs together with the silence in the house that was so thick you could cut it with a knife almost cost me my sanity.

Teaching together with my spouse did not make things very easy, but I soon learnt and knew how to be silent everywhere I was. I had great fun being with my students and whenever I was teaching I came back to life. Humour was woven throughout my lessons and my students did well in both Mathematics and English, the subjects I taught. I had the opportunity of also teaching Bible Knowledge and that was glorious. I was not meant to preach, but the truth is the truth and cannot be stifled when it is in plain view. Most of what I now regard as preaching or sharing Christ to my students stemmed out from the questions that arose from our discussions. Some of those moments of sharing were outside class.

In 1984 there was a very serious squabble that was leading to a deadly fight between two groups of boys in the school. There was a gang from Golela which served as the town part and those from around the school. The head teacher and all of us, teachers were informed about the problem and that some of the students were carrying very dangerous and illegal weapons. The teachers claimed they could do nothing about the problem because apparently it was something that had started outside the school. In my privacy I began to pray about the situation, but after my prayer I felt a very strong urge to do more than just pray.

After asking from some of the students I identified the leaders of both gangs. Without telling anyone including my spouse, I called the leader of the gang from around the school. I spoke lengthy to him about the repercussions of what they were doing. He listened to me and by the time I had finished I could see deep within the 'brave' and 'dangerous' boy another weak and insecure boy who was searching for something of value in life and felt like playing the tough guy was going to help him. DJ, the gang leader told me that he could talk to his boys to drop it and they would listen to him if the other gang would be prepared to drop it too. I promised DJ I would not tell anyone and I kept that promise. My assignment was just beginning.

Getting the leader of the Golela gang to come and talk to me was a bit difficult. It had been easy for DJ to come to my house afterschool when I was alone with the girl who helped me in the house, because he lived close to the school quarters. God supports anything done in obedience to Him and He made it possible for me to talk to the other boy from town. After repeatedly assuring him that DJ's gang would drop it the Golela leader agreed to settle his boys too. To complete my assignment I privately called both leaders and the squabble was settled without any of the teachers knowing how. It is true I felt really suffocated and bound in my home life, but God used me privately with no one even noticing.

I believe some of the students I spoke to shared with their friends because there were times when some girls would come to me and seek counsel on what they were facing as girls. One girl in particular asked me to talk to her friend who wanted to commit abortion and she was concerned about her friend's life because a number of people who committed abortion died in the process. Before I could talk to the girl she disappeared and returned to school after a number of days. She had already committed the abortion and survived. The other teachers did not know about it. I ministered to her and she received my message of Christ.

In my little private world I saw my significant difference, but what I found more frustrating was that the students were already aware of the strife I was going through. Sometimes humiliating things happened and when the humiliation went beyond what I thought I could bear I had a strong desire to leave the earth. What helped me conquer the enemy when he coerced to commit suicide is that I had been taught the truth in depth about suicide and I knew the curse that fell on Judas Iscariot when he took his own life. Immediately I remembered that suicide would separate me forever from God and I came back to my senses and just cried bitterly.

When I saw my marriage not being what I thought it would be I got very frustrated and started seeking help from all accessible pastors and their wives close by and those back in the cities, Mbabane and Manzini. A pastor and his wife, from a church in Golela were very skilled and attempted helping us, but there was no success because soon my spouse stopped going to church completely. Once I asked to go for a weekend to one of the Assemblies of God leaders in Mbabane. For the whole weekend I lived in the house of the president of women's wing of the church. The women of God were so good with all the advice which I took religiously and kept to the dot. The trouble is that we were dealing with one side of the equation. We hoped to make a two-man effort work through only one person. What killed me the most in my spirit was the realization that I was on my own in the 'church and God business.'

As a young person I had abstained from many things which my peers indulged in. I was taught about the benefits of abstinence and the chief one was that one day I was going to have a Godly family of my own. I had learnt about the consequences of wrong decisions and when I made my own decision I was convinced that it was the best I could ever make. I had seen many women come to church without their husbands, but with their children only because they were not born again when they got married to their non-believing husbands. I did not like to fall into the same pool with those women. On the other hand I saw other women who came to church with their husbands and children and my dream was to be like the second lot of women and come to church with my family when I eventually have one. To some people this may be a trivial matter, but to me it mattered a lot!

Sunday, July 31, 1983 was a devastating day for me as I sat all alone in the house because I did not know how to get to the few churches that were very far from the school and I was alone because my spouse had gone to watch a soccer match. I grappled with God and reminded Him of my commitment to Him. By that time I had got a negative report from some

Italian gynaecologists. I had shared the sad news with my mother who said nothing of the sort was going to happen. She said through prayer God was going to reverse the report. So, on that Sunday morning, rolling on the floor and full of tears and all the stuff that accompany tears as you pour your heart to God, I asked Him to give me a baby. He answered my prayer and that 'child' is a great blessing to me like his name Sibusiso (blessing). 'We' dedicated the baby to the Lord on his first birthday. 'We' threw a big party and invited many children within the community near the school we taught. 'We' also invited a pastor to our house. His church was far. He honoured the invitation and held my first child in his hands. I believe God did something amazing in that dedication.

My unfulfilled and God's fulfilled promises

The year 1987 came with some significant events in my life. It was in April and we were already asleep when we heard a knock at the door. It was my sister, Busisiwe and her friend. When we opened the door my sister just burst into tears breaking the sad news that our father had passed on. I have no way of expressing what a blow that was to me. My father was my hero. He is the one man so far that I am definitely sure ever loved me, as I am writing this testimony now. I say a lot about our bond in the manuscript for one of my coming book, *My Dad and I*. Well, as his first born I had to leave Lavumisa right away that night and head for home at Khalangilile, Manzini.

Receiving the news of my father's passing on was like a deep stab in my spirit, because I remembered how I had failed to keep my promise to him. Most men, especially from my home area did not value the education of girls, but my father did. I have distant cousins who never even went to school at all, but my father even sent me to a mission boarding school. For that, I was so grateful in my heart. I realised that my finishing school, still pure when many girls in my home area were getting pregnant left, right and centre and therefore dropping from school was as a result of my salvation which was enhanced by the exposure to Christianity at Mankayane High School. School fees were exorbitant in my school and my parents sacrificed a lot. I greatly appreciated that gift.

When I got my first salary I wanted to give my father something significant, but he said he was fine and only asked me for a bottle of London Dry Gin. I did not want to go into that kind of liquor store, but in my spirit I heard very well that I had to buy it and give my father as a way of honouring him because that is all he had asked for. After that I promised my father that I was going to help him by paying my youngest sister's fees. She was in Form 1 in 1983, the year I got married and I started off my journey of paying her fees well. I had actually told my fiancé before any marriage plans that I wanted delaying marriage because I had made that promise to my father. He had said there was no problem with that, but later after we got married I was not allowed to fulfil the promise. Oh, that killed me. I cried and cried until I accepted. My father understood because he had not asked me in the first place anyway. Then, knowing that he had gone and left me with this kind of burden in my spirit really hurt me.

At the vigil, the night before the funeral, Mr Nkumane, a pastor of one of the local churches stood up to speak and revealed that just two weeks back my father had come to him holding a bottle of beer, saying he was abandoning that kind of drink for good and wanted to accept Christ into his life. Mr Nkumane said they prayed indeed and when this happened my father was on his way back to Mhlume Sugar Company where he was working. He was returning to work after the Easter break. As Mr Nkumane sat down and the congregation was singing, a bus full of people from Mhlume was just parking outside, between our house and the vigil marquee. The people from Mhlume came in already singing their own chorus. When the singing stopped, a number of them started testifying how my father had gone to their church meeting and told them he had decided to take the Christian way.

I cannot express the joy I had. That was supposed to be a sad moment, but knowing that my father, for whom I had prayed, fasted and even organized outreach services was already at Home made me leap with joy! He gave his life to Jesus on Easter Sunday 1987, went to introduce himself to the believers on the following Sunday and had a headache which translated him home on Monday evening! God fulfilled his promise to answer my prayer. As they lowered my father's casket I collapsed and passed out. What was stabbing me was my unfulfilled promise. It was one of my aunts (father's sisters) that consoled me and said I can still keep the promise by looking after my mother well. I thank God when I had multiple streams of income later I did not ask for permission to give money I had laboured for. I still felt guilty whenever I listened to some women in women's meetings, but for once I decided to follow my heart.

Singing rekindled

It was the same year of my father's passing on, 1987 that my 'then spouse' started a part time adult education course with the University of Swaziland. Whenever he was away for his residential course in the city I saw it as an opportunity to take care of my passion to sing which could not be quenched. I decided to sing solo during morning assembly before students and teachers at Lavumisa High School where we taught. Whenever he was away I became a vibrant person; the other part of me that was stifled within always came alive.

After morning assembly one day the deputy head teacher of that school asked me why I did not sing on other days. I simply smiled it off without answering him. It was at that same time that I leaped forward and identified an evangelical church to which I walked a very long distance. I went to the church with my young son and the child minder who helped me look after the boy when I was at work teaching. It was in that church, Mgampondo Evangelical Church that I started ministering to the congregation through singing.

The same year, 1987, I fell pregnant, but that pregnancy did not stop me singing and that was the time I sang like never before. In 1988, when my son was four years old I had a second child, a baby girl, whom I carried on my back whilst holding the hand of the four year old boy walking by my side. I remember like yesterday how I stood before the pastor, Mr Isaiah Mbhamali as he received my daughter from my hands when I dedicated her to God. I was glad I was in church and I was dedicating my daughter, but growing up, I had seen couples dedicate their children together. In most of those cases I had seen the man being the one who hands the baby over to the man of God and I liked that kind of scenario, so being there alone touched a nerve in me.

An answered prayer

In 1989 God answered my prayer in an amazing way. I know he had long heard my pleas, but to me that was the time when I saw His move. My spouse was returning from the city for his residential course at The University of Swaziland when he broke the news that he had got a new job and was not going to teach anymore. He had got a competitive job in the city. When he told me we were leaving Lavumisa for Manzini I could not believe my ears. In my private prayer I poured tears of joy unendingly! In Manzini it did not take long to get a teaching post in one of the new secondary schools, Ngwane Park Secondary School. What a breakthrough!

There were numerous churches in Matsapha where we lived. When we moved to the city my in-laws entrusted me with the care of three children which I did not find to be a problem because I love children. I actually preferred being called Mama by all of them. There was no aunt. Although I enjoyed going to church it still devastated me to go there alone with my two children and three nephews I lived with. Sometimes I would see my friends from youth coming to church with their husbands and children. I hoped to once again enjoy interdenominational church meetings like I had done in my youth back there in the city. It never happened. I was allowed to go to the Sunday main church service only.

There were times when I heard gospel artists from outside the country were coming to minister in gospel music bonanzas and hoped to go, but I was not allowed. I was also not allowed to attend any evening church service. I could not be outside home after 6:00 pm and it pained my heart to hear of special church events I could not be part of. One of my great sources of pain was seeing on TV and hearing over the radio a gospel group I had been part of in my youth. I badly wanted to sing with them again and they were eager to have me sing with them again that I was back in the city, but I was not allowed to.

Evangelism

Another part of me that felt stifled was the passion for evangelism. As I have related above how I established the Mankayane High School break time evangelism ministry before going to teacher training college and also how I was part of the Dabulamazwe Outreach Group, the urge to tell people around me about the Good News increased. Telling my students about Christ was never a problem and opportunities for doing that were always in abundance. Although I told my students about Jesus Christ, I still felt the urge to reach out and talk about Him also among the people in my neighbourhood. Where we lived at the Prison Staff Quarters there was a house close to ours where on weekends I saw many people sitting outside drinking beers and just having fun, their own way. My heart went out to those people and I saw them as good ground to sow the seed of Jesus Christ's love.

On Sundays my spouse always went to watch soccer games at the national stadium or trade fair grounds, so I took advantage of his absence and asked the lady in whose house people assembled to drink to allow me to come over and sing and talk to them. When I told her I could bring an electrical piano to play she allowed me, saying that may be entertaining to her friends. My experience with my father asking me to play my guitar and sing for his friends had somehow introduced me to such ministry.

That opportunity to minister to people who did not go to church reminded me of an experience I had whilst still at William Pitcher Teacher Training College where the president of the Students' Representative Council (SRC) invited members of the Student's Christian Movement to come and sing in an event which had nothing to do with preaching. Since it was a circular gathering the rest of the believers in the choirs refused to go and sing there. I wanted the people to hear me sing for and about Christ. I was ready to take my guitar and sing alone there, but my friend, Hazel agreed to come with me. We sang and at the end of the event a woman came to us and told us she wanted us to pray with her because she wanted the Jesus we were singing about. It was such a glorious experience and later in the week another mature student came to tell us he was going to start attending our services because he liked what we were doing.

With all enthusiasm and excitement realizing I was going to do what I had not done in years and had always wanted to do, I carried the musical instrument and went to the neighbour woman's house. She told the men and women who were drinking there that I wanted to sing for them and also say something. They listened attentively as I sang and spoke about Christ. In response one of the men told me I was doing a good job and he said his own wife had been a Christian as a young person and she stopped going to church after he married her. The man was bragging about his 'achievement' of separating someone from Christ. Some said they liked the music and said they would consider going to church to get more and others simply laughed. I knew there was no other way of reaching people who never went to church apart from going to them. I did not have any arguments with those who were excited and wanted to start arguing, but I felt like I had done my part of going out to 'tell' as our Saviour said we should 'go and tell.' Worrying about the results was not part of the deal.

Stealing money from myself

Coming back into the city and expanding in my income generation helped independently earn money from which I could tithe without any restriction. Ever since marriage, my salary was not like my own anymore because it was budgeted for before it landed in my hands. I could not even tithe from it. Tithing was one of the major losses I accrued due to my decision. My spirit suffered a great deal because as a young person I had seen the manifestation of God's word related to tithing such as Malachi 3:

"Will a man rob God? Yet you rob me.
"But you ask, 'How do we rob you?'
"In tithes and offerings.
You are under a curse—the whole nation of you
—because you are robbing me.
Bring the whole tithe into the storehouse,
that there may be food in my house.
Test me in this," says the LORD Almighty"
and see if I will not throw open the floodgates of heaven
and pour out so much blessing

that you will not have room enough for it.
I will prevent pests from devouring your crops,
and the vines in your fields will not cast their fruit,"
says the LORD Almighty.
"Then all the nations will call you blessed,
for yours will be a delightful land,"
says the LORD Almighty.
(Malachi 3: 8-12NIV)

From the early days of the marriage I was not allowed to tithe and the main reason was that 'the pastors misused the money anyway'. I struggled because to me this new order was like someone strangling me and taking away from me an element that is vital for my existence. I remember even before the wedding how I had literally run out of funds for the part that I had to finance personally, how I went to my pastor, Mr Simelane.

"Oh, Betty, my daughter, we will just pray to God to show up because you tithe and God will provide," he said with a smile.

That had been a powerful word and we prayed. Amazingly, a few days after that prayer, I got a phone call from my uncle, my mother's younger brother, who had just returned from Washington DC (USA) where he had been serving as the ambassador for Swaziland. He asked me how the wedding preparations were going. I told him that a lot had already been taken care of, but there was still a shortage of money on one particular area. My uncle told me to make a list of everything I still needed. Oh God is so faithful! Hallelujah! I made the list! Later, we praised God with my pastor, Mr Simelane for swiftly answering our prayer. God answers our prayer before we even ask, but waits for us to ask and then endorse the provision or release of blessing.

I got the teaching of the importance of tithing from my church when I was young and also from men of God who carried special anointing and could teach about this subject in a special way. Pastor, *Mkhulu* (Grandfather) Ndlovu was known countrywide for his clear and effective teaching about tithing and he could deeply massage this truth even using figurative language to show how a believer who does not tithe steals from God. In my local church, Encabaneni AEC, offering time was a celebration time. We did not have people coming around collecting, but the congregation danced their way to the front where they laid their tithes. By the way, tithes and offerings were not just monetary! They were in the form of whatever people had. Harvest time was the climax of bringing back to God what belonged to Him. We sang relevant songs such as *Ngenisani* (bring it in):

97

Ngenisani! Ngenisani!
Ngenisan'okweshumi konke
'Zinkomo 'zimbuzi
Namabele nawumholo
(Bring it in! Bring it in!
Bring in all your tithes
Cattle, goats
Food and earnings)

Being married to someone who had not been taught the same way about tithes and offerings led me to stealing. As I was not allowed to tithe I started pinching or 'stealing' money to tithe secretly. I was torn between forces. I had no idea which way to take. In order to wean myself from 'stealing' money from the family money to tithe as well as give offerings I ended up reviving my extra income generation skills. I worked very hard and earned money that could not be strictly accounted for because it was from little things I did on the side outside my teaching career.

Income generation skills and talents

I developed most of my income generation skills as a result of mere interest and money was not the issue when the whole thing started. I have already mentioned above how I developed an interest in designing and sewing clothes, but this later grew to include millinery. The hat and hairpiece production skill brought me a lot of money because many women did not want to cover their heads with scarves as the culture dictates. My fancy hats and hairpieces helped them get away without being accused of going bareheaded. Whilst still at Lavumisa, every evening I was alone as my spouse drove his friend to a drinking place at Golela, although he himself did not drink. I sat there making the hats and hairpieces of various kinds and then deliver them to the numerous primary schools that fed our school, the only high school in that area.

The more money flowed in was the more the family demands rose. I cannot elaborate on that one here, but the main thing is that it still pleased me to be known as the Proverbs 31 Woman and the pride of my husband. I worked even harder and made it easy for 'us' to purchase cattle, goats in large numbers as well as residential plots and portions of a farm. I focused on my hand work and it gave me joy such that my eyes were blinded from any other thing that could have been of concern! I was happy, but that was as far as the happiness went.

Getting money and more and more of it is a good thing because it enables you to do what you want to do without any stress. Soon I realised that there were more ways of generating income apart from sewing clothes and millinery. As I was a teacher in Lavumisa, I saw the students queuing up to buy bread sandwiches and juice from market women. Sometimes the market women's wares would get finished leaving some students without food, so I joined the wagon, but I provided different wares. We bought an electric generator and a gigantic freezer in which I could store loads of 'ice block' as we called them. These were made by freezing juice that was poured in plastic bags like lolly pop.

I also baked cakes, iced and decorated them. Both students and teachers bought my sliced cakes. The cakes were a big hit and soon some of the students ordered full cakes to take home or their rented places for those who rented their dwelling places, such as what they called *Ndishini* Hostel. I taught some of the girls from the school how to bake and ice cakes, so they made money doing this for me. Basically money was never a problem, but the problem was that I did all these things covering up a void part of my life. I had grown up in an environment of joy and laughter all the time and I liked company, so the loneliness I experienced was unbearable. The busy hands helped me divert my focus from what I could not change.

When we moved into the city in 1989 things changed and I had to drop the smaller income generation activities and focus on something bigger. I got reconnected to people who knew I made my own bridal regalia and within a short period of time I was busy making wedding gowns. As I had hired some women to help me as seamstresses whilst still at Lavumisa, I did the same in the city. I hired a woman who worked for me as a seamstress. I designed and cut all the work she would do every day. She did all this in a spare room in our house, but that could not continue because people were coming from all corners of the country and the demand could not be satisfied from that kind of environment.

I registered my business and soon moved to the city. I then hired more people and trained them. All this was easy to do because teachers had more free time than most professionals in my country. Apart from the three lengthy school vacations, weekends were free and school ended by 3:00 pm. It was for that reason that by 1993 Betty's Bridal Boutique stood at the heart of Manzini, the hub of Swaziland and Betty's Own Creations, the workshop where all the manufacturing was done was also situated a street away at The Central Chambers. Those years I tasted first-hand what the Bible means:

He is like a tree planted by streams of water,
which yields its fruit in season
and whose leaf does not wither
Whatever he does prospers
(Psalm 1: 3NIV)

Betty's Own Creations was not just about sewing of Bridal wear. I had men and women working for me, some of whom were from Mozambique and they were highly skilled in tailoring. They made men's suits of all sorts. We had changing outfits for the brides after removing their wedding gowns as well as outfits for mothers-of-the-bride. We had hats and bags that went with those outfits and we did shoe decoration. Beads, pearls and sequins were in abundance and in all assorted colours for clients to pick from. I would go to Johannesburg, Durban and Pietermaritzburg, especially the Oriental Plazas to get bales of silks, satins, organza, laces, feathers, hat veiling, gut, buckram and all that kind of stuff.

By early 1994 the country was hit by a wave whereby teachers in many schools started using uniforms like the staff in banks. Some of the ladies skirts and dresses were pleated. I could not be left behind and I used my privileges as a member of the Swazi Business Growth Trust to have loans and afford pleating in Durban at a macro scale. My staff would go from school to school getting clientele and whenever we got deals we just smiled because that meant huge cheques paid at a go by the Swaziland Government (Teaching Service Commission), as the teachers' employer. Many people asked me why I was still teaching and not focusing on business. I just had no peace to do that especially because I still wanted to get a degree! All along I had Education Diplomas. At the time I did not fully understand it, but the one who made me knew what He was doing with me and where He was eventually taking me!

Here comes a writer

I heard my pastor, Matthew Ashimolowo talk of working smart as opposed to working hard and at first I did not understand what he meant, but then when comparing my streams of income and writing, I then understand. From my school days I liked writing compositions, short plays and poems, but it was not for money. Whilst still at Lavumisa High School where, I was often alone in the evenings I used to think a lot. In my lonesome hours I became very creative and wrote a lot of poems and short stories most of which were never read by anyone apart from the writer. In those poems I expressed my inner feeling. It was not the best thing to do, but I had tried what I could and having got no answers I resorted to writing. It was through pen and paper that I wept, laughed and even fought! I used to fight and if you happened to read and listen carefully to each syllable of my poetry you could see a warrior right there! I enjoyed reading the Book of Joshua in the Bible because it revealed to me the warrior side of God. Now I fully understand why we have many songs that address Him as the Man of war!

It was a great opportunity for me to hear the radio announcement that as a way of promoting the SiSwati language, Mrs Thembi Mthembu, the Senior Inspector of SiSwati in Schools had invited the legendary author of Zulu literature, the Professors, Sibusiso Nyembezi, D.B.Z. Ntuli, C.T. Msimang and other acclaimed authors to come to Swaziland and teach the Swazi people who were interested in writing SiSwati literature. Over a hundred people attended the weekend workshop. I only made it for the last day, but I thank God I happened to be one of the first ten writers whose short stories made it to publication level. That was the beginning of a lifetime passion that has since arrested me! When my first cheque of Royalties came, 'Madam' gave it to 'her man' to invest because that was the right thing to do. He invested it indeed!

Looking at all these streams of income in addition to the teaching salary, it is obvious that money has not been a problem in my life. I was financially doing well, but please do not ask me if I was happy. I know I had inner joy resulting from my relationship with God, but my knees were on the floor continually because I needed answers to prayers I had made from the very first year I got married. The prayers were ongoing because instead of answers there was an escalation of the situation. Also, do not ask about the situation because some things are better not mentioned at all, especially if they will not build up anyone. It is very easy to wonder why on earth one person has to do all this. My answer rests in God's word which I regard to be having all answers to human enigmas. It is there that we are told people are gifted differently:

> *Nevertheless, each one should retain the place in life*
> *that the Lord assigned to him*
> *and to which God has called him.*
> *This is the rule I lay down in all the churches*
> *(1 Corinthians 7: 17 NIV)*

This verse is not necessarily about our life occupations, but about our various gifting in the work of the Lord. It is also the Bible that specifically spells out clearly the differences in people's abilities through Jesus' parable of talents:

To one he gave five talents of money,
to another two talents,
and to another one talent,
each according to his ability.
Then he went on his journey.
(Matthew 25: 15 NIV)

Who are you?

It is very important to live life according to what your vocation in life is as an individual. Some people may regard this as a minor issue, but the truth is that all depends on your God-given DNA and who God really wants you to be. If you know the stories of Samuel, Samson and John the Baptist, to name, but a few you will understand that God does set apart for Himself some people to use in special missions. The Bible states clearly that much is expected from a person to whom God has given much. It may be easy to take things lightly and say what is the big deal about experiencing a few changes after marriage, but experiencing change in all these key areas of my life was like uprooting a gigantic tree and planting it in a flower pot where it does not last but withers and eventually dies. I withered to a certain extent, but I thank God I did not die!

More conflicting belief systems

My commitment to the Christian faith from childhood made me stand against all that appeared evil. As a child, things were made easier by the fact that I had support at home and at school. Whilst growing up, I remember when my father's younger brother lost children at early infancy. They were all sons. My uncle's only child that survived was Sindi, whose name means the saved or rescued one. Sindi was a girl. My father and his brothers were convinced that the loss of children was a curse that could be corrected by slaughtering a cow for *emadloti* (ancestors). Although my grandfather had pronounced clearly before he died that he did not want any recognition and honouring of ancestors in that home, my father and the extended family slaughtered a cow against my grandmother. A woman came to brew the traditional beer which my grandmother strongly detested. I remember like yesterday how my grandmother, mother and myself did not touch that meat and that was the last my father ever did it.

Now, having stood firm by my faith to stay away from a feast prepared in appeasement of 'angry' ancestors the decision I made in marrying a man who had a belief system different from mine led me to actually being one of the women who had to cook when a cow has been slaughtered for *abangasekho* (those who have gone). To many people, this is no big deal, but to me it is everything! It was my choice that did not only strip me off the things I valued the most, but it added those that I detested the most. I had to submit and I did! As a young Christian I was taught against compromise, but the choice I made compelled me to compromise! Whenever I read the following scriptures my inner person had a tingle:

Abstain from every form of evil.
(1 Thessalonians 5: 22 NKJV)

but that we write to them
to abstain from things polluted by idols,
from sexual immorality
from things strangled, and from blood
(Acts 15: 20 NKJV)

Consider the people of Israel: Do not those who eat
the sacrifices participate in the altar? Do I mean then
that a sacrifice offered to an idol is anything, or that
an idol is anything? No, but the sacrifices of pagans
are offered to demons, not to God, and I do not want
you to be participants with demons. You cannot drink
the cup of the Lord and the cup of demons too; you
cannot have a part in both the Lord's table and the
table of demons. Are we trying to arouse the Lord's
jealousy? Are we stronger than he? "Everything is
permissible"—but not everything is beneficial. "
Everything is permissible"—but not everything is
constructive.
(1 Corinthians 10: 18 – 23 NIV)

The mental picture I have of myself sitting there before huge containers of meat and taking my portion against my will reminds me of Samson whose decision to lay his head on Delilah's thighs led to his loss of eyes. The mental picture I have of Samson right now is equally pathetic. Samson, the Nazirite was ordered to dance for the Philistines as they celebrated and offered a great feast and sacrifice to Dagon their god. Samson was a man through whom Israel had experienced great victories. Beloved, please note that the Philistines could not do to any other person what they did to Samson. The enemy targets the anointed one, those with a special significant assignment to fulfil on the earth. I am grateful I have lived to tell this testimony. I know Satan's plan to stop me and destroy me did not have what is happening right now. These experiences and others which are not suitable for this platform made me desperate and then remember the word:

> *and call upon me in the day of trouble;*
> *I will deliver you, and you will honour me*
> *(Psalm 50: 15 NIV)*

Also, as things got tougher I remembered the song my bridal party sang on the day after my wedding day, as I distributed gifts to my in-laws which said *Noma indlel'inameva ubothantaza* (Even if the pathway has thorns pray). What a song! I don't know whether it was good they sang it or not, but the pathway had thorns indeed and 'Betty Girl' had to pray, so pray she did. Disclosing what kind of thorns I had to tread on cannot help anyone. Most of the time I had no proper time and space to pray, but somehow manoeuvred. It did not take long for the Mankayane High School girl and William Pitcher College young woman to 'die.' The vibrant Miss Betty of Mankayane High School 'died.'

I thought my dreams were completely shattered! Hold on, and hear me well again, Satan thought he had done away with me. He thought that was my end. He is such a liar. I cannot carry on without stressing that the devil is a liar and whatever he says will not happen will actually happen as long as we fix our eyes upon the Lord the Author and Finisher of our faith. The seed that was sown in me cannot be easily uprooted. I was taught the Word and I embraced it fully. I may have made the silly mistake of marrying a man I did not really know. He was not a bad man at all, but the truth is that marriage is about bringing together two pieces that belong together; pieces that will rise and fall together, pulling each other up. I mean people that promote and add to each other, not those who will bring down and subtract from each other.

I need to stress that hoping into a tight fitting shoe or an over-sized one with the hope that it will be okay with time never works. What normally happens is that the feet sometimes develop corns. If you have literally had corns on your feet like me you know what I am talking about. Sometimes you may try to be brave and walk on those sore feet, but I bet in no time the face shows there is trouble 'down there.'

The decision I made in 1981 which I finally sealed in 1983 when I got married cost me my identity. I lost even who I really was in God. What I became can also be portrayed by the woman in Luke 13: 10-17, who had a spirit of infirmity for eighteen years. She was bent over and could not raise herself up. In verse 16 Jesus states that she is a daughter of Abraham and also that Satan had bound her. The other striking fact about this woman is that although she was bound by Satan she went to the Synagogue. It was only Jesus who loosed her and made her well again! I am thankful to God because I am telling you this testimony now because I am loosed too.

Chapter 10

Beginning of a new day!

o o o o o o o o o o o o o o o o o o o o o o o o o o o o o o o

The dawning of my new day as I started a new life in the city meant a change of life and events altogether. It meant more opportunities and I am not one who allows golden opportunities slip by if they are available. Ngwane Park Secondary School was still new and only its second year. The buildings were still under construction, so we used the primary school buildings and we shared other facilities with the Ngwane Park Youth and Training Centre. At the youth centre they needed a business English teacher and as someone who had studied Teaching English as a Second Language as well as English for Special Purposes they asked me to teach Maths in the morning in the secondary school and Business English at the Youth and Training Centre in the afternoon. The two heads worked together to make my schedule fit into both schools.

Teaching at the youth centre gave me more opportunities such as having fellowship with the people there and sharing some of my creative skills such as playwriting and acting. I had always helped students improvise skits and short plays, but working with those young adults was very different. I also got the opportunity of advising them about possible occupations after graduating. My connection and relationship to the centre was a foundation to help me later establish a women's development group when studying at the University of Swaziland.

Taking a bus to work was not convenient at all. One of the teachers who lived in a township close to school drove to work. 'We' had already had two cars but I did not have a driver's licence. I decided to go to a driving school and I even got my licence before the appointed time because I was determined to liberate myself from using a bus to work. I was very excited to get my licence. At that time 'we' sold the smaller car that I had hoped to use. However, the

Lord continued blessing everything I did in terms of business and I afforded to buy a car cash. To my great disappointment I was not allowed to drive that car. Although I was still very skilled at playing happy outwardly, whenever people asked me why I was not driving to work when we had cars I did not know what to say in response. My frustration was unbearable and once when I was witnessing about Jesus Christ to one woman who had observed my life closely she told me that she did not need Christ in her life because she knew Christians to be miserable people.

The words of the woman I was witnessing to hurt me and I did not have anything further to say to her, because even though I knew of Christians who were not miserable I could not quote them and leave myself out. People want something that is working. They do not want to jump into a bus whose engine is not even running. Witnessing to students about Christ worked better for me because they saw my academic excellence as well as my professional occupation which were things they aspired to achieve in life too.

Although I was restricted in my movements and activities for the Lord I became very happy when we lived in Manzini because I was allowed to take on a part time Diploma in Adult Education course at the University of Swaziland (UNISWA). The opportunity to study again was a big thing to me, so at the end of the two years in 1992 I graduated and got a distinction. Seeing this positive and more fulfilling change of events made me feel good and celebrate God in my life. That was the time when my sewing and bridal business was growing. Realising that anytime money was needed I could produce it in my household made me feel great. This kind of inner fulfilment made me not focus on the more intimate challenges I was facing. When the going got tough on those unsaid areas I prayed even more. To enhance my prayer and get more practical help I read a lot of books on marriage some of which I list here:

- *Lord Change Me by Evelyn Christenson*
- *Prayer that moves mountains by Gordon Lindsay*
- *Fight for your family*
- *To have and to hold*
- *Love and Marriage*
- *Imperfect partners: perfect marriages*

In 1993 I got my third child and it was a boy. When he was a year old, at the beginning of 1994 I really felt like a piece of steak in a grill! At that very time when I felt like the heat was increasing God intervened. I saw His hand move on my behalf when later in the year my then spouse announced to me that he was going away to pursue a degree in another country for three years. To add icing on my cake he told me that I could apply to go to the local university and pursue a degree too, if I wanted. Oh my Lord, 'if I wanted?' I had been hungry for education! My Father, the on-time God orchestrated things such that in that same year the Ministry of Education was just initiating a scheme where teachers who had served the government for over five years could get a government scholarship and be paid in all four years of study, but with a twenty five percent reduction each year from the second year of study. What a breakthrough! I got in!

At university I decided to drop Mathematics because there was no English and Maths combination. My interest in writing all four genres of literature made me choose English Language and Literature. Educational Psychology, Philosophy of Education, Curriculum Design and a lot more other education related courses were part of the deal and I was elated! I was fascinated by all my lecturers and I just gulped down my mental throat everything they gave me. I remember how I obtained a clean one hundred percent for the very first multiple choice test in Educational Psychology. Almost the same thing happened for my first English literature assignment. It was an essay and could not be one hundred percent, but it was a good grade, A! I know that the natural, God given ability had a lot to do with that kind of excellence, but more than anything I was focused and excited to be finally getting the opportunity I had wanted for such a long time.

Positive confessions about the future

One of my lecturers, Dr GC looked not very far from my age and seeing her academic achievement motivated me to get a PhD too. I discovered that there were some 'doors' I wanted to enter which could only open for me with a PhD in my hand. From the very first semester of my first year of study I started telling my friends that I was going to get a PhD someday. Most of those who heard me simply laughed and said I was saying all that because it was just the beginning of my educational pursuit. They told me things were going to be tough soon and I would change my mind! Oh, my Lord those people helped me. By talking negatively to me they were only 'quenching my fire' with petrol! It burnt more.

I used to take the same mini bus with Mfundo, a young man who was fresh from high school and could have been my student if he went to the school I had been teaching. He was a Christian too and since I have a passion for youth and easily get along with them, we soon became friends. I told him about my dream to be Dr Betty someday and he said he wanted to be Dr Mfundo someday too. Whenever we met along the corridors of UNISWA we addressed each other as 'Doctor.' Amazingly, although Mfundo does not have his PhD yet, he is not where his classmates are. He has climbed his own ladder in an amazing way and that PhD is along the way!

Free to drive that car at last

As I took public transport to and from university the car I had bought two years back was still sitting in front of the house. One of my friends asked me why I was not driving that car. I told her I was not allowed to, and she laughed and said I was joking. She asked me how I could be scared of someone who was away in another country. I was convinced I had to obey him even in his absence. After much talking to me and explaining how she felt my kind of emotional abuse had made me very naive under the camouflage of loyalty, the truth came out and I decided to drive that car. I had got my licence two years earlier and had driven it for a short while and stopped when I was ordered to stop. To wake me up from where I was sitting like a hen brooding over eggs that would never hatch, God used my friend SM who never left me alone. It became clear indeed that I really needed to drive, especially because I stayed off campus with my children and I had my business in town. By the time my spouse came home for his vacation I was out and about 'cruising' in my Peugeot.

Madam in a hat - come rain or shine

As a young woman I had been very stylistic and did all sorts of styles with my hair. My students at Mankayane High School used to complement my styles a lot, but from the time I got married I was not allowed to comb my hair like some women in town did. I had to cover my hair and that made me look a little senior than my age. I did not like tying scarves, so I opted for fancy hats and overdressed even when going to work such that you would think my relative was getting married. In weddings I would sometimes '*mourn more than the bereaved!*' I mean, I would overdress and I carried this kind of lifestyle and hat wearing to UNISWA. Everyday my classmates, especially the younger ones who were fresh from school would ask me where I was going that day and when I asked why they were asking they would say they were asking because of my dress code. Overdressing was a trend among the education women students, but my young classmates made a comment which showed me the odd thing about me was wearing those 'Lady Diana' and 'Queen Elizabeth' hats to class. One woman senior lecturer also made a comment that freed me and off came the hats from my head. My spouse's degree pursuit at the University of Botswana proved to be a great blessing for me.

More creative explorations

One day my English Literature lecturer, Dr Oyegoke told us about a creative writer's workshop that he conducted with interested students. I saw an opportunity and I went for it. That was a marvellous group to be among. We supported one another in an amazing way. Before coming to UNISWA I had already been actively involved with the Umdlandla Swaziland Writers and Authors' Association where I was a member of the steering committee first as the Public Relations Officer and then I was currently the Secretary General. I had been involved in helping aspirant writers although I was and still feel like I am an aspiring writer myself. As members of the Writers' Workshop we wrote creative work such as poems, short plays and short stories and then made presentations at our Friday workshops. At the end of each academic year we had a Creative Writers' Collage, where we made presentations for the whole university community.

The last time I had acted before an audience of that nature had been in 1980 at William Pitcher having started from when I was about six years of age. My acting again at UNISWA was literally like bringing back to life a dead person. The old young Betty came back to life. I performed my poem *Ntfombi YeliSwati* (Swazi Woman) with passion as the whole lecture theatre applauded and laughed all the way through. I was doing what I really enjoyed. It was through the same workshops that I got motivated to write a collection of short stories that I entitled *Hills and Valleys*. Three of my short stories from that anthology won prizes. On one of the creative collage events I acted a one woman play, *Please Don't!* The play was partially based on my real experience. It was about a woman who had experienced extreme disappointment to the point of committing suicide. Before the woman dies she regrets and wants to live, but it is too late and she dies.

At the end of the play I took the role of another woman who comes into the death scene and then cautions the audience against suicidal attempts. I concluded that performance by singing a song with my friend, Hazel and a few other participants as my son Sbusiso played the electro-organ for us. The main message of the song was directed at anyone frustrated to the point of thinking of death, advising them to talk about their frustration to someone else even if it that someone goes on to talk about it later, because at least, that way the death may be stopped.

It did not take long for some of my lecturers to identify my difference. Some of them encouraged me to work even harder, telling me that they saw great things happening through me in the near future. At the time I regarded being a university lecturer as a great thing and it was therefore one of my ambitions and I wanted to lecture at the University of Swaziland. They told me that one route toward lecturing was getting exceptionally good results which often led to the university recruiting you as a teaching assistant. The next step would be to be sent to a university abroad for a higher degree. A majority of the local lecturers with MA and Doctoral Degrees had got into the system that way. Since I wanted this so badly I did my part and excelled in all my four years of study at The University of Swaziland, getting the Sino-Swazi award for best the best first year student in the faculty of education and the Dean's award for the best final year student in the faculty of education.

Getting my desired results did not come very easily. I had to be focused and wax my ears to all naysayers. There were times when some of the people I regarded as friends would make fun of my pursuit for excellence in everything I did. Whenever I heard unkind words hurled at me I used to speak to my inner self. Being my best was the main issue to me. I was not competing with anyone, but I wanted to be satisfied whatever grade I got was the best possible I could get. It was my father who kindled my pursuit for excellence from the time I was young. He amazed me one day as I was getting an outfit ready for a customer, by telling me that I should aim at presenting my work such that it is hard for people to tell whether it was a ready-made outfit from a shop or sewn using a domestic machine. He coached me there in a way that was to stay with me all my life.

In my final year of study I had to stay on campus and I used to lock myself in my room and put an ambiguous sticker note on my door written "Check later at..." That note did not say whether I was in or not and that way I avoided distractions. There was a lot of work to do within a short time, including an educational research project. An academic year is nine months, so from the beginning of the final year I wrote a poem and put it on my room notice board. The poem stated that all I had was nine months to deliver 'my baby.' It implied how a pregnant woman has to live differently from other people in order to deliver a healthy baby. Sometimes I had to cross night and sometimes I went with no TV and even news for days on end! It paid dividends.

Children discovering more about God

The three years I was left alone with my children brought many changes both at home and outside. I started conducting evening prayer time daily and we used to sing and share the Word. The two older children Sbusiso and Nqobile had already accepted Christ as Lord and Saviour, so I gave them the opportunity to share the Word too. Sbusiso would play the electro-organ as we sang before prayer. I taught them many songs most of which were about the *faith* theme. I started ministering in song at church and very soon when

I was given the opportunity to minister that way I sang with the children. Twice as we were singing, a prophetic word was given over my life and the children. One was given by one of the church elders or deacons and the second one was given by a man of God from Canada who worked for The Trans World Radio. I received those prophetic words and I am glad I have lived to see them come to pass as the years go by! More is still happening. Amen and Amen!

One day, in the morning I discovered that as we were asleep the house had been broken into and a lot of things including electronics, video tapes and even food from the refrigerator were stolen. I reported the case to the police and they came to do what they could do, but they did not have any clue. In the evening when we were just about to pray and we were taking out the organ we discovered it was also gone. Oh, that was a blow on my side. I literally cried and just did not know what to do. My daughter who was about eight or nine then did not cry at all; she became a charging rhino. She made a very aggressive prayer and I saw **FAITH** right there in front of me, but I was too confused to get it well:

"You devil are a liar! We want our keyboard back," she said, as that is what we called electro-organs.

"We want our key board back, right now. We use this key board to sing for God at church!"

For a while Nqobile did not pray to God, but she was giving a command to the enemy to return what he had stolen. I had taught my children and had demonstrated this kind of commanding and binding before I release something, but that night it just did not occur to me to do it. I was in great shock because of all the recent events. My daughter went on to call the musical instrument,

"Keyboard, wherever you are, we are calling you back! Come back home! We use you to serve God at church!"

Nqobile started crying as she then asked God to bring our musical instrument back and she just poured out her heart stating how much we loved to sing in accompaniment of our electro-organ. She said her prayer and boldly concluded by stating, she was praying in the powerful name of Jesus Christ of Nazareth. That is what I was taught and that is also what I had taught those children. As we went to sleep we were all upset and somehow very down in our spirits. On the next day at university I shared this catastrophe with other believers at the lunch fellowship where the Lord had opened a door and I sometimes preached. They prayed with me. In the evening as I was parking the car I saw a shiny object on the lawn. I stopped the car and went to check the shiny thing; Oh Hallelujah, it was our YAMAHA! It was back. What a joy it was to see God moved by a child's prayer of faith. What the enemy did as an attempt to frustrate us hit back on him because that incident engraved in me and my children what nothing else can ever erase!

What we established with the children could not be stopped anymore. When their father had finished his studies and was back in the country we had to pray in the girl's bedroom because we could not use the living and dining rooms anymore. It was a bit abnormal after what we were used to, but we prayed there because we could not pray with the television or other entertainment means on. The good news is that God was in the house and that was all that mattered to me.

Graduation time!

Hearing my name called to go and receive the Dean of Education's Award was a dream come true. I bowed as I went to have my hand shaken by the King Mswati III. That was a big thing to me. My main dream had been to work for the university as a teaching assistant. I had got the required results and there was actually a need for teaching assistants in the English department, especially Literature my area of interest, but to my surprise, that year the university had decided to stop taking teaching assistants for reasons I never got to know till now. In my heart I felt a sense of disappointment. I knew most of my colleagues were aware of the possibility of my getting a job with the university, so it was demoralising to start looking for a job in schools. There were no vacancies in the city where I lived.

I went to the Teaching Service Commission (TSC) for employment and they told me I was 'lucky' to get a post at Lavundlamanti, one of the schools in rural Swaziland where they needed an English Literature teacher. I could commute from the city to that school or live there and come home on weekends, so I took the offer. Many of my colleagues who had not put that extra effort and had got average results were already in good schools in the city. I began to feel like God had let me down after all the hard work. Every morning I had to wake up very early and get a bus to work at about 5.00 am and return home in the late evening. Driving there proved to be almost impossible because apart from the distance the road was also not very good for use every day. I took my new situation graciously, believing God for something better. I got my courage from God's Word which was my daily food. I liked this special one:

> *And we know that in all things God works*
> *for the good of those who love him, who*
> *have been called according to his purpose*
> *(Romans 8:28 NIV)*

Soon I heard that some of my English Literature colleagues who were there when our lecturer made comments that I was going to be a lecturer someday were making fun of me. One of them sneered behind my back sarcastically saying that she did not know that there was 'a university at Lavundlamanti.' Hearing this made me to trust God more and believe for a better job. I had applied for an advertised post at William Pitcher Teacher Training College, but I got a 'regret' reply, and felt very shattered. I decided to hold on to the above verse believing that something was to come out of the situation. It was when I was almost comfortable with my hard situation that God showed up and that was one of those 'and suddenly' cases, where God shows up with something good for you when you least expect it.

One afternoon I left school early because it was half day and as I just came off the bus from Lavundlamanti, I jumped into a Christian lady, Mrs DM who was one of the teachers at Lozitha High school and her husband was a government minister then.

"Betty it's been a long time since I last saw you, where have you been?" Mrs DM said as we hugged each other.

I told her my sad story of commuting to Lavundlamanti everyday because there were no vacancies in the city schools. Not even at Ngwane Park High school, the school I had taught in before going to university for my degree course. I related to DM how things were hard to the extent that my situation as a teacher with a teacher's diploma was even better than my having a degree and teaching in such a remote area. The difference in my salary was consumed by my commuting expenses. DM just smiled in a way I failed to understand at first.

"Look here, you don't have to worry now," she paused, smiled and continued,

"You know God's ways are amazing Betty. I was just debating how I will deliver my case to my Head teacher. We are going to Switzerland. My husband has a post which he has to take up there urgently," she continued with a smile.

She told me hearing my story was a miracle for her as well because she was still thinking of how to tell the school head teacher of her sudden departure, at such an awkward time of the year, the third term. To cut the long story short, with Mrs DM's permission I went to her head teacher and told him of her sudden move. The head teacher wrote me a letter to the TSC, applying for a teacher to replace her. I had my own letter applying for a transfer from Lavundlamanti to Lozitha. The officer at the TSC had no chance of even reserving the post for anyone he may have had in line because he did not even know that Minister M was leaving the country. By the time the news came on TV and radio, and teachers flocked to the TSC to apply to replace Mrs DM my case was already set and done.

Beloved, this is not just a tale, but my aim is to encourage those who feel like carrying on having faith in God seems not to bear any fruit. I want to say this thing called **faith in God** really works, but sometimes there is a certain period of **waiting** involved, and when your time comes you never regret. God saves the best for last. He is ever so faithful. I taught at Lozitha High school for only one school term, from September to early December.

When I realised my lectureship dream was not working yet I had sent an application to the TSC when they advertised deputy headship posts in several schools in the country. Whilst I was at Lozitha the TSC called me for an interview. At that time I had even forgotten that I had applied for the post of deputy head teacher in one of the schools in the Manzini region. I got the job. Amazingly, in the school I was posted to, there were squabbles among some of the teachers and the TSC ended up sending me to Ngwane Park High School, the same school I had taught in before going to university in 1994. I was surprised to learn that my salary as deputy head teacher of a high school was more than that of a college lecturer. In my heart I felt like singing "Look what the Lord has done…"

When God closed the door towards lecturing at William Pitcher College, He wanted to open the bigger door of deputy headship. It is true; God closes small doors to open bigger ones and sometimes doors which are as big as gates. Now with my new job as deputy head teacher of Ngwane Park High School, well placed in the Manzini city, where I had my businesses I felt like I had finally 'arrived' and had to sit and enjoy life. However, with us children of God things are not like that. We do not 'arrive' here on earth. Things keep getting better and better. We will arrive when we get to heaven. However, before we get to heaven there is some life to live here on earth!

Chapter 11

A New Life indeed

○ ○

My four years of study at UNISWA were packed with life changing experiences as I have stated above as well as the home-going of one of my family members. My family lost my father's younger brother, *Babe* Bhekimpi Abednego, but that left me with a testimony because God accorded me the opportunity to nurse him whilst hospitalised for a few days at the Raleigh Fitkin Memorial Hospital in Manzini. He gave his life to Jesus the night he was to go home. I had prayed for him so many times and that special night, whilst changing him and feeding him like a baby I asked him if he heard what the evangelist had been saying. He agreed and when I asked him what his response was, he accepted the invitation. As everybody was wailing at the night vigil before his funeral I had the privilege of being the one to stand up boldly and announce the unexpected news of his salvation. I still had tears fall down my face, but I had the comforting truth that I would see him at Home someday.

Although toward the end of 1998 I had the blessing of being promoted to the position of deputy head of Ngwane Park High School, the years 1999 to 2001 were the peak point of my grilling. If I had been an expert in wearing my make up to look good on the outside and hide the inner pain, the heat in the grill walloped me and I could do it no more. As I hopped into the New Year, 1999, I felt like I was the happiest person ever. I had seen most of my dreams coming into realization. Whilst on my third year of my Bachelor of Education studies at the University of Swaziland I had taken it upon myself to make plans to excel in my educational research project which is what most of our forerunners had told us could be a challenge. So, I wanted to take a page or two from 'wise ant' and prepare for the winter in the summer.

Further Studies

I looked for a supervisor early and I was happy to make an agreement with Dr A. Nxumalo to be the one. I asked him a lot of questions regarding what I had to do to excel. One of his pieces of advice which I regard as gold up to today was that I had to start associating with veteran researchers. He advised me to join the Swaziland Educational Researchers Association (SERA). I did and in a month's time Swaziland was hosting a symposium. Apart from the Southern African region there were representative from abroad such as England and America.

In that symposium I got connected to a professor from Sussex University in England. I went to talk to her about what I wanted to research on and she gave me good advice. When she was back in England she started sending me Sussex University prospectuses whilst I was still pursuing my Bachelor of Education Degree and from our connection I fell in love with Sussex University. I was determined when I study further I would do my Masters Degree there. I started applying right away whilst pursuing my B. Ed degree. Sussex University told me I had to possess an Honours English degree before I pursue their MA program. I was determined to go to Sussex University, and therefore, as a way of complying with their demands I decided to apply to the University of South Africa (UNISA) to pursue an Honours English Degree part-time. They accepted me and my program was to commence in February 1999. I made all these plans for further studies prior to my appointment as deputy head teacher of NPHS.

As 1999, the New Year showed its face, I braced up to start work even before schools reopened. January is the most hectic month of the year for school heads because that is when they make their admissions. It is very demanding to be involved in students' admissions in a city school like NPHS, where parents and guardians start queuing up as early as 05: 00 am, when the very first buses going there start operating. Seeing the pleading faces looking at you with eyes of hope for a place in Form 1 and Form 4 when you know very well there is limited space is difficult. Some parents would say the weirdest of things:

"*Deputy*, I understand there is no more space left, but I don't mind even if you squeeze my child in a very small corner of the classroom...."

Others would even say the least expected:

"Madam, please plead for me with your Head. I can bring whatever you name..."

Those are the ones used to 'greasing' or bribery. Others would even promise to buy their child's own desk and chair. From that experience I discovered that one of the hardest things for a school head to do was standing firm to tell somebody to go home with their child because there was no more space in the school and telling them to try other schools in remote places. Through the wise guidance and mentorship of the head teacher, Mr Zwane or *M'Era*, as we used to call him, I learnt how to stand firm without hurting the already hurting as, well as dexterously deliver the sad truth that they had to honestly try elsewhere.

On the very first day in my office, whilst attending parents who were queuing up to seek a place in Form 4, I encountered a woman who came crying, saying her son did not want to return to school and was threatening to kill his father with a gun. As I saw tears fall down the woman's eyes, something welled up in me and I held her hands and told her that things were going to be fine. From our conversation I gathered that she was a Christian and I told her how strongly I believed God could change the situation. Holding the woman's hands, we both closed our eyes and I prayed in the name of Jesus Christ of Nazareth. I told her to send the young man to me on the next day and indeed the young man came on the following day. I had a very relaxed conversation with him. God gave me a way of reaching to the young man's faculties and by the time he left my office he was ready for school in a few days. His mother could not believe her son had agreed to return to school and had given up the idea of killing his father.

The office of the deputy head teacher had multiple functions, ranging from general school administration, counselling, students discipline and sometimes in-house discipline of teachers if need be. The latter was tough to carry out, but God had yoked me with Mr Eric Zwane, a well sizzled school administrator who, prior to his promotion to head NPHS, had been the chief deputy head teacher of Matsapha Swazi National High School, the largest school in the country, which was not different from many schools brought together. *M'Era* mentored me until I fitted into that hot seat.

Sometimes my office became some kind of mini-prayer room. God gave me the opportunity of ministering to parents, students and some teachers who brought various issues and problems. From the onset God had revealed to me that He was the one to show me how to perform in that position. There were people with conflict issues as well as those who were struggling to get school fees, books and more. There were times when all I could do was pray with the person and indeed help would come even where I had no idea it would. The staff members had an amazing spirit of sharing. Together we established funds to assist those who desperately needed help. We established the Lend a Hand Fund, which was a contribution from everyone including students and teachers. During my two and a half years in that office we were able to pay school fees, buy books, uniform and we even shouldered all funeral expenses when one of our students passed away.

In the same office some students gave their lives to Jesus Christ as I led them to God in prayer. It was amazing to see a dramatic transformation in some of my students. One special example was Abraham Bulunga, whose name I write in full here with great confidence because in spite of being a genius and qualifying to study whatever he wanted at university, he accepted God's call to Bible College in South Africa. Initially, Abraham belonged to the Muslim religion, but after hearing his brother Abdou tell him what I shared about Christ he made a decision too. Like the brothers, Andrew and Peter the two Bulunga boys brought each other to Christ. Similar to Peter and Andrew the one who was brought to Jesus later ended up being the prominent one:

Andrew, Simon Peter's brother,
Was one of the two who heard what John
had said and who had followed Jesus.
The first thing Andrew did was to find his brother Simon
and tell him,
"We have found the Messiah"
(that is, the Christ)
And he brought him to Jesus.
Jesus looked at him and said,
"You are Simon son of John.
You will be called Cephas"
(which, when translated, is Peter)
(John 1: 40 – 42 NIV)

One of the serious decisions I made as I took on my new responsibility was to initiate internally steered revivals. In the school there used to be revivals once or twice a term (trimester) where we used to have a man or woman of God from outside the school come to preach in our morning assembly for the whole week. We came into agreement with the other teachers involved with the Christian Students Fellowship as well as the students themselves that it would be a good idea to have weeks where for the whole week we had preachers from within the school. The head teacher supported the idea and then those of us who felt led to do this, took turns to preach before both teachers and students. That was a dream-come-true for me. As you already know, this was partially because of my Mankayane High School background and upbringing.

I had the wonderful opportunity of establishing a drama club and the students responded amazingly. We had numerous theatrical performances within the school which addressed serious issues such as drug and alcohol abuse. My drama group performed marvellously and I decided to expose them to performing for larger and outside audiences such as at UNISWA. At the university my students performed very well in both Siswati and English. We felt like we were just a small family. Up to now I cherish the pictures we captured whilst out to perform at UNISWA.

As a way of promoting English proficiency among my students I brought heaps of magazines, both old and new into my office and the traffic into my office was always busy with students coming to borrow as well as returning old ones. We also improved the school library as much as we could. I established writing competitions among students and the event that really motivated them was the Speech and Prize Giving Day. The very first year we were appointed to head the school with Mr Zwane, the staff members wanted to have this special day in the school. We were also going to have our first issue of *The Laurel*, the school annual magazine. Both teachers and students' talents were sharpened because we were all involved every step of the way. I was elected by the teachers to be editor-in-chief, but students entered a competition in poetry and the naming of the school magazine, thus we got *The Laurel!*

Reflecting on my life now I realise that I had differing lifestyles. At school I was a vibrant woman who just unleashed all she had within her, but at home I was a timid and voiceless zombie! In my businesses I was *Mama* to my staff without considering age and we had a lot of fun especially when the business was doing well and money was flowing in. Surprise packages both at month end and Christmas were determined by the productivity of the staff and the money we made. The atmosphere was often brilliant!

On weekends I taught English at UNISWA's Institute of Distant Education and to my students I was 'Mama Motivation' who demystified 'the thing called Literary Theory.' It really boosted my self esteem to hear those hundreds of students say "we wish you were our full time lecturer, not just our tutor, because you make the thing so easy to understand!"

In spite of the conflicting life at home and work my daytime life seemed to be taking over and I felt happy. I got more fulfilment from seeing the happy faces light up whenever I had helped someone. Two of my very brilliant students could not even afford paying their exam fee. As I saw the need before me, God reminded me of a decision I had made even before I was married. As a young girl, when I discovered what happened to a woman called Dorcas in the Bible I purposed to do acts of kindness to those who cannot help themselves. I wanted something similar to what happened to Dorcas to happen to me too:

In Joppa there was a disciple named Tabitha
(which, when translated, is Dorcas),
who was always doing good and helping the poor.
About that time she became sick and died,
and her body was washed and placed in an upstairs room.
Lydda was near Joppa;
so when the disciples heard that Peter was in Lydda,
they sent two men to him and urged him,
"Please come at once!"
Peter went with them,
and when he arrived he was taken upstairs to the room.
All the widows stood around him,
crying and showing him the robes and other clothing
that Dorcas had made while she was still with them.
Peter sent them all out of the room;
then he got down on his knees and prayed.
Turning toward the dead woman,
he said, "Tabitha, get up."
She opened her eyes, and seeing Peter she sat up.
He took her by the hand and helped her to her feet.
Then he called the believers and the widows
and presented her to them alive.
(Acts 9: 36-41 NIV)

I helped those students pay their exam fees. It was such a delight to see their good results with credits in English language and literature the subjects I taught them. It was at the same period of my life that I had a very strong urge to help a child who had no one to support and was brought to me by a woman asking for work. I took the child to help play with my young one, but I could not stand seeing a child stay out of school when her age-mates were in school. I took that child in and asked my mother to stay with her and go to school the following year.

It was at that same time that I went to the funeral of a woman who was a close relative of my in-laws. I watched as her two young daughters were just collapsing as they saw their mother's casket lowered down. I heard so clearly as in an audible voice that I had to fully mother one of those girls. I felt like that was just impossible because two of our own children were in a private school with exorbitant fees. The voice persisted. I cried and cried and knew it would be difficult to even express what I had just heard. Still crying, I went to another elderly woman and shared what had happened. She encouraged me to obey. When I told my children's father about this he said he did not mind as long as I would be able to pay the money. That was a huge responsibility, but I knew God had spoken and there was nothing to do, but obey. One thing I like about God is that He brings to completion whatever He starts! The songs we used to sing from childhood kept me encouraged:

Let's love one another
Let's love one and all
Let's love one another
And God will; bless all.

Be kind to one another
Be kind to one and all
Be kind to one another
And God will bless us all

Let's do for one another
Let's do for one and all
Let's do for one another
And God will bless all

In the years 1999 to 2001 my plate of responsibilities was full indeed. Although to an outsider it may look like I had deliberately designed things myself, the fact was God was setting me up for the lift-up that came to me as a very ugly picture. Anyway I believe you also know God's ways better, especially if you are familiar with life stories of the likes of Abraham, Jacob, Joseph, David to name, but a few. He sets you up and then sticks by you to reveal His faithfulness. At that same time I got a mysterious illness. One night I thought I was dying and I was ready for it. On the next day I asked NFN, one of my children's aunt (Big Mama as we say in our culture) to please take good care of my three children when I was gone. God used KN, my children's cousin who was already married to assist me. She shouldered all my medical needs and I finally got back to life. Miraculously, I also got that Honours degree at UNISA!

My celebration was short-lived and more challenges came like a flood. I somehow felt hopeless then, but the good news is challenges or no challenges we are winners as the Bible states:

When the enemy comes in like a flood, The Spirit of
the LORD will lift up a standard against him.
(Isaiah 59: 19b NKJV)

I sat on my lovely black leather swinging chair with my hands and head despondently placed on the massive mahogany desk. There were big leafy indoor plants and everything that I had designed and put in there to make my office in the new administration building resemble the person I felt I really was. The office was quite beautiful and very spacious, but something was just wrong. Again I had been crying all night long asking questions whose answers seemed to be adamantly refusing to come my way.

I could not talk about the internal turmoil. Finally, I decided to call one of my prayer partners whom I regarded as a friend. She was much younger than me and taught in my school too as well as co pastor a church with her husband. There was no need to say much. She read the story on my face and then prayed with me. Some issues are not just to be prayed about; they require action. I felt like I was at the edge of a cliff. I had been well groomed about keeping private things private and for me even a looming death had been taken as a private matter. All I could tell '*Mkhokheli'12* Khulile was that things were hard and I felt like I was done and over with! I still feel like mentioning details will help no one, especially because the aim of this testimony is to build and not destroy.

We prayed, but I completely lost hope because I had realised that God had always answered my prayers pertaining to my personal development except for the thing that mattered the most to me. Marriage was and still is very important to me. I just did not understand what was going on because God used me to minister to people who were having problems in their marriages and things worked amicably thereafter. In the cases where God used me both parties were ready to work things out. At first I thought the reason I was involved with helping married couples was that I owned a Bridal Boutique. Later I realised God had given me deep understanding of how relationships work, but the sad truth is that marriage is not one legged. You do not sing solo there, but it is a duet and actually it works even better in spite of challenges if you sing a trio, with God being the central pillar!

The turmoil from my private world was embarrassingly interfering with my work. I saw no hope. One day I walked away from school during school hours, and in my head I heard voices telling me to keep on walking and never stop. Then suddenly a small still voice in my heart asked me what I was doing. I remembered that I am a child of God and I am not desperate at all because my Father promises in His Word to never leave nor forsake us:

> *For He Himself has said,*
> *"I will never leave you nor forsake you."*
> *(Hebrews 13: 5 b NKJV)*

I hated my life, and this was close to hating myself too. Basically, I was a very rich-poor woman, because we had property in excess, but all that could not help me. The enemy hastily brought suggestions to me, but Holy Spirit never kept quiet either. He spoke in a very steady voice reassuring me that He was always there for me.

Just let Jesus know about it

One Sunday morning things just went really bad and that morning I was going to minister in song at church with the children. We had many songs that we had sung and felt ready to share with the congregation, but that morning I just saw no point of singing for the sake of singing. I needed answers. I went into the bathroom and prayed silently, asking God to help me out of my situation. God had actually revealed the reality of the situation from the onset in 1983, but I was in denial. He had used so many avenues including dreams. Once, I had a dream and then when I woke up from the dream I went to use the bathroom, but coming from there discovered that what I had just seen in the dream was actually happening in the living room.

The enemy thought he had me on the hip because he was employing emotional pain rather than physical pain. Emotional pain is deadly, because people see you without any physical bruises and they think you are okay. They do not realise that you could just be at the verge of a permanent mental breakdown. Also, no one can really see what is going on because in spite of the internal damage the outward presentation can give a contrary picture. At that time the bathroom was my sacred place of prayer, and I could sit there and tell it all to my heavenly Father, as quickly as I could, before anyone wanted to use the room. By the time I came out my eyes would be dry. I looked a little bit normal and sometimes one would anticipate I was a little bit ill or something like that. I tried to do my Sunday morning businesses in the house normally, but there was no way I could be normal where abnormality prevailed. When I came out of the bathroom God had given me a new song.

Sbusiso, the first born child had been playing some music which I really liked and we had to work on lyrics soon. God gave me the lyrics in a split second and I wrote them down. I asked him to get the keyboard and he played. I fitted the lyrics and the song was right there. My daughter came and there we were with a new song. As we sang my daughter even had a way of coming in after one of the stanzas in a way that made the song just beautiful. Using the words of the song I encouraged myself and refused to go down. We sang it again and again that morning, and I strongly felt I had to give my testimony at church. The children agreed they were confident we could sing the song and we went to sing it that Sunday morning.

Before that we had never composed a song and sung it at church the same day, but that was not just a song; it was words from my heart. At church I asked to sing with the children during testimony time, as we normally did. Before we sang, as Sbusiso was still playing the music I started speaking to the church congregation right there. We had not planned this with the children, but I went ahead and spoke as I felt led to:

There was once a woman who was troubled because she had no children and her husband's other wife despised her. Her name was Hannah. Hannah had been crying for years in her heart, and one day she decided enough was enough. She went to the temple and poured out her heart to God. The high priest, Eli thought she was a drunken woman, but she was not. God heard her prayer. She got the son she needed, and called him Samuel. I believe there are many Hannahs this morning who are going through various experiences. Whatever it is that is wearing you down in your heart you have to tell it to God right now. I have also told God my own issues and he has given me this song which we will share with you now. I stopped, and Sbusiso played on to a good point of starting the singing. We sang:

> *God answers prayer whenever you let Him know*
> *God answers prayer whenever you let Him know*
> *God answers prayer whenever you let Him know*
> *Whenever you let Him know*
> *Whenever you let Him know*
>
> *Whenever you get to crossroads*
> *Whenever your sky seems dim*
> *Whenever all seem so dark*
> *You better let Him know*
> *You better let*
> *You better let Him know …*

I remember so well that Sunday morning immediately we finished singing, one of the church elders prayed for me and the three children. People thought we were a quartet, because four of us stood up there to sing, but with the youngest one just standing there looking at us. We were actually a quintet with only three audible voices, four physical bodies standing there with the fifth member neither seen nor heard, but heavily felt as one received the singing in spirit! The church elder had a prophetic word for us, and I embraced it. It was a confirmation of things God had said to me as a young lady teacher of twenty years of age. The elder said God just gave him a picture in the future where my family was used by God especially the girl. He went on to describe the picture God had given him.

Giving of prophetic words was not a usual thing in that church, but there it was. It is so wonderful to say that today as I am writing this testimony part of the prophecy has actually come to pass, and we believe for more to come. Just like Hannah decided enough was enough, I said my own 'enough is enough' in my heart and I believe the seed to pursue God in a different way was birthed at that very time which the enemy had orchestrated for destruction. Something good came out of that!

Well, good things do not always come just like that; they take processes and some of those processes require the death of something such as the death of a seed before the birth of a plant and plenteous fruit. As I have just said, things had become really bad, I mean very ugly! I went to God in a way I had never done before. I was a bit daring and asking Him questions I had never asked Him before. I was somehow accusing the Creator of the universe for abandoning me. I was accusing Him for not answering my prayer. I was asking Him where He was. I told Him what I was tired of doing. After throwing all the temper tantrums before my Heavenly Father I was a bit exhausted and had nothing more to say. When I was quiet and just lay there like a dejected little girl He then spoke to me. He was steady and I knew He had spoken. I knew it.

My Heavenly Father told me that He never leaves His own which meant He had always been there. I did not get the whole point because at the time there was a lot I was holding on to, thinking He was the one who placed it all in my hands. I had been crying to Him for things to change and He gave me my answer, saying everything was already there and I could only realise it fully if I engage in a walk of faith with Him. I thought I was already in a walk of faith, but He gave me Hebrews 11 verses 1 and 6. It was like I was seeing those verses for the very first time ever in my life! Wow!

Chapter 12

A Walk of Faith

Now faith is the substance of things hoped for,
The evidence of things not seen…
But without faith it is impossible to please Him,
For he who comes to God must believe that He is,
And that He is a rewarder of those who diligently seek Him.
(Hebrews 11: 1 & 6 NKJV)

No pleasing God without faith

I looked over and over again at the above scripture and then eventually I got the point. When I said enough is enough I had just received a threat that shocked me. It was not the first time I had got such a shock. The first time I got a shock was when I noted things were not as I had thought they were. I was just discovering that in my marriage we were viewing God and going to church differently. I thought it was a mandate from God, but the response I got was "no one can tell me what to do!" It was the first time I ever heard someone I believed to be a Christian express that they did not care what God had said. More than anything I was shocked because I had always known the fear of God as the force that brings order into life. Although that was hard at first, I eventually came to terms with the reality that I was on my own in the church going business.

The second major shock I got was the realization that the concept of marriage and joint parenting I had always thought I was in was an illusion that never happened. It was a show for the world, but reality was "girl, you are on your own!" Although I had seen the reality happen I still held on to the illusion that someday things would change, but when I was told that I could bring up the children on my own I almost lost it and just did not know where to go. Going for help from men and women of God had not helped me because they all told me what I already knew, and there was no person with a voice of authority that could say something and help me in my situation. In my limited thinking, in that hour of darkness I saw working full time for the University of Swaziland as the closest way out of my dilemma.

I looked ahead and realised that getting a Masters Degree would be my quickest entry into the university. I knew a part-time pursuit of a Masters Degree at UNISA would take what I regarded as 'ages'. Mine was a case of 'do or die'. The question was how on earth I was going to see this thing happen. Now God brought His master scripture Hebrews 11: 1 and 6. In verse 1 He told me clearly what faith is and in verse 6 He told me a new aspect which spelt clearly that although having faith was going to benefit me, having no faith was out of question for those who claim to belong to Him. The sixth verse pronounced clearly that if I did not engage in the walk of faith as described in the first verse, I would not please Him at all. Pleasing God was always my mission from the time I gave my life to Jesus. As I pondered over the verses I saw crystal clearly where the connection was. I was in a bad situation where no one on earth knew what was grilling me and I was not ready to disclose anything, so I was hoping to get funding to go and study in England for a year and then come back to lecture at UNISWA.

It all came out so clearly that the object of my desire was a scholarship to study abroad and faith required me not to just wish, but to count it as already done; not only by believing in my heart, but by practically living like it had already happened! Father told me that He wanted me to engage in a walk of faith with Him like He did with the Patriarchs such as Enoch, Noah and Abraham to name, but a few:

And after he became the father of Methuselah,
Enoch walked with God 300 years and had other sons and daughters.
Altogether, Enoch lived 365 years.
Enoch walked with God; then he was no more,
because God took him away.
(Genesis 5: 22 – 24)

By faith Enoch was taken from this life,
so that he did not experience death;
he could not be found, because God had taken him away.
For before he was taken,
he was commended as one who pleased God.
(Hebrews 11: 5NKJV)

By faith Noah, being divinely warned of things not yet seen,
moved with godly fear,

> *prepared an ark for the saving of his household,*
> *by which he condemned the world and became heir of the righteousness*
> *Which is according to faith.*
> *(Hebrew 11: 7 NKJV)*

> *By faith Abraham obeyed when he was called to go out to the place*
> *which he would receive as an inheritance.*
> *And he went out, not knowing where he was going.*
> *By faith he dwelt in the land of promise as in a foreign country,*
> *dwelling in tents with Isaac and Jacob,*
> *the heirs with him of the same promise;*
> *for he waited for the city which has foundations,*
> *whose builder and maker is God.*
> *By faith Sarah herself also received strength to conceive seed,*
> *and she bore a child when she was past the age,*
> *because she judged Him faithful who had promised*
> *(Hebrews 11: 8 – 11NKJV)*

After having heard about the above highlighted examples I asked God what He meant by a walk of faith that was different from what I was already engaged in. He brought quite a number of aspects of the walk which I had never looked at, the same way as what He showed me. Firstly, He told me it was a solitary walk, where I will be able to hear Him better without the clattering noise made by the 'Madding Crowd.'

A walk of solitude

I wondered why we need to have a solitary walk with God and I got the answer from the fact that His ways are higher than ours indeed. It is so amazing how He works out things in ways we never anticipated before. He always speaks in a still clear voice. This voice can only be heard when one moves *Far From the Madding Crowd* as Thomas Hardy's novel goes. Sometimes I wonder why Hardy's novel's title labels the crowd as madding. Is the crowd really 'acting in a way that suggests or reveals the presence of a psychiatric disorder'? I don't mean to compartmentalise people, but like it or not, every one of us at one point in time find ourselves being part of a crowd. This could be something we never even plan. Moving in agreement with the crowd requires being clever, analytical, and being able to use common sense. So dear friends, I want to make it clear once more that hearing God's voice and getting this message well means you have to move away from the clever and analytic crowd. This is not always easy to do because it sometimes means having to do 'foolish' things that do not really make sense. It means having to behave in a ridiculous way.

What do I mean by all this rigmarole? May be to clarify a bit I have to bring some scriptures that God has used to deal with me. Firstly, we need to get some lessons from our Saviour, Jesus Christ himself. As a girl growing up I used to like singing the song *I want to be more and more like Jesus.* I liked this song more for its melody than the message it carries. As I grow in Christian living I realise that there is more to the song than the melody. To be more and more like Jesus means sometimes accepting being misunderstood, hated and opposed by the highly religious of the time.

During Jesus' time there were times when even His own disciples had to be aloof. The Bible states clearly that crowds followed Jesus, but there were times also when He had to leave them and be with only his chosen twelve. Furthermore, there were times when He had to leave the twelve and pick only three from them; Peter, James, and John. That was when He had to experience things at a more elevated level like when he was going to be transfigured. To show that God's way of thinking is higher than ours, even the three chosen disciples proved to be spiritually limited. Peter said they better build tents up there on the mountain. That was not time for settling down and enjoying the glory, because Jesus had work to do. Peter could not see all that.

Jesus wanted to do His father's work, which was to die for the sins of the world (all of us), therefore when the time for Him to carry out that mission came, things became tougher and there were times when he could not even take the special three disciples with him. He had to do it all alone. The case was then between Him and God the Father. Jesus left all His disciples and went on to a hill to pray. When He went to check on His disciples He found them all dozing. He asked them if they could not even be there with Him for an hour. They loved Him and wanted to be with Him, but the assignment ahead was for Him alone.

One could ask why the disciples let Jesus face the challenge alone if they were loyal to Him. The Holy Bible reveals that His sweat was blood, which shows it was a very tough time in His life. The period for performing miracles such as healing the sick, changing water into wine and multiplying food, had passed. Having all the crowds admiring and following Him for the good works was very good and sort of comfortable. It is true that the religious were always opposing Him and making false accusations against Him, but still the crowds were on His side. When Jesus had to do His father's will, things escalated and there was a sudden change.

Beloved, when you sing, *I want to be more and more like Jesus,* remember what that means and sing it with great understanding. Being more and more like Jesus is not really 'nice', but let me tell you, it is good. It is the best, thing that can ever happen to a human. It entails a lot of tear shedding. It means going through severe earthly loneliness. I mean unbearable loneliness but, in that loneliness you are never alone. Holy Spirit is with you every step of the way. The words of reassurance grace the Bible in both Old and New Testament:

....I will never leave you nor forsake you
(Hebrews 13: 5b NKJV)

Be strong and of good courage,
do not fear nor be afraid of them;
for the LORD your God,
He is the One who goes with you.
He will not leave you nor forsake you.

And the LORD, He is the One who goes before you.
He will be with you; He will not leave you nor
forsake you; do not fear nor be dismayed."
(Deuteronomy 31: 6& 8 NKJV)

No man shall be able to stand before you
all the days of your life;
as I was with Moses,
so I will be with you.
I will not leave you nor forsake you.
(Joshua 1: 5 NKJV)

This experience is very good, but it is very different from the comfort we get when things are all fine with us. So, learning from Jesus we have to move on to the zone of walking 'alone' and sometimes shedding tears, 'sweating blood' as well as 'drinking vinegar'. What is great is that at the end we can also say 'it is finished' or 'it is done'. I have shouted many times "Praise God, it is done!" This is a continuous process. After each "Praise God, it is done again" there is a phase of rest and whilst you think "what a nice comfy zone" you then hear the Father's voice saying, "more, child. I have better and greater things in store for you." I have learnt, whenever He says "better things" He means better and unparalleled things indeed.

A walk of irrational living

The second aspect of the walk of faith that Father gave me was that of living an absurd lifestyle. Oh, that really squeezed and crushed me because from childhood I was labelled 'brainy' and that was kind of 'cool', but getting into the faith walk was snatching away my smart part. The scripture God used to deal with me into understanding how I had to stop analysing issues when He speaks is the one about the wedding at Cana when Mary, the mother of Jesus told the disciples to do whatever he told them to do:

> *On the third day there was a wedding in Cana of Galilee,*
> *and the mother of Jesus was there.*
> *Now both Jesus and His disciples were invited to the wedding.*
> *And when they ran out of wine,*
> *the mother of Jesus said to Him,*
> *"They have no wine."*
> *Jesus said to her,*
> *"Woman, what does your concern have to do with Me?*
> *My hour has not yet come."*
> *His mother said to the servants,*
> *"Whatever He says to you, do it."*
> *Now there were set there six water pots of stone,*
> *according to the manner of purification of the Jews,*
> *containing twenty or thirty gallons apiece.*
> *Jesus said to them,*
> *"Fill the water pots with water."*
> *And they filled them up to the brim.*
> *And He said to them,*
> *"Draw some out now, and take it to the master of the feast."*
> *And they took it.*
> *When the master of the feast*
> *had tasted the water that was made wine,*
> *and did not know where it came from*
> *(but the servants who had drawn the water knew),*
> *the master of the feast called the bridegroom.*
> *And he said to him,*
> *"Every man at the beginning sets out the good wine,*
> *and when the guests have well drunk, then the inferior.*
> *You have kept the good wine until now!"*
> *(John 2: 1-10 NKJV)*

The instruction given by Mary reminds me of a game we used to play as little children, where in order to be part of the game the participants had to do whatever the leader said and did. For instance if the leader said, "someone say I am a cow," the one whose turn it was to respond would say, "I am a cow."

That really sounded very stupid, but as children we would say the silly things and stay in the game and have fun anyway.

When Jesus was invited to the wedding at Cana, His mother knew that His presence meant everything was going to be alright. However, they soon reported a problem. They had run out of wine. From this story we learn that problems will still occur in our lives even though Jesus Christ has already been invited. It is so amazing to see the sorts of reactions people have whenever they encounter crises. Some panic, others run for the phone to tell a friend, and others do a whole lot of frantic forms of behaviour. Mary, knowing who Jesus was gave them this advice, which many may regard very stupid, "whatever He says, do." How on earth can someone say such a statement? What if the person concerned tells the other people to do something odd like Jesus did?

Well, I meditated and did all that I felt I had to do about my situation and the walk of faith with God, but it became clear that God was not impressed by mere meditation. Meditation needs to be followed by practical living in a similar way that theory and practical application relate to each other. Theory is good, but learners grasp better when they see its practical application. Now the next step was for me to take my first 'toddler' step in my walk of faith with my Father!

Chapter 13

A Practical Walk of Faith

o o o o o o o o o o o o o o o o o o o o o o o o o o o o o o o o o

The good and perfect will
Is yours my God and King
Bring me closer to you my Lord
Holy Spirit
Conquer what is my will
So that I may be fully yours
(a translation of the Zulu chorus, Intando emnandi...)

Embarking on the walk of faith with God requires full surrender. All my five years in boarding school we used to sing the above song which marks full surrender to Holy Spirit to guide our every move and to most of us it simply became our hostel anthem without full spiritual understanding. However, as God instructed me to take a walk of faith with Him in order to get what I hoped for, I interlocked with the song!

The practical walk of faith I engaged in was not an easy endeavour. It cost me a lot of what I had held very dearly. I became a solitary person and found that there were very few people with whom I exchanged meaningful and agreeable conversations. To the majority of people I had crazy talk. To some I appeared as some kind of weirdo, who could mentally lose it anytime. My 'crazy' talk was accompanied by matching actions. I purposed in my heart to follow in Christ's steps:

To this you were called, because Christ suffered for you,
leaving you an example,
that you should follow in his steps.
(1Peter 2: 21 NIV)

Whilst we were at William Pitcher College, my friend Hazel Magagula read the book, ***In His Steps*** by Charles Sheldon and shared it with me. It set us through a revolution! The same spirit got revived in me and I was determined to walk through until I saw a manifestation! In order for this to work out, I had to disconnect from many 'friends' who were naysayers and connect to those who talked my kind of talk. Holy Spirit was the one who divinely showed me where to disconnect and also where to connect to. Whenever some people who thought themselves as smart challenged me and asked me questions I saw as spiritually stupid I decided to emulate my Savior and not argue or even answer:

> *But Jesus made no reply, not even to a single charge*
> *To the great amazement of the governor.*
> *(Matthew 27:14 NIV)*

Holy Spirit showed me that my point of taking off was to be more submissive to Him than I had ever been, to a point of appearing 'stupid'. Whenever the emotional pain struck, I focused on the light at the end of my tunnel. I did not want anything that would sabotage my going to study abroad. I asked for permission from my spouse and I also decided to unquestioningly submit to him even in the oddest of situations. That had always been my lifestyle anyway, but this time around, I had a stern purpose like Daniel. My request was granted, but it was conditional. I was to go to the UK only if I had funding and I would have a study leave with pay which would enable me to continue paying the children's fees. To me that was a confirmation I was going because I already believed beyond the shadow of a doubt that God was going to grant me the necessary funds!

My next step was to apply to two universities in the UK, Sussex University and Kent University. I also applied for the study leave from the Ministry of Education. From my years of service to the government I qualified for the study leave and to be appointed for funding through the Ministry of Labour and Public Services. I also applied to the World University Service for a scholarship. The proposal I wrote and the support I got from my referees made me feel like I had already got that scholarship! Using email was not a common thing then, so I opened an account with the Manzini Post Office and would drive there during my lunch break to communicate with the universities and make more searches for funding.

I heard clearly that God wanted me to start telling people I was going to study abroad. That was a bit weird because I had no proof of funding yet. The reminder came so loud and clear in my spirit that 'by the way, girl' ***faith is the substance of things hoped for, the evidence of things not seen.*** I could not question that, so I obeyed and started talking about it to everyone I happened to have a conversation with. Stella, a friend I had recently met when we were awarded by the opportunity of representing Swaziland as Young Researchers by a German Foundation heard me and believed I was going. She understood very well that I had nothing in my hand, but my faith. She encouraged me and also spread word to people that 'Betty was going to the UK soon in August/ September. Many of those who had already studied abroad before laughed and explained how things worked! Oh my Lord, little did they know that my Father does not do things the people's way! He has His own ways!

For a while there were no responses from both UK universities and the funding bodies. When anxiety attacked me I started confessing more and telling people more. One day at work, I called into my office two boys, Thulani Thwala and Sandile Dlamini who were Christians and I was a guardian for one and sometimes supported the other. We had a special prayer and to this day I have not forgotten that prayer. We called on Father. These young people loved God and to them I was a *Mama* that has been supportive, so when *Mama* was stuck there had to be an intervention! As we prayed one of my 'sons' declared God's supremacy and said that as a child of the King of Kings I could go wherever I desired whether UK or USA. What on earth brought the USA to that young man? How prophetic! Well, Father heard, but there was nothing tangible to show. Faith was all I had in my hand and my 'big mouth' was not shutting up! I spread word of my going abroad more than ever before!

Whilst still believing God and waiting for responses a British couple that had left Swaziland in 1992 visited to show their adopted son where he came from. I told them about my coming to study in their country shortly. As their son played with my youngest, VB, the mother expressed how she felt like it would be nice for their son AB, to be with my son when I eventually come to the UK to study. She told her husband and the agreement was made there and then that when I go to the UK they would help and stay with my son and enable me to call him every day. To me that was a big sign from God right there. From that encounter, Mazulu, my son already knew he was going abroad with his mother and he was very excited. Anything negative would demoralize the child, so I knew God would not promise and then decline!

The enemy never gives up. In the next few days following God's blessing of the provision for my son, the World University Service replied and it was negative. Sussex University responded at the same time with a positive response that was accompanied by the exorbitant fees required for International students. Tuition fees were going to be about £8 000 and general living expenses were to raise that figure even more. Did I stop confessing? No!

Did I not feel a bit weak in my spiritual knees? Of course I did, but I had a powerful weapon, my mouth:

> *Death and life are in the power of the tongue,*
> *And those who love it will eat its fruit.*
> *(Proverbs 18: 21 NKJV)*

I confessed even more. I regarded Sussex University's accepting me as a sign from God. I applied for their studentship online and the response did not take long. They told me they fund PhD scholars only, and to me that was a 'yes' from God. I thought, 'So, Lord it means I will embark on a PhD immediately after the Masters, Wow!' Holy Spirit said 'if you believe it tell people about it!' That was tough. How could I talk about that whilst still believing for the MA funding. He gave me an instruction to tell my church about it. That was a steep hill, but I obeyed. I stood up to tell the church at EBC that in a short time I was going to pursue an MA in England and my family was to follow me soon as I pursue a PhD.

After the service many people came to congratulate me and the question everyone was asking was 'who is funding you?' I did not know, so I told them I did not know yet. Oh, my, my, my, that was when people thought 'Betty has lost it upstairs.' I mean, people were seriously concerned about my mental state. As if that was not enough, the second instruction came; 'sell you business!' That was a big business. The boutique had over eighty wedding regalia sets each comprising a wedding gown, bridesmaids' dresses and all accessories such as flowers, gloves, baskets, cushions, Men's suits, ties, bow ties, you know the whole lot involved in that kind of business. We had expanded to even wedding cakes. I had a lady who helped me with those. She was a member of the Manzini Christian Women's Club and we had monthly meetings at the George Hotel. She was amazing!

The word I was given had been to sell the business, so I advertised, but got no buyer. The next instruction was to sell it in small parts at low prices and give away the rest. People came from remote parts of the country and bought the stuff for almost nothing. A young lady who had just started a booming business of decorating in weddings, especially decorating marquees bought the license and the larger part of the business, but the price I charged was ridiculously low. The business had to go. One pastor showed interest and was ready to buy and God said, let him select what he wants to buy and when he had done I was told to give him. I did. Some concerned friends and relatives spoke openly, telling me I was making a great mistake because I could start my business again on my return from abroad, 'if I was going there in the first place'. In their tones I could sense that they did not see me going at all. I could not blame them because I could have felt the same way too being in their position. I did not waste time to argue with anyone. I simply did what I had to do as instructed by Father.

The money I got from the sales was mere peanuts and I could not do much with it. Apart from the purchase of the two tickets, mine and my son's, I had to divide the money into two and do something special for my two mothers, my mother and my mother-in-law. Amazingly I managed to answer their special different needs; electricity installation for my mum and a big water tank for my mother-in-law. After each of these deeds I felt inexplicable peace. I could still hear God's still and very clear voice in my heart, telling me to go deeper and do things which were proof I believed that I was definitely going abroad.

Having wiped away all traces of my bridal boutique business, I felt great peace, and knew in my heart that indeed a great miracle was coming. I knew something unusual, and something that I had never even conceived in my heart was going to happen. The business and its majestic growth had been a miracle on its own, and it was beginning to be my countrywide identity even over my professional occupation and status as an author whose contributions were studied in schools and all the other equally important aspects of my life. So when all of a sudden I realised that what had taken me almost half my age to build up had been completely dissolved, the enemy gave me a sense of loss and I thought I had finished filling 'my water pots', but I heard God's Holy Spirit firmly tell me that what I had done was only the beginning and there was more ahead.

Another instruction was to give away my valuable clothes and Holy Spirit gave me specific names of two women of God to give to. I did, but I did not give my suits I had brought from England in 1999 when I visited my sister and aunt in London. God told me to release them. I did, but held on to a leopard skin coat I liked. The voice said, 'let it go too!' I obeyed. He instructed me to also give away the young children's computer I had brought from England for my young son during my previous visit. It seemed as if I was cleaning away all personal valuables. The song which my mother and aunt Esther (my father's youngest sister) had taught me whilst very young became my motor:

> *When we walk with the Lord*
> *In the light of His Word*
> *What a glory He sheds on our way!*
> *When we do His good will;*
> *He abides with us still,*
> *And with all who will trust and obey.*

Trust and obey,
For there's no other way
To be happy in Jesus,
But to trust and obey.

The hymn has more verses, but I dwelt on the chorus and just trusted Him and obeyed! One of the student teachers from the university, who was doing teaching practice in my school was a Christian and had heard me talk about my going abroad. She told her mother what she had heard me say and she told me her mother had said she had proof I was definitely going. The mother said she got it very clearly from all the confessions people were reporting. At the time I had never heard of Bishop T.D. Jakes, but many people who were free to access what I was not able to access within the Christian spheres knew about him. The student teacher's mother said I speak like Bishop Jakes and I told the daughter I did not even know who they were talking about.

On the following day, Sindy, the student teacher brought me copied tapes of Bishop Jakes and Dr Myles Munroe which her mother was giving me to listen to. I played the tapes in my car and Oh my Lord, something broke loose! There was such a deep connection right there! The man of God was saying things I had never heard anyone say yet I had always had in my own spirit and spoke to those I ministered to one on one or small groups. The man of God made me realize I was not insane. I felt like if I was insane he was even more insane. That just threw a bucket of gasoline on my inner fire. I went more ablaze. In one of my gift tapes Bishop Jakes was talking about dreams and the importance of unwrapping all our gift packages from God whilst still here on earth. I decided there and then that no one was to stop me achieving what God meant me to achieve whilst on earth.

The other man of God, Dr Munroe was talking about the 7 Principles of an eagle. What did God expect of me when He brought such people when I was already 'crazy?' Dr Munroe confirmed my being an eagle right there. Some of those principles were already evident in my life and some more were to manifest later, but I had no clue at the time. I was already 'a lone flyer'; I had a very strong vision; was fully set and already flying in the storm; I was prepared for training; I will not even say much about the fact that eagles do not eat dead things; I was going through the 'plucking off of my feathers, filing the beak and talons', but getting Dr Munroe's precise wording is the best thing to do here:

1. Eagles fly alone...;
2. Eagles have strong vision...;
3. Eagles do not eat dead things...;

4. The eagle is the only bird that loves the storm...;
5. The eagle tests before it trusts...;
6. The eagle prepares for training...;
7. The eagle...retires to a place far away in the rocks.
While there, he plucks out every feather on his body
Until he is completely bare.
He stays in this hiding place until he has grown new
feathers, then he can come out.
We occasionally need to shed off old habits
And items that burden us without adding to our lives
(Dr Myles Munroe: Inspiration on the 7 Principles of an eagle)

I may have had aspects of some of the principles of an eagle, but evidently, when I was young I did not have the fifth principle of 'testing before trusting!' It knew it was not too late to learn. I believe reading this testimony will help you to personally develop this principle in your own life: ***Test before you trust!***

God was not through with me. We had a real long walk ahead. After the negative response from World University Service funding, my hope was with the Ministry of Education. My days were getting fewer and I had not heard from the MOE, so I drove there to find out what the outcome of my case was. The officer in charge of applications pertaining to further studies had always been promising that things were fine, but that day he said someone had misplaced my application form and it was nowhere to be found. He told me to apply for the following year. Oh beloved, I think you can already imagine, I completely had no room for a negative response, not to say other people ever have. I tried all I could and the only thing he said was he was sorry they had misplaced my application form.

The enemy started gloating over me telling me that I had to forget about it. I drove down the notorious Malagwane hill like one who had received death news, but I am glad I could still focus on driving. I do not remember exactly what was going on, in both mind and heart, but what I remember very well and know like I know my Name is Betty Sibongile Dlamini, is that when I was driving past Ezulwini Valley and I was about to pass by Ezulwini Caravan Park, I heard like an audible voice what I had to do next. The enemy had announced to me that I was shattered, done and completely over with; what a shame, but Holy Spirit swiftly reminded me of the Biblical story of the wedding at Cana. He asked me questions whose answers I knew very well. So, having answered well, a voice told me to take the instruction Mary, the mother of Jesus gave the disciples at that wedding and then apply it to my situation. Mary's advice was, "Whatever He says do."

As I tried to figure out what that meant for me, Holy Spirit told me that since I had run out of wine, I had to pour water into water pots like they did at that wedding. I did not lose hope in my search. I could not go to Manzini without trying something else. I headed for Ludzidzini Royal residence and I thank God, ZTG, the acquaintance I was looking for was there. I thought she was still in charge of one of the country's funding bodies. She told me she had just handed over to a successor. Well, I do not want to kill your reading appetite by relating every step of the way, but I tell you I left no stone unturned. I even tried a financial institute owned by the Swazi Royals. There was no help, but as I was leaving, one of the officials called me aside and advised me to try another route I never thought I could pursue.

As I was thinking of knocking on all the other possible doors, I got my next instruction. That one was about was my part-time job as a tutor at The University of Swaziland. I loved my job and it made me realise that I could soon be a lecturer after getting my Masters qualification. The next instruction was to resign and not renew my contract with the University of Swaziland, so I stated that I could not renew it due to my going to England for my Masters degree. Immediately I had done that I heard that gloating voice from the enemy mockingly saying, 'Well done, and if you do not go what are you going to do? Fool you have lost it this time'. At times I literally had to speak back to the devilish voice, and tell him I knew who I believed in, 'My God is able, so I am going to England no matter what, so shut up devil!'

God was still holding my hand in that walk of faith and He told me that I had to take yet another step of faith at Ngwane Park High School where I was the Deputy Head Teacher. I had a great debate in my heart about this next step, but Hebrews 11: 6 spoke clearly again "Without faith there is no pleasing Him". I did not want to disobey God in any way, so I decided to follow the instruction and have a small farewell function with the teachers. They had heard me talk of my plans to study abroad, but to them it was not a certain issue yet, because up until the end of term in August I had not secured any source of funding. I had conquered the devil in my own internal battle, but now I had to deal with the outside world as well.

I went into the Head teacher's office, and told him of my plan to have a small get together and refreshments where I would officially announce to the teachers my departure to England. Mr Zwane is a very wise man, and I feel very privileged to have had the experience of working closely to him. As soon as I had finished talking I saw that 'smile' which was packed with multiple unsaid questions. He gave me his sound advice of not saying anything at the time until such a time when I was definitely sure of my departure. Mr Zwane's advice made me realize he genuinely cared for my well-being. He told me that life could be a bit uncomfortable for me in the school, if I was to have that little party and find myself back in the school at the beginning of the next term. I realised too, that being in his shoes I would give similar advice to someone I cared for.

I felt like I was at cross roads because I knew very well that it was a bit stupid to buy those refreshments and summon my colleagues to tell them I was leaving for England when I was not sure at all. I knew better; that was no rationale matter. I obeyed God and told the teachers about my departure. Some had a private laugh about the whole thing, but I dismissed it all because I knew the one I was dealing with. I emptied my office of all my personal possessions. I still remember the last day I left the office for which I had been the first occupant, and an office in which, tears had been shed in prayer with a student, teacher or even parent in need. That was a chapter closed for life, but I was not so sure at the time.

In 2001, I had no second term vacation at all, but God who plans things perfectly did it such that the three weeks school vacation was my time to run my faith marathon. When schools closed, my spouse went to China and he left having granted us full permission with the boy to leave for England if things worked out. His one month trip enabled me to run as demand arose without worrying about cooking and all that comes along with a wife's responsibilities.

I had no time to waste. I followed the advice I had been given by an official when I went to one of the finance institutes. The woman there had given me a few names of offices I could go to and get help. I negotiated my way through to the offices of various government ministries including the Prime Minister's office. At the Prime Minister's office they referred me back to the Ministry of Labour and Public Services. There they wanted a letter from the Ministry of Education. I had to go back and face the official who said they had misplaced my application. When he saw me he hurriedly got into the elevator. I followed him and as we were in there he told me he had no time because he had to go to another region. When we came out of the elevator, he met another officer and gave him an order, "hey Mr. G, please help this woman. I am in a hurry"

Beloved, this may sound a bit too detailed to you, but I want you to pay attention so that you may understand God works in mysterious ways. Mr. G did not even know what he had to do because the Big Man had not elaborated on what had to be done. Mr. G asked me what I wanted. I told him I needed a letter recommending me to go and study so that the Ministry of Labour and Public Services may consider my application. Although I did not see it happen right away, God showed up there and then. Mr. G told me he had other urgent businesses and asked me to draft the letter of recommendation. I was panicking not really understanding what was happening. No one understood except for God who can set you up for your very uplifting!

To cut the long story short by the end of the day I had submitted the recommendation letter, but they told me it was impossible to do anything in weeks. The lady there handed me an application pack and told me the Commonwealth Scholarship is quite competitive, but the good thing about it is that favoritism does not apply as is the case in other places in the country. That gave me a smile because I knew God assists me obtain excellence when I ask Him and He had done it before. When the woman told me my application was going to be submitted the following year a waterfall of tears gushed from my eyes. I had thought that was my provision right there, but God was setting me up for a whole cake not just a piece. I asked for a second application pack and they gave me. I was so committed to building up my marriage and still believed for things to be better, so, I thought, maybe we could both get the scholarship.

During the days that followed, I was led to engage in a seven day fast. God revealed Himself in a fresh way and more powerful way than I had ever experienced before. I think I was on day five when as I was in the bath tub something hit me incredibly and I got the victory message in 1 Samuel 17 where David kills Goliath! As if I was in a rollercoaster God showed me all He can do with me if I trust Him the same way as David. I saw vividly the David part of me. David had fought and won private battles which no human on earth ever witnessed. His only witnesses were the flocks he looked after. Oh, beloved I am just enveloped by God's presence right now as I am writing this because I know where I have been and no human will ever know because I have decided not to expose things and fight what only God can fight!

Beloved, I have seen God empower me to kill 'bears' and 'lions'! I have done it with Him covering me. Right there, in the bath tub, I blacked out. When I recovered from what He showed me I summoned my three children and started speaking to them. It was terrific. Those three children have seen a lot! Through their being mothered by a 'crazy' mother they can tell you some things about God! They know His works first hand.

I spoke to them about the victory ahead. God made me tell them something that sounded very strange even to me, but I said it not really knowing what I was talking about! I told them God was saying we would never be together in the same manner in that house ever again. I had no funding yet and my younger son did not even have his International passport yet, so I did not have any idea what was to happen to me next. I just moved and spoke as God commanded. I preached that powerful sermon to the three children. They just listened and prayed with me when I said we should. What I said to them has now literally happened. At the time I had no clue whatsoever!

God gave me another ridiculous instruction; to have a farewell function in my house and preach the David and Goliath message to the church ladies' group. I was a member of the Manzini Christian Women's Club and most members were from EBC, my church. As EBC ladies, we also had a fortnightly Saturday women's meeting in which we took turns to host in our houses and we had different speakers. I told the chair of our church ladies' group that the next meeting was my last one in Swaziland, so I volunteered to host it, but to confirm God's instruction to me she said I had to be the speaker. I was amazed because God had already told me I had to preach the David and Goliath sermon He gave me during my seven days of fasting. Hosting the meeting did not necessarily mean the host had to be the speaker, so I knew God had orchestrated the whole thing!

That meeting was very unique. I invited people who never came to our meetings. My long time friends, Hazel and Dudu came as well as my sister who comes after me. Khulile from my school came too and Holy Spirit told me that was my send off party. The ladies brought a lot of food and it was an EBC thing to have potluck meals. Oh, the cooking in that church was fabulous; I mean the ladies had fantastic gifting when it comes to catering! More than food for the stomach God covered me up and I said what He said to say.

One striking thing God revealed to me was that although Hebrews 11 does not elaborate much on David's own faith his name is there. God showed me David's major act of faith which I see contained in this story! The giant, Goliath had been menacingly challenging Israel when David came into the camp. He asked more about it and they told him, but as they were talking Goliath came. Read the story if you want or just skip it:

> *As he was talking with them, Goliath, the*
> *Philistine champion from Gath, stepped out from his*
> *lines and shouted his usual defiance, and David heard*
> *it. When the Israelites saw the man, they all ran from*
> *him in great fear.*
> *Now the Israelites had been saying, "Do you see*
> *how this man keeps coming out? He comes out to defy*
> *Israel. The king will give great wealth to the man who kills*
> *him. He will also give him his daughter in marriage and*
> *will exempt his father's family from taxes in Israel."*
> *David asked the men standing near him, "What will*
> *be done for the man who kills this Philistine and removes*
> *this disgrace from Israel? Who is this uncircumcised*
> *Philistine that he should defy the armies of the living God?"*

*They repeated to him what they had been saying
and told him, "This is what will be done for the man who
kills him."*

*When Eliab, David's oldest brother, heard him
speaking with the men, he burned with anger at him and
asked, "Why have you come down here? And with whom
did you leave those few sheep in the desert? I know how
conceited you are and how wicked your heart is; you came
down only to watch the battle."*

*"Now what have I done?" said David. "Can't I even
speak?" He then turned away to someone else and brought
up the same matter, and the men answered him as before.
What David said was overheard and reported to Saul, and
Saul sent for him.*

*David said to Saul, "Let no one lose heart on
account of this Philistine; your servant will go and fight him."*

*Saul replied, "You are not able to go out against
this Philistine and fight him; you are only a boy, and he
has been a fighting man from his youth."*

*But David said to Saul, "Your servant has been
keeping his father's sheep. When a lion or a bear came
and carried off a sheep from the flock, I went after it
struck it and rescued the sheep from its mouth. When it
turned on me, I seized it by its hair, struck it and killed it.
Your servant has killed both the lion and the bear; this
uncircumcised Philistine will be like one of them, because
he has defied the armies of the living God.
The LORD who delivered me from the paw of the lion and the
paw of the bear will deliver me from the hand
of this Philistine."*

Saul said to David, "Go, and the LORD be with you."

*Then Saul dressed David in his own tunic. He put a
coat of armour on him and a bronze helmet on his head.
David fastened on his sword over the tunic and
tried walking around, because he was not used to them.
"I cannot go in these," he said to Saul, "because I am
not used to them." So he took them off. Then he took his staff in his
hand, chose five smooth stones from the s
tream, put them in the pouch of his shepherd's bag and,
with his sling in his hand, approached the Philistine.*

Meanwhile, the Philistine, with his shield bearer in front of him, kept coming closer to David. He looked David over and saw that he was only a boy, ruddy and handsome, and he despised him. He said to David, "Am I a dog that you come at me with sticks?" And the Philistine cursed David by his gods. "Come here," he said, "and I'll give your flesh to the birds of the air and the beasts of the field!"

David said to the Philistine, "You come against me with sword and spear and javelin, but I come against you in the name of the LORD Almighty, the God of the armies of Israel, whom you have defied. This day the LORD will hand you over to me, and I'll strike you down and cut off your head. Today I will give the carcasses of the Philistine army to the birds of the air and the beasts of the earth, and the whole world will know that there is a God in Israel. All those gathered here will know that it is not by sword or spear that the LORD saves; for the battle is the LORD's, and he will give all of you into our hands."

As the Philistine moved closer to attack him, David ran quickly toward the battle line to meet him. Reaching into his bag and taking out a stone, he slung it and struck the Philistine on the forehead. The stone sank into his forehead, and he fell face down on the ground.

So David triumphed over the Philistine with a sling and a stone; without a sword in his hand he struck down the Philistine and killed him.

David ran and stood over him. He took hold of the Philistine's sword and drew it from the scabbard. After he killed him, he cut off his head with the sword.

When the Philistines saw that their hero was dead, they turned and ran. Then the men of Israel and Judah s urged forward with a shout and pursued the Philistines to the entrance of Gath and to the gates of Ekron. Their dead were strewn along the Shaaraim road to Gath and Ekron. When the Israelites returned from chasing the Philistines, they plundered their camp. David took the Philistine's head and brought it to Jerusalem and he put the Philistine's weapons in his own tent.

(1 Samuel 17: 23 – 54 NIV)

The striking fact God showed me about David is that there was a big, big man whom everybody feared, but that was just a person. David knew God to have enabled him to take on and kill dangerous and deadly animals, a lion and a bear! Basing everything on his past experience, David believed he was going to be the one to remove that gigantic human being. I understand that David had seen God perform miraculous deeds before, and He knew he was coming in the name of the Lord, but then in the first part of verse 46, David says the weirdest statement in that chapter. He says, "I'll strike you down and cut off your head." That part did everything for me. God told me to tell the ladies that David had no weapon that could chop off the giant's head he claimed he was going to chop!

On that Saturday afternoon, on the 8th day of September, in the dining and living rooms of our house at the Correctional Services College, where women of God were packed, I declared with tears falling down my face that what I was doing could be seen as crazy, but God was telling me I was going to England. At the time there was still no funding and tickets yet, but by faith I **BOLDLY** declared I was going! I told the ladies that with no weapon in his hands David declared he was going to chop off Goliath's head, and yes, as we know the story well, he actually chopped off the giant's head! At the time I said and did all I did I had not yet met people who speak what I spoke and still speak. God knew where he was taking me and I have lived to encounter some mighty men and women of God who talk and walk a similar walk and talk to the one God took me through.

The ladies prayed for me and gave me their blessing. The enemy does not want to stand and watch you take what belongs to you. He attempts to discourage you and make you feel like you have made a mistake when you obeyed God. When schools reopened I was still there with no funding in my hands. We have a saying that 'those who have white teeth laugh until the last molar tooth shows!' The enemy and his crew laughed, but I know God to have the last laugh.

One night I felt like I was half asleep and half awake the whole night. The whole night I had in my spirit the song, *avulekile amasango,* (the gates/ doors have been opened). It was like I was singing it in my sleep. For the first time in my life I got another meaning to the song. I had always taken the song to mean that the gates of heaven have been opened, so sinners can come in through Jesus Christ, as we know the veil of separation was torn in two when Jesus won our victory. The other implication of the song that I got so clearly that night was that the doors for entry into my desired future had been opened and all I had to do was walk right in.

When I had the dream-like experience, I was going through the most crucial and intricate time of my life. I desperately needed God to intervene.

Time was running against me. I had to get God's provision there and then or simply go back to Ngwane Park High School and assume my duties. When my mind was becoming 'confused' I clearly heard God's voice saying "no backing off! Move on, for the doors are opened!" Incredible hey!

The whole thing was becoming difficult for me to understand. God presented me with what I took to be contradictory messages in the sense that in the spirit world He was saying to me I should move on because the doors were opened yet in the natural everything was shouting, 'Back off! Drop it!' At that time there was not a single vivid possibility for funding. All those sources of funding I had banked my hope in had finally spelt it very clearly that there was no funding for my studies. All the devastating news had come at the eleventh hour as far as I was concerned. There were also some close people who seemed to say, "Aha, we told you this thing will not work."

What began to concern me was the fact that I was not the only one affected by the suspense of God's provision. My son, Mazulu was also expecting the answer and as schools reopened it became hard for him to concentrate at school. He did not want to go there because he had told all his friends and his teacher before schools closed that he was soon leaving for England. My son would ask me everyday if I had already got the scholarship I needed in order for us to go to England. In my spirit I knew I was going, so I would always tell the boy that I had not got the scholarship yet, but definitely we were going. He would then give me a long stern kind of look and I would notice the eyes welling a little bit with tears. Whenever that happened I would have a big smile and tell my son not to worry because we were going soon.

The way God operates is just amazing. When His child's faith is put into a test there are always third parties involved apart from God and His child. The believer has to demonstrate the belief in God to all those third parties. For me the third parties came from all angles; my immediate family, the friends to whom I had already shared the news, my colleagues, my business associates, my university students and many more. All those people were watching me because they had been told **by me** that I was going to study abroad.

Out of all those few who still believed God was going to move soon, one voice meant a lot to me; my mother's. On the day following the night of my song, 'the doors have been opened' my mother gave me a telephone call, and told me that the answer to my prayer was around the corner because she had seen it in a dream. I really got excited because she was one of those who were battling in the prayer with me. Sometimes she joined in chain-fasting with me and my other prayer partners. My eyes brightened with excitement as she related her dream over the phone.

In her dream, my mother was at the top of a dangerous and high rocky cliff. If she could fall from where she stood it could be the end of her life.

On either sides of the cliff there was no way of coming off the cliff. As she looked further on she saw a safer, flatter place very close to the cliff, but it was difficult for her to jump to that elevated safe place. She told me how she suffered in her dream trying to get herself to that safe place. Right in her dream she cried for help, and before she could see it happen, she found herself having landed on the safer place. My mother emphasized that she did not see how she moved from the deadly cliff. She confessed to me that as she woke up and realised it was all a dream, something in her spirit told her that the dream was about me and what I was going through. Right there over the phone she excitedly shouted 'Sibongile, my child your problem is solved!'

My song, 'avulekile amasango (the gates/doors are opened) and my mother's dream made me more positive and go ahead with my preparations for going to England. God had pointed me toward another place of great importance for help. Access to the royal place of residence had been difficult. Soldiers prevented me for days on end. At that point in time God brought my father's cousin into the picture. She was much younger than my father's generation, so I called her my cousin. God divinely connected me to Agnes Gule-Mtetwa to be His voice in my life then. I was almost all dry, but she kept telling me that I would overcome, and suggested that I always sing the chorus:

We shall overcome
We shall overcome some day
Deep in my heart I do believe
We shall overcome someday.

I cannot really say I was happy and excited to get all those encouraging messages. The noise from the natural world was quite loud in my ears: 'You are going nowhere! There is no scholarship for you!' The noise sounded very logical. I understood its message so loud and clearly. In the natural, really there was no available scholarship for me, as I had already been told. My mind then engaged in a battle between the natural and spirit worlds.

I literally had two teams. The natural side had multitudes and fighting that natural world and all logical messages were my mother and cousin Agnes, who said my prayer was already answered. There was also my other long standing friend Hazel would never stopped to make brief phone calls to me with messages such as ' Betty, my friend, this is God's battle, just watch and see, bye love.' When Hazel made those calls sometimes she did not even give me a chance to respond, and quickly hung up. There were some of my friends, whom I had told about my situation who called me once in a while, checking how far things had gone and also encouraging me, telling me that

God would never leave me alone, but the Big Three were positioned to see me hit the winning point!

There was a time I got confused and thought it better to simplify my life and give up the whole madness. God then gave me anew the story of Peter walking on water. He showed me that when Peter focused on Jesus, he managed to walk on the water, but when he shifted his focus from Jesus and started analysing the situation, things changed. Analysing made Peter realise he was actually walking on water, which is not really in agreement with science and nature and he started sinking. Peter then immediately turned to Jesus for help. Jesus was there for him. God's message for me in this story became very clear. I had to focus on Him and believe Him every step of the way without bringing my own reasoning into the situation. To further instil the importance of my focus on God I got the verses:

> *Trust in the Lord with all your heart,*
> *And lean not on your own understanding;*
> *In all your ways acknowledge Him,*
> *And He shall direct your paths.*
> *(Proverbs 3: 5-6 NKJV)*

I found this to be very tough for me. How could I separate myself from reality? Oh yes I could, by simply focusing on Jesus Christ and then in turn moving on without any doubt. In the midst of this whole confusion, my cousin Agnes came to me in a very uncompromising manner. She told me I could not have it both ways. She said I had to either take God at His word and stop bringing in my reasoning, or just disobey Him by analysing my circumstances to work out whether it was possible for me to go or not. I realised that the second was not really an option for me, so I held onto God and believed Him to keep His promises.

The ways of God are so amazing! He brings into our lives people at certain seasons and for specific reasons. At the time I did not know Dr Mike Murdock and I had never heard his Wisdom Key, *when God wants to bless you He brings in a person into your life!* How noble! My cousin, Agnes had not been so close to me before this particular time of my life, but she literally became my guardian angel and checked on me in an unusual way. One day as I was still running around in my pursuit for funding, she called me, to only give me two verses of scripture that talk about God's faithfulness and His everlasting mercy (Psalms 36: 5 and Psalms 100: 5). She extracted all the relevant scripture I needed such as the story of Jael who was only a woman, but killed the enemy who was a man using a nail and hammer. "Cousy, take your own spiritual nail and hammer and kill the enemy who makes you doubt

God's promises." Those words greatly encouraged me and I started focusing on God's promises once more. Through Agnes God had provided me with my *Rhema* word.

God spoke very clearly to me and I knew I had to obey Him by moving on from what I was familiar with and knew so well, onto what I knew nothing of. God then literally took me by my hand and led me from point to point, and making halts in various places. Some of you may not understand what I mean by that, but I mean exactly that: God led me by my hand. If He left me to start moving on my own I would not have done it. When God calls you to a specific destination, He tells you where He is calling you to, and also what good things are in store for you over there, but He does not show you what you will go through before reaching your destination. I think the reason for our not knowing every part of the journey, which includes turns, stops, leaps, staggering, sitting, lying on the stomach, sleeping and a lot that takes place along the way is that if we could see all this as it is, some of us could blatantly and flatly refuse to take even the first step towards our calling.

The Lord God almighty made us, loves us, and knows us more than we know ourselves, so He makes things bearable for us by showing us our future in small bits, which our little minds can handle. He has done that with me and He still does, therefore, I now like it and understand that it is all for my good to know little by little.

Like most people, I like to know what is ahead of me all the time. If I have to set off to be at a certain place at a certain time I like to know everything before I embark on my trip. Things do not always go this way with God. He wants us, His children to trust Him completely; He wants us to trust Him with all our heart and lean not on our own understanding (Proverbs 3: 5). When God took me on my walk of faith I trusted Him with all my heart, because I absolutely had no other way of dealing with my situation.

What I have realised is that the human mind can never conceive fully, what God really has in store for the believer. The scripture, 'Eye has not seen, nor ear heard, nor have entered into the heart of man the things which God has prepared for those who love Him' (1 Corinthians 2: 9) spells it so clearly. I have learnt some of the things God has for us can be understood as we go through some stuff that God is leading us through. Even as we go along the way heading for our destination, we can never perceive fully what that destination is exactly like. No matter how hard you may try and even believe God, the best future you can think of is nowhere near what God has intended for you.

I have known God to be a good leader who knows the end from the beginning. He knows that your destination is point *Z*. He knows it can scare you to death to be shown that you will need to go from *A* to *B*, to *C*, and move all the way to *W, X, Y* and then land at *Z*. That is what I call God holding me by His hand. When standing at point A and looking ahead all I can see is point B and God tells the believer, that is where we are going. Before landing at point B the believer's hope is very high and they may think 'oh yes this is it, finally we are landing at our destination, what a relief'. When we get to point B and throw ourselves down as a way of resting after the **very** long walk from point A to B, God just smiles at us, and He allows us to enjoy the rest, but tells us that we have more walking to do because our destiny is towards 'that direction' and that is pointing towards point C. The rest that the believer gets at point B is important and as the walk towards point C starts, the believer has more stamina and heads on for point C. By now you all know the story and can tell me what happens when the believer gets to point C, and point D and E, and so on until we get to Z.

Before my departure from Swaziland things happened real fast like I was in a rollercoaster. I had two more places I hoped to get help from. One was a governor I had been waiting to meet, but he got stuck in America when the September 11 calamity happened. Whilst waiting for him I still went to try entry into the palace where I was beginning to feel in my spirit my answer was waiting for me. In spite of the young queen's summoning me over the phone, some of the soldiers would not let me through. When the governor came, it was easy to meet him at his home and he asked me where I wanted to study. I told him, Sussex University. He burst into laughter and told me I was too ambitious because that was a good university and the last Swazi they sent there was a son of one of the former ambassadors of the country in England. The governor did not give me any hope. When he heard I was a deputy head teacher, he advised me to forget and go back to work.

On the other hand the head teacher told me that it was difficult for him to let me stay off work without filling in the official absent from duty forms which every civil servant had to fill in when they go on study leave. Basically he was recalling me to work if I still did not have official leave to go. I could get that official form signed only if there was proof I had funding to go and study. I told him I would bring my signed form soon. My last pursuit was the palace where for many days over the vacation I would go and be told to wait by the gates only to be told it was too late for the young queen to see anyone. Together with Agnes we headed for the palace. I had done that trip umpteenth times, but I still went.

The day I entered the palace appeared to be like all other days yet for me it was not. I will not say much, but like one man of God in America always says, you are one person away from your answer I was actually that queen away from my answer. The God who paved a way for me to teach at Lozitha High School was divinely connecting me to the queen who was then a student and when I was promoted to Ngwane Park High School she transferred to be a student there. She was a Form 4 student in my school when she got the call to royalty. Before my need to study abroad she already honoured me to grace my sister's wedding in 1999 on the virtue of my being her former teacher. The queen's honouring me and seeing all the royal escorts at my baby sister's wedding had been a big thing for me, but this time my meeting the queen was for a more personal need.

Waiting to see the Her Royal Highness was not a joke. There were times when I would have spoken to her over the phone and she would have said I could come and see her, but when I got to the gate to the palace, the soldiers on duty would tell me that I could not see her because she was still taking a nap. On other days I would be told to wait, and by waiting they meant one had to do real **W A I T I N G.** God was training me for a life skill, I have realised I need until the day I leave this world. The car park for guest to the palace was a good distance from the royal residence, and sitting down on the ground outside the gates, for hours. By hours I mean **H O U R S**, and that sometimes meant sitting there from morning until sunset, only to be told to go home because it was already too late for Her Royal Highness to be seen. Agnes offered to go through such a taxing experience with me.

We sat with Agnes by the palace gates encouraging each other about Godly issues. I even remember us sharing from the book *If you are not growing you are dying*, which came very handy at the time I was experiencing my growth, where God was shifting me from my comfort zone, and removing all the soft cushioning materials from my nest, like eagle parents do when it is time for the little one to learn to fly. To build their nests eagle parents do it in two phases, the frame and the cushioned parts. For the frame they use thorny wood and then fill it in with soft grass, cotton wool and all sorts of soft material to make the little eaglets comfortable after being hatched.

When time to fly has come the eagle parents then dismantle the nest by removing the soft parts of the nest. The poking thorny and rough parts of the nest's frame force the little eaglet to fly. A similar practice used to be found among the Swazi people who used to teach a lazy toddler how to walk using a hard way. They would leave the toddler next to a nest of red stinging ants. The toddler would sit for a while and start crying, but when seeing no *mama* come to rescue, the little one would start standing up and exercising those lazy legs into the very first step of walking. I do not know whether this really happened or not, but many times I have heard adults tell it and I get the moral of the practice. That is what our Heavenly Father does to make us grow to new levels.

When I was there, the young queen hand wrote a note, put it in a royal folder and gave it to me to present to one of the ministers. Getting the minister was not as difficult, but he pointed us further to the King's office where people's petitions and similar issues were addressed. My high hopes were a bit brought down when I realised there was no instant help from the king's office. I thought I would be seen by the council responsible for such cases and get my help the minute we get to Lozitha Royal Residence, but more shock was awaiting me. We went to Lozitha with Agnes again, and I have not seen such a patient person. If she is not patient by nature I believe God got hold of her and made her so for the mission He had for her. Agnes was with me and was again subjected to long hours of waiting with me, only to be told to go home and come the following week, just when our turn to be seen came. That was such a frustrating experience.

I had no more days to use in pursuit of the matter let alone days and yet another week. By that time at the University of Sussex new students were already having their orientation. I did not mind missing the orientation and hoped to get all necessary information as soon and I got there, even if it is a little later than everyone else. Agnes spoke to one of the men who were there to usher in the people who were to be interviewed by the council. She pleaded to the man, asking him to please address my case that day because at Sussex University they had said I could not be registered if I got there after the registration date for the MA programme which was the 8th October. That meant I would lose my place.

Our father, God operates in amazing ways! The man talked to another man and they said we should come again on the next day. Early in the morning when the Lozitha Royal Residence gates were opened for visitors, we were there waiting with Agnes in order to beat the queue. It did not take long for us to be seen. The man who addressed me said my case was going to be looked into. He spoke in a very promising tone. Agnes was doing all the talking by then, and told them how our case was an emergency one. Finally the man in charge said he thought I had to go to England in order not to lose my place, and he suggested I leave someone who will go before the council on my behalf. Agnes offered to do that. I left with an official note that my case was going to be discussed in my absence. I was made aware that before I am allowed into England as a student I had to have someone committed to helping me with my living expenses before I get my financial help, through the king's office.

All of a sudden things had taken a different direction. I called my youngest sister who worked as an administrator in another university seeking her help with my living expenses, my voice was partially excited because I could see the light on the other end, 'seeing so clearly' that I was going to be granted financial aid at the king's office. My sister was quite hasty, and electronically sent me her letter of commitment to helping me whilst waiting for my funding from the king's office.

Within two days I had purchased the flight tickets and my son's passport was released after the proof of flight tickets. On the day I was to leave I went to sign the study leave with pay forms, gave them to my head teacher and waved good bye to the few teachers who happened to be in the staff room at the time. I was on my way! Agnes offered to give me a ride to the Johannesburg Airport for free. I still do not understand God's ways. He brought Agnes into my life for that particular season, and all that was for a specific reason. Now I know God chooses some people to go and carry out specific duties for him. When they have done that He lets them go peacefully. Sometimes I look back and realise that there are some people with whom I used to have such good relationships. Some of these people were of great help to me and I was also of great help to others, but when I try to force the situation back to where it was, things just do not work. Whenever that happens we may feel a bit guilty and think maybe something is wrong. Now I know, no one has to feel bad about themselves, because 'There is time for everything' (Ecclesiastes 3:1).

When God's clock has clicked 'O'clock' for something it has just done that and all those concerned should come to terms with it. Sometimes we feel like the separation is loss, Oh no! It is not. Why?

And I know that all things work together for
good to those who love God, to those who are called
according to His purpose
(Romans 8: 28 NKJV)

I have just disclosed a lot of personal information, which is regarded as hanging one's dirty linen for the world to see. Why am I doing that? For you! It is for you my friend. People never talk about such things, and that is why there are so many suicidal cases. I want to encourage you and make you aware that God never leaves nor forsakes His own, when they turn to Him. He is there for each step of the way. Our mistake is that we want Him to pour out to us everything He has for us at a go. God's way of doing things does not go that way. He gives us 'our daily bread' and we eat it one day at a time. He does not give us our weekly, monthly, yearly or lifetime supply all at once.

When we have all our supplies we tend to forget God and sometimes stop trusting in Him. I now understand why the Israelites in the wilderness were given their daily food (*manna*) one day at a time. As I got into the plane on Friday, 5th October 2001, I thought, wow! Everything is fine now. My son, Mazulu was by my side and yes, God had honoured our faith in Him and made our departure possible. As I sat there reminiscing on the recent past events I was excited to finally enter my season of proper rest; little did I know that the real walk with my Heavenly Father was just beginning!

Chapter 14

Arrival in England

○ ○

By midnight on Sunday, 7th October, my coach arrived in Brighton, Poole Valley Coach Station. I was already from Newcastle in North England where my son was to reside. As I stepped out of the coach I could feel the stinging chilly air of the city. Probably this was a combination of the location of the city which is by the sea, as well as my being from warm tropical Swaziland. The coach driver who was probably looking forward to his union with his bed quickly gave me my luggage and turned to get back into the coach. I looked left and right, back and forth and there was no sign of anyone who might be in a similar situation as mine.

"Excuse me Sir, Can you please show me where I can get taxis to The University of Sussex?" I said beginning to understand the reality of my situation being alone with several pieces of heavy luggage in the centre of a big city.

"You need to call a cab love", he said heading for the door of the couch.

"Do you know where public phone booths are," I asked, trying to maintain my confidence and composure.

"Over there," he pointed as he got inside the coach.

Inside the phone room was a tall woman who had come off the same coach as me. She was ordering a cab too and she was going to Mouse Coomb which was on the way to Sussex University. She said if I did not mind we could use the same cab. I was relieved and thanked her. In no time our cab was there. The God sent angel helped me pass my luggage to the cab driver who carefully packed it in the cab. At the back of my mind I was expecting the cab to be at the University within a few minutes as a taxi from Mahhala Shopping Complex in Matsapha would take to get to The University of Swaziland. I was very tired and looking forward to a good night's sleep in what was to be my new bed.

After what felt like decades to me, the cab stopped and my God sent angel paid and alighted. After a few minutes I saw the big sign post Welcome to the University of Sussex. My face brightened up and the jolly little girl in me came to life. I became all smiles. The driver took me to York House where I had been told to collect the key to my students' shared house. The driver waited for me. As I walked there I was so excited thinking, 'yes I am here where one of the governors said I could never go.' That was the university of my dreams, where people such as the then President of South Africa, Thabo Mbeki studied.

The two security guards in uniform were on duty. After I had given the one in charge my name and all other relevant particulars, he gave me my two keys, one for the main door to my new house, number 101 Coomb Road and the other to what was to be my special space in Brighton, my bedroom. I was shocked to learn that the cab had to take me back towards the city centre where we just came from. I had thought my house was within campus as is the case in other universities I knew back in Southern African countries. They told me post graduates students were assigned houses outside campus as opposed to students' blocks within campus.

I realised that I was going to need transport to get to university which was an expense I had not anticipated. After what felt like ages to me the cab driver stopped outside my new home. He told me how much I had to pay and with trembling hands I handed over the £20 note. He gave me some change but it was all no use because I was still far from mastering my new currency. Moneywise, I was still thinking in terms of Rands and Emalangeni currencies. I felt like my paying more than R 100 was a clear and severe rip-off, as the exchange rate was £1 to R11.50. I had no idea the rate exchange was still going to cut deeper into my flesh than I had ever known.

Inside the house I locked the main door behind me and looked for my bedroom. I was looking forward to a good night's sleep. I had not eaten much earlier on due to anxiety, so my stomach started complaining. In trying to attend to the two pressures at hand I shoved down a sandwich I had not eaten along the way and washed it down with coke; at the time I had not cut off those kinds of drinks from my diet. When I eventually threw my exhausted body on my bed, I lay there like an infant who had been playing all day long does when sleep time comes. A heavily scheduled day waited ahead of me.

"Everyone has already been registered my dear. I'm afraid you have been left out due to your waking up very late," the lady at the counter of the registration room said.

"How could I do this to myself? How could I travel all the way from Swaziland only to enjoy sleep and miss registration?" I asked myself as tears started falling down my face.

"Please help me! This can't be! Please help me. I need to be registered. Oh please! Somebody help me!" I started screaming. What a way to wake up from a bad dream on one's very first day. I was relieved to realise it was only a dream. I also heard there was a knock at my door. The knock at the door must have rescued me from being late on my first day at Sussex University because it was when the knock became louder and also accompanied by a voice that I woke up.

"Is anybody in there? Alright then, I just wanted to check if I can use the shower", the voice went.

I sprang to my feet and staggered to the door.

"Hi! I'm very sorry I must have been fast asleep, I did not hear you," I said rubbing my eyes and yawning simultaneously.

At the door before me, in a full-length dressing gown was a longhaired woman. She had a very calm voice. She apologized for waking me up saying that she thought it would be proper to check if the latest housemate needed any help or to use the bathroom at the moment. We quickly introduced each other. Sociability was written all over her face and it made me even share my dream at which we both laughed copiously.

"It's clear that you are worried about being registered on time, so why don't we have a quick wash up and go to *Uni* together," Cathy suggested.

She offered me to use the bathroom first but I thanked her and declined, because I still had to do a little unpacking. It did not take long for us to get along. She told me she was Swedish and had come to do her PhD. She explained what her research was all about, but dear me, I cannot even remember now because it was one of those fields far from English literature, or just arts in general. I was amazed to learn that a young 'girl' was already in possession of a master degree and now taking specialised research. Cathy was God sent to me because she explained a lot of things I needed to know such as how to get to university from Coomb road, as well as the different options of bus ticket purchasing. I learnt that one could save any purchasing long-term bus tickets called weekly, monthly or even three months savers.

When we got to Sussex University I discovered that what was before me was completely different from the university I had seen the previous night when fetching my keys. There it was before me, the buildings among very tall trees. Exactly as it was in the Postgraduate Prospectus I got whilst still in Swaziland. On entering, there lay Falmer and Bramber Houses. I felt like screaming saying, "Finally, I am here at Sussex! Yes, the very Sussex University I have been told I was too ambitious even to apply to. For a minute the words of all the pessimists I had encountered in Swaziland came to me in a flush:

"Hey *ntfombatana* (girl), you are over ambitious. Why don't you go to universities in South Africa? Sussex is a prestigious university."

It is even unfair to label this old man a pessimist because he had been telling me reality and in that case it was the ugly reality. If things were only in my control at that stage, I could have easily forgotten about the whole thing of going to study in England and waited for two more years to study in South Africa as suggested in the ministry of education. However, I could not reverse at that stage because I had already seen and heard a lot from God showing me that I had to pursue the dream and by faith it was all going to work. After getting very well and clearly the message in Hebrews 11: 6, I knew that having no faith was not an option for me. Doubting Him meant offending Him and I did not want to do that.

All said and done, I was a student at the University of Sussex. Ask me, how as I was not registered, I will still insist I was. My name was found in many of those offices. In the postgraduate office in Bramber House, they knew I was one of their own with my registration number clearly printed 20111582. Ask me more about this number; all I will say is that it was a registration number I had to reproduce in many of the offices. In the Accommodation Office in Bramber House, the records were clearly written with name, number as well as my special domain, my bedroom in 101 Coomb Road. In the international students' office situated in Arts B Building, my name and number were recorded as well. One floor above this office, the school of English and American studies my name was there too, together with the programme I was to pursue. Now, tell me; how could I accept anything contrary to these records? I am sorry to say, but no, I just could not think otherwise. That was it! I had finally arrived at Sussex University where I was a postgraduate student, but then order had to be followed.

As Matron Mndzebele used to say "First things first" at Mankayane high school during those early years, this really got stuck in me. Who could start with the last things when our mother '*Make* Mndzebele' as she was called had said? I had to deal with first things first. Although I wanted to get acquainted with the place, I had to attend first things first by going to the registration office. With Cathy's help, I had done very well and I was one of the very first few on the queue. My turn came and the guide showed me where to go. I had to go through a number of hands. The first was a table where you had to produce documents giving the name of your sponsor/s.

As I walked there I had this awkward feeling in my heart and for a moment or two someone next to me could have heard the horses racing in my chest. I quickly remembered how to deal with this and took a deep breath, similar to deep breaths, Mrs Douglas my antenatal instructor trained me to take in 1992.Those breathing exercises were meant to help me deal with the labour pains I was to go through during the birth of my son, Mazulu, but to my surprise they were now coming quite handy. After that very deep breath, I felt like I had regained composure. I do not know if anybody noticed anything. I therefore walked confidently to the table, wearing my all weather trademark; my smile with great confidence.

The lady on the other side of the table smiled in a way that made her teeth flash. This triggered a real broad smile from me, which lasted only a minute. I sat down at what was my chair at the moment. I sat upright; making sure that an angle of 90 degrees was formed where my torso met the table before me. I held in my stomach, pushing my bust a little out and tilting my shoulders a bit back. My chin went a bit up as if to elongate, my neck. My eyes were focused on those of the lady on the other side of the table. Being a loyal student, how could I betray Mrs Guma? That was my time to display having been groomed by Professor Guma's wife. She had been a very special lecturer to most of her students.

"*Bantabami* (my children), especially you girls, when you walk, walk with life, don't drag yourself, as if your body aches all over. When you sit down, you don't just tumble down like baked Alaska. Sit up…" I reminisced on my College English lecturer's mentorship.

I liked Mrs Guma and she actually became one of my role models. How could I therefore forget what she had taught me, all those years back? The lady in the office told me to produce my paper about my finances. I did not have much apart from the mail I had from the university, the letter from my sister stating that she was going to help pay my fees in instalments if all came to worst with my hope for financial help from the king's office. To this, the lady smiled again.

"Lovely! Now, Betty how much deposit are you paying now?"

The 'horses in my chest wanted to start galloping' again, but this time I had full control. My response pointed back home where my expectant eyes were looking. The lady told me they were giving me what was called 'refused' registration, which was actually not as bad as it may sound. What it meant was I could go on with all university activities, such as meeting my tutors, lecturers and fellow colleagues, at the scheduled times. However, I had to be back in the same office in two weeks to report the development of my case, or probably to pay or submit a letter from an organisation or a board of some sort, promising that my fees would be paid. Their giving me two weeks was a breakthrough to me because I thought my cheque or letter to affirm my funding was to arrive anytime soon. Being in my shoes what would you do? Rejoice and give praises to your God, yeah? Exactly! That's what I did. What I had to do was settle in Brighton like every other student and wait for the funding issue to be sorted in Swaziland.

Something made me feel like I had to search for possible funding whilst waiting for the outcome at The King's Office. That very first week, my diary entry for Thursday, 11th October, 2001 reveals what those early days meant for me:

> *This wonderful Thursday morning I have still not been registered at this University, but I am allowed to attend seminars. This morning I will submit my application to the Mandela Fund and then search for funding in the Career Development Office. There, they have a facility called Funder-Finding and I have already made numerous applications to educational trusts accessible to international students which I learnt about through the Funder-Finding facility.*

I had no clue what the precise outcome was going to be and how it was going to happen, but as in the case of Abraham of the Old Testament, I was sure God was going to provide for my studies. When Abraham's son Isaac asked his father where the sheep for the sacrifice was, as he saw the firewood and the lighter. Abraham told his son that God knew. I also had that confidence that God knew and He was going to show up at the top of my 'Mount Moriah' (Genesis 22). I would be lying if I can say I had no anxiety attacks. They came, but I fought them with the truth I knew. My knowledge of God's provision from the Biblical stories as well as my own personal experience made me sing with boldness:

> *God can do it again and again and again.*
> *He can do the miracles.*
> *Like He used to do*
> *Yesterday, now, forever He's always the same...*

The rhythm of this song greatly appeals to my feelings, so as I played it in my mind and sang along I would close my eyes and make my slow moves, dancing with side sways. When I look back at this now I know, its melody married with the message made me love it and use it as my battle axe not only for my 2001 battle, but all recurring ones!

On my first Saturday I walked by Lewis Road looking for a Christian Book Store because I had accidentally left Our Daily Bread, the devotional I used then. I had no idea that God wanted to introduce me to another devotional which became so practical to me. I tumbled into a small book store that was heavily packed with all the good stuff I like. The store belonged to a woman who told me she was a Christian and told me where all the churches were. I opted for The Connaught School of Missions which was also along Lewis Road. The lady told me she did not have *Our Daily Bread*, but *A Word for Today*. I did not know it then, but God was beginning a new ministry in my life. The devotional was amazing and a year later I found myself having introduced the man of God, Bob Gass into many households in Swaziland.

Chapter 15

The way up is the way down!

○ ○

I counted it a blessing that I was attending all seminars, although I was not registered yet. I was waiting to hear from Swaziland. I had a lot to do whilst waiting. It was difficult for me to live away from my young son. Before I left Swaziland the older two were already in boarding school, so I was a bit used to speaking to them over the phone, but I wanted to see the young one. When I kept missing seeing my son although I spoke to him over the phone whenever I wanted, I realised how good God had been to me to make the Bennett family offer staying with him. It was a great relief to hear him speak in an excited voice telling me of his first day at school and all the good things he has received from Uncle P and Auntie V, ranging from his new uniform, new clothes, toys, a bike and more. He also told me of his new friends from school and at the Cubs club he had just joined. In the middle of his excitement he asked if my scholarship was sorted yet. I confidently told him I was sure everything would be fine soon.

I was right about everything being fine, but I am afraid I was not that accurate about the time factor. The reason for that being that God's time is not our time. He operates in ways too high for our small minds to conceive well. My wallet was beginning to tell me stories. It was getting hungrier by the day and the only way I could put something in it was through getting a job. I discovered I could get help from the Students' Advise Office regarding employment opportunities. I had limited time to do all these things because as I was hopping from office to office seeking advice and help my classmates were already goring their eyes on the bulky handouts our tutor had given us. I wanted to read too, but the order remained; first things first! Each morning as I lay in bed knowing that I was not so sure what the day brought for me I felt very humbled, but I counted it all a blessing because I knew when I left

I was at a point when I was running on my last drop of gasoline to go yet another mile in that house.

Materially, everything in the two houses I left in Swaziland was so gorgeous, with even royal colours such as the deep maroon and black colours in the bedrooms and the royal blue velveteen curtains trimmed with gold and matching sofas. The gigantic pricy dining room suit and all its accessories as well as the marble and ceramic tiled floors and walls in the bathrooms were nowhere near the glorious atmosphere that filled that tiny winy bare bedroom. As I lay in bed reading my Bible it became clear that God had been so good to me. I prayed whenever I wanted with no restriction. I revived my long lost habit of conversing with Father anytime and without even closing my eyes all the time. There was still time for that kind of eye-closing ritual, but I literally lived with Him and talked to Him like one would to a room-mate. It was a humble room, but I enjoyed it all. I never stopped exclaiming, "God you are good to me!" His presence filled my room!

By Sunday, 21st October a lot had happened. I was still not registered, but studying. I had been in and out of a number of offices including the Postgraduate Office, Study Abroad Office, International Students' Office, Students' Finance Advisor, Education department and a lot more. I had done a lot of funding search through funder-finding. That morning I went to church and it was marvellous. God gave me more reassurance and promise as He did the previous Sunday, but this time it came out full force because it was woven throughout the service from the songs we sang to the pastor's sermon. My Rhema word was 'hold onto the vision and dream ahead, and know that God Himself will see it come to pass'. There was also the special song which went:

> *Something good is gonna happen*
> *Something good is coming to me*
> *Something for me from the Lord Jesus*

Sister Pamela simultaneously hit the keys of the piano/organ and poured out her spirit into the microphone as she led the singing. I believed that the song was true for me. Amen! Yes, something good from the Lord was on its way to me. On Sunday evening, 21st October I went to the Christian Students' Union. It was fabulous there too. The message was still hitting on target, 'God is with you and He will see you through!' Remember, on the following day was the two weeks I had been given to come back for registration. On Monday I called home and they told me that the negotiations were still going on and things there tended to take longer time. I could not complain to anyone, because when I left I had been told they were going to look into my request.

I went to the registration office and they understood my situation and told me to focus on my studies whilst waiting. What a relief! I had thought they would just stop me right away if I had not brought the money. They did not give me any specific date to go there again, but said I should take my time doing all I can do to get the money. I was still allowed to attend all seminars. That was a new life I had never lived before. Some of the things that happen still baffle my mind up to now. The prerequisite for entering a university owned house was a down payment in the accommodation office. I have no idea whether God dealt with it by making me arrive after midnight when the offices were closed and I had to be given my key or what. My rent was going to be paid together with the rest of my fees. So I waited.

It became clear that I had to get a job and get it soon. I made many telephone calls, looking for part time jobs. Everywhere I applied they asked me the same question, "What is your National Insurance (NI) number?" I did not have an NI number. One could only get an NI number if there had been a job offer and I could not be offered a job without an NI number. What an awkward position! I needed things that I could not get without the other. At the same time I was getting responses from my funding application. Most were saying they had already made their allocations earlier, and my application came very late. That Tuesday afternoon I got a call from one agency saying I should come and register on the next day, Wednesday, at 2.00 pm. It was for a cleaning job which would commence at 4.00 pm.

I praised God for that job! I was offered a part time job by Hays Montrose. I worked from 4.00 pm to 8.00 pm at British Telecommunication (BT). I would be paid £5.50 per hour. When I got paid my wages for my eleven hours that first week I counted it as such a miraculous provision because my finances were drying up. That day I literally had only £2.60 left, but then I knew I was going to get my wages of £60.00 soon. God never leaves His own people who trust fully in Him and He keeps His promises. It was a humble experience, but I had amazing peace knowing well that what I was going through was for a purpose. I felt in my spirit that, like the children of Israel I had stayed too long in that wilderness and had to move on and claim my promised land.

I strongly believed God was bringing my provision of money for my studies. Strangely, I had no idea how I would get the money, but I was very sure He would not lead me out of Swaziland, to abandon me in England. I made daily journal entries and most of them were statements that revealed my strong faith that things were going to work out in an incredible way to a point that anyone who saw me go through what I went through could find it hard to believe that kind of documentation! My journal statements were like this one: "I am writing this down today so that whosoever reads this later when everything has come to pass may know that God is very faithful. God will never fail us. Praise Him Hallelujah!"

I **ministered to myself** in songs and when things looked really bad, I sang the song Tony Saiden used to sing as he travelled with Evangelist Reinhard Bonnke. I was not just singing, but I was truly filled with joy:

> *I just feel like something good is about to happen*
> *I just feel like something good is on its way*
> *I just feel like something good is about to happen...*

I agreed with Tony and felt like my own good thing could happen any day then. In all that excitement and expectancy the following Monday they told me I had to stop work at BT because the person I was covering for was back. That was a bad report naturally and, the normal thing to do would be to complain or feel bad when such a thing happened, but I did not. The situation looked very bad, but I knew who my Father is, and therefore praised Him whatever the situation was. I wrote in my journal, "Soon I will be back to bring some positive report, because that is how my Dad operates." The confidence I had in God regardless of what I saw before me was amazing.

I remembered the Biblical story about how the Israelites praised God before the walls of Jericho went tumbling down. I fanatically started praising God for the answers I was expecting. This may sound crazy, but I knew I was not crazy at all. By faith God had miraculously answered my prayer as I left Swaziland. By sight my prayer had not been answered yet, but then I did not go by sight and I still do not. I had seen my answers in the Spirit and I only had to wait to see it happen in the natural. As I praised God I knew He was tapping his foot to my praises; really enjoying it. I knew He was soon going to open His bag of goody-goodies and take out something especially for me. As I was thousands of miles away from my thirteen year old daughter, then, her words of encouragement kept ringing in my ears, "God will never disappoint us Mum." I feel like even interjecting and asking you to praise Him for what you believe Him to do for you. Praise Him before you see it manifest! Let us shower Him with all praise! Amen! It is no coincidence that you are reading my testimony. Praise Him for what you believe Him to bring to you if you do have something you expect Him to do for you. Amen!

Chapter 16

Divine Connections

○ ○

...... I know who holds tomorrow
And I know He holds my hand
With God things don't just happen
Everything by Him is planned
So as you face tomorrow
With the problems large and small
Just trust the God of miracles
Give to Him your heart.
(Swazi Gospel Singers)

All the faces in the seminar room looked friendly. I gave my name to quite a number of my new colleagues, and in turn I got a few names to associate with faces too. In that class were like family, but out of all those students, one had something special about her that drew us together. With time my friendship with Hailey Daniels began to grow. We discovered we were both Christians. Hailey had just given her life to Jesus through the Alpha Course at her new church. One Saturday night she invited me to a gospel concert at her church, Church of Christ The King. She thought at the concert I could possibly meet some people from my country, Swaziland because her church was very big and had many nationals.

The concert was fabulous. The music was great and I danced all the way through. It is very nice to dance to music that is about your passion. I love God and I love music that lifts His name high. At the end of the concert Hailey tried to connect me to some African people, hoping some of them would say they were from my country. One young man whose name I have forgotten said he was from Rwanda, and he said he knew a couple from Swaziland that goes to that church too. He took my mobile phone number to give to my country people. I looked forward to hearing from them, but no one from Swaziland called me that week.

You know sometimes when we want something; we expect it to happen 'sooner than yesterday'. If nothing happens at our time we sometimes give up hope. In my walk of faith I have learnt that God operates according to His heavenly clock. Truly, with Him everything goes according to plan. I believe it was for that same reason that Isaac did not come at Abraham's time. When God knows it is time for something He does it. He does things to fit them into larger pictures or larger plans. I have also learnt that God's plan is always too big for me to understand all the time. Sometimes He delays things to prepare us because if they happen at our time they would just hurt us or spoil the whole process of what He is doing in our lives. As I spend time with Him, I eventually get what He wants for me or get to where He is taking me, but He does not reveal all the steps He will lead me through and the duration of the whole journey there. This can sometimes be frustrating to some of us who want things happening fast, but as His child I am continually learning to trust in His perfect acts and stop being anxious. His Word tells me what makes me relax once I have obeyed knowing that He orders my steps:

The steps of a good man
Are ordered by the LORD,
and He delights in his way
(Psalm 37: 23 NKJV)

By the time Hailey invited me to her church concert I had been through severe testing. God was teaching me what real faith is about. In my experience I thought faith was about believing in God to do the impossible, and then seeing Him actually do exactly what I believe Him to do. I did not really get clearly the role of God's timing in our walk of faith. I had no idea that the walk of faith is more about aligning me with God's will for me than His giving me all that I want. This reminds me of how I have heard some preachers slash biblical verses and leaving out the vital elements of those verses such as praying in His will. If we ask for something that He wants to give us because He deems it good for us, we get it, but if we ask for something that He does not want to give us He does not. The secret key again here is that He never withholds anything good from us. If He holds it back He knows it is not good for us. Check this:

For the LORD God is a sun and shield;
The LORD will give grace and glory;

No good thing will He withhold
from those who walk uprightly
(Psalm 84: 11NJKV)

Mark that last clause in the verse, "for those who walk uprightly." Anyway, when I left Swaziland believing God for a miraculous provision of a scholarship I had heard God clearly promising me to do it for me. In my little mind which is far less than God's own:

For as the heavens are higher than the earth,
So are My ways higher than your ways,
And My thoughts than your thoughts"
(Isaiah 55: 9 NKJV)

I thought God was going to provide my need as soon as possible. I felt the same way as the two sisters of Lazarus felt when they sent for Jesus because of their ill brother. They expected Him to come soon before it was too late (before he died). Oh, God is neither late nor early. He is always on time. His timing may not always align to what we expect, but it is always the best!

In a way similar to Lazarus eventually dying, being buried and beginning to stink, my scholarship situation had started to stink. There was completely no hope. I had visited the student's Career Development Unit of Sussex University to a point where the whole exercise almost lost meaning. I had tried all possible sources of funding and had got the same responses, 'Not eligible to this kind of funding' or 'too late; apply for next year'. I needed money for my fees that same academic year 2001- 2002. I know, you may be asking why I had to get into the trouble of making applications everywhere, but remember how things were when I left Swaziland. I was not guaranteed a scholarship. They said they were to look into my issue. I have learnt to walk, one step at a time. I knew in my knower that God wanted me to go and study, so the King's office was definitely instrumental in pushing me to the 'ice cold swimming pool I would not dared dive into, had I known how cold it was.' I hope you get my picture here.

Well I tried to call the people back in Swaziland and I was told they had removed Agnes from the whole equation. My spouse was the one representing me there. He was the one who delivered the dreaded outcome to me over the phone. They had finally decided they could not help me so my spouse had to recall me. That was supposed to be shattering news, but honestly when I heard such a report I had already gone a long way with God and I had already been baking long enough in God's oven to agree to be taken out before I was well cooked. I wanted to go all the way and see Him give me that Masters

Degree He had promised. The fact that all along the people in Swaziland had said they were still discussing my case was a sign for me that God wanted me to stay believing. So, I heard, but I rejected that negative report and believed God for my provision.

Faith is an amazing 'thing'. You keep on believing God when everything around you says 'there's nothing to believe in here'. I knew God had promised me and so He was going to do it. Whenever people asked about my fees I completely had no explanation to give but said help was along the way. One day I got the call I had been waiting for. The Swazi couple from Hailey's church called and I cannot explain the excitement of hearing my language in a place where I least expected it. Although I was happy to hear from these people I hated the idea of anyone having to ask me about my student status and finances. I believed God was working on something, but I was not ready to be interrogated about the *hows* and *whens.* By that time, I solely survived on my four hour evening job at BT. I even managed to do a daily four hours because my time table was favourable for that!

As Swaziland is a very small country it is every possible to know most people, especially those in one's profession, so I realised that apart from the fact that those two had been teachers like me, they had been my clients in my part time business at 'Betty's Bridal Boutique'. The woman had her engagement outfit designed and made in my boutique. We were all excited. They invited me over to their rented flat in the city centre one evening after work. I was excited and looked forward to meeting the couple, but a part of me was reluctant because of the possibility of questions about my finances. As you already know before I left Swaziland, everyone asked who was funding me; I knew that question was bound to come again.

I had a very good time that evening at Andrea and Thandz Dlamini's place. Soon the dreaded question of my scholarship was asked. I simply told them the truth. Amazingly, something in me just grew and I confidently told them that I did not know yet where my fees were to come from but I was definitely sure that God was going to provide and at the end of the academic year I was getting my MA qualification. Oh, I have to tell you now I know God likes it when you trust Him that way, and just speak **FAITH** even when you have no facts to support what you believe in. Thandz, the wife was in a similar situation as mine because she had also started doing her MA without a proper grant. However, her case was different in that her husband had a grant from the Swazi government and she greatly hoped to get it too. Actually, later things worked well for her and we praised God.

A New Ray of Hope

Whilst still in Swaziland I had heard from my sister Zanele and VB, who helped me look after my son that there was something called being a supply teacher in England and those who got into that programme were paid very well, but I had no clue what one had to do to become that. I had been a High School teacher and Administrator in my country but did not know where to start from in trying to get a teaching job. Actually I did not even know I could possibly teach whilst studying. Thandz told me she worked as a supply teacher one or two days a week when she had no lessons at university.

Thandz explained the concept of being a supply teacher and gave me three phone numbers to call in order to be registered. I will not get into details here, but the good news is that the first number I called was to Teaching Personnel. They sent me an application pack. I sent it back with all my certified copies of my four certificates: Secondary School Maths and English Teacher's Diploma, Adult Education Diploma, a Bachelor of Education Degree in English Language and Literature and an Honours Degree in English. Before I knew it, the agency called and informed me that they received good references from the University of South Africa so they were offering me a job with them. I had no idea God had started putting pieces together to work out His plan for my life.

Like all other nights, as I came off the bus in Lewis Road and walked up to my shared student's house in Coomb Road I had a talk with God. You know if anyone was to be invisible and watch me closely they would bet I was crazy. I used to talk to God. I mean talk aloud. I used to cry in the dark winter night. I used to tell God how I felt about things, but I declared to Him I still believed Him for financial provision. I would talk like He was a human body walking by my side here on earth. Sometimes I cried. I shed loads and loads of tears, but the good thing is that God collects our tears. He also collects our words to use them in the creation of what we need. I was not aware that my time had come. I was expecting God to show up in a way that I would understand easily. God being God had other plans. Oh what a good God!

This might be difficult to understand well, but by the time Teaching Personnel offered me the job it was December 2001. I was going to start work when schools re-opened in January after the Christmas holidays. As I have said earlier the university had allowed me to attend seminars whilst waiting for my grant from home. As the year 2001 came to an end and the Christmas vacation was approaching I began to receive letters that really scared me, from the Finance office. I had to pay fees or else leave the university completely. They were going to stop me from attending seminars unless I was a registered student. In my courses I had started writing two term papers which were due for submission on 9th January 2002. I was already working hard on those term papers even though my BT job did not allow me enough time in the library.

With my inadequate funds I photocopied what I needed from the library. I could only read books in there and not borrow any out, because I was not registered. You know when you walk with God and He deals with you, He sometimes assigns angels to be there for you. I was the only student not registered in my group. God sent those 'angels', my colleagues to offer me help. I could not complain about library books. Immediately my colleagues knew about my shaky situation, they took out books I needed. The support was amazing! Although I was not registered, my term papers were taking shape. Whilst in Swaziland it had always been my principle to be the best I can be in my academic work. At Sussex I was not happy with my performance. I did not have enough reading time and preparation for seminars, so I was not even productive in discussions. I knew very well that given the time to read I could do better. I felt so humbled because I was not used to being a passive student in class discussions, but I found myself being that way in that current situation.

A few days after meeting my fellow Swazi people I got a letter from the registration office notifying me that I would not be allowed to submit my term papers unless I was registered. I had already poured myself into that work, so I prayed and trusted God to make a way. I made an appointment to see the Students' Finance officer, Mr M. You know God's angels began to take varying forms in that University. I laid my case before Mr M and asked to pay my tuition fees in instalments. When Teaching Personnel offered me the three days a week job and told me how much I would earn I realised that if I did not spend a single penny of that on anything else I could pay my fees. Mr M looked me in the eye and told me I could only be registered and pay my fees in instalments after paying a £1 000 deposit and showing proof of where the instalments would come from. My eyes brightened and I praised God. For me that was a miracle, right there in front of me!

When I look back to that time of my life I still find it hard to understand, let alone, explain to another person, how I really operated. I seriously do not understand how God made me do all that I did: Reading and writing my two term papers, doing my work at BT and wondering how to raise £1 000 immediately. Everything had to have materialised by 8th January 2002. Time was against me, **BUT** God was on my side. Whilst still in that maze I remembered that I could get money from my account with the Swaziland National Association of Teachers Cooperative (SNATC). I applied to withdraw E10 000 hoping it would be about £1000 as the exchange rates had been about three months earlier when I arrived in England. I had to make unending calls to Swaziland and jump from office to office at Sussex University to get my money before the appointed time. God assigned more angels through staff in the International Students' office and many more others.

By the end of the year, before the university closed for Christmas in 2001 I have furnished Mr M with all the necessary documents. I had faxed letters from SNATC and my bank in Swaziland stating that a sum of E10 000 would be sent over by January 2002. Teaching Personnel also sent me correspondence, confirming that I was guaranteed to get a three days teacher's wage, every week. What I had to do was come back before 8th January with £1000, be registered and then submit my term papers on the 9th January.

Satan never gives up. He tries to fight although he was defeated long ago. When the E10 000 was converted to UK Pounds, it happened to be the time when the rates were at their worst on the side of the South African Rand side. That rate has remained the lowest I have ever heard of to this day. My E10 000 (R 10 000) became £499.56 because the exchange rates had gone up to £1 to about R20 (E20) yet when I arrived in October it had been £1 to about R10/R11. Within two months things escalated so much. Later the rates changed and continued fluctuating, but they have not gone back to that £1 to R 20. When I had to transfer my money for fees from South Africa, my money was almost devalued by half. Looking back at the whole situation, I realise that was what my pastor, Ps. Matthew Ashimolowo calls a **Set-Up for a Lift-Up!** When a situation looks bleak, that is when His Hand over the situation becomes more magnified.

I was disappointed to recognise that I still had to raise an amount of £500 before being registered at the beginning of January. In the natural realm, there was no way I could raise that money in the amount of time left, which was basically less than a month. I prayed to God for an answer to that problem and **strongly** believed that He was going to do it. I encouraged myself with scripture and songs including the following:

Being confident of this very thing,
That He who has begun a good work in you
Will complete it until the day of Jesus Christ;
(Philippians 1: 6)

****

I shall overcome
I shall overcome
I shall overcome soon, soon and very soon
Deep in my heart
I do believe

I shall overcome soon, soon!
(A chorus)

****

He is able
He is able
I know my Lord is able
I know my Lord is able
To carry me through!
(a chorus)

****

God will make a way where there seems to be no way
He works in ways we cannot see
He will make a way for me
He will be my guide hold me closely to His side
With love and strength for each new day
He will make a way
He will make a way
(a chorus)

During the last but one week of the term there was a Student's Employment Day for that vacation period. Many employees flooded into the Students Employment Unit. I registered with quite a number of them, but I ended up taking a job to be a waitress at The Royal Albion Hotel. This was the job that later gave me my needed £500. God's angels took over the hotel management. I had favour in the eyes of almost all the managers. The Restaurant manageress, Mo always asked me if I needed extra shifts in addition to the official allocated ones. I took everything I was offered. Sometimes I did double shifts non-stop. This was the case also on New Years day. In addition to the many hours I worked that day was doubly paid. I could not work on the days around Christmas because I had to go up North to be with my son for that special time of the year.

My wages from the hotel were not going to be due until after the deadline at university. What was I going to do? God assigned His angels again and they took the form of the hotel finance manager. God's hand of Favour was upon me. The hotel agreed to pay my $500 cheque in advance so that I could be registered at university. On the 8th January I presented the Finance Officer, Mr M with my cheque of £500 from The Royal Albion Hotel and cash from SNATC in Swaziland.

On the 9th of January 2001 I submitted my term papers, but those papers were 'written by God Himself.' As my colleagues were polishing their term papers I polished mine in between Royal Albion shifts and BT shifts. As if that was not enough pressure on me, that was the time my spouse decided to send my daughter to me. He withdrew our daughter from Waterford KaMhlaba United World College because he felt it could be too much for him to deal with it whilst I was away. I left having paid for the two children up to December 2001. My daughter joined me within three months. The devil thought he had loosened all hell but praise God I did cry a lot but also sang my praises through that hard time. I had already learnt to sing praises through the storms!

When I got my results I could not believe it. I got a B+ for one paper and a C+ for the other. In UK universities an A is something you need to hire a Limo to bring home! For me getting a D would still be a miracle considering my circumstances, but this! That B+ grade after I had been writing in the wee hours of the night and dragging a tired body deserved a party! I shouted praises even louder making calls to all who cared about my achievements. Really, this is what I call a Divine Connection: Hailey Daniels, Rwandan brethren, Thandz & Andrea, Teaching Personnel, BT, Royal Albion Hotel..... you name it!

Chapter 17

More Heat in the Refiner

○ ○

I will refine them like silver
and test them like gold.
They will call on my name
and I will answer them;
I will say, 'They are my people,'
and they will say, 'The LORD is our God.'
(Zachariah 13: 9b NIV)

Christmas with the Bennett family and my son in Newcastle was fabulous, with a lot fun things and games as well as more food to eat than we had room, but I had to return to Brighton on Thursday, the day after Boxing Day. On Friday, 28th December I was getting my daughter from the airport. Although it was only three months since I had last seen her, seeing my daughter there felt like it had been ages. We were happy to be together, but it was very clear to both of us that the days ahead were uncertain. We had nothing but faith in God. Coming off the bus in Lewis Road and turning up into Coomb Road my feet really felt a bit heavy because I knew my daughter would be shocked to see the small room we were going to squeeze ourselves into before things got settled. The days that followed were a great challenge and on my side I did not like to see the child going through the trouble of having no proper place to call home. One of my housemates made it very clear that she did not want any extra person in that house and a teenager for that matter!

The challenges that followed exposed my daughter to a life of faith in a way she had never experienced before. She had only had glimpses of a life of faith when I lived alone with them as their father was away studying for three

176

years. During the first week of January 2002 we got to understand better what the Bible means by walking through fire and deep waters:

> *When you pass through the waters,*
> *I will be with you;*
> *And through the rivers,*
> *they shall not overflow you.*
> *When you walk through the fire,*
> *you shall not be burned,*
> *Nor shall the flame scorch you.*
> *For I am the LORD your God,*
> *Fear not, for I am with you;*
> *(Isaiah 43: 2, 3a &5a NKJV)*

The challenges we faced made us see more parts of God we had never seen before. We had to leave the university house and look for private rented accommodation, but my circumstances were not favourable of taking that venture at that time when I had to work hard taking on three jobs as a BT cleaner in the evening, Hotel waitress on weekends and some late evenings as well as being a supply teacher on three days a week. I still had to be at university for seminars, two days a week. Those were long days for me, but God gave me the grace to survive within that kind of abnormal living. When I got a room to rent as I share all other house amenities with a Muslim family I was pushed by the affordability of the room, but later I realised God was training me more. Although at first I did not like living with that family, it turned out to be a blessing in disguise because I could be away working in the evening knowing that my daughter was with the couple and their two young girls.

My daughter became one of the worship team at church and therefore attended special bible study sessions and prayer meetings which I could not attend due to my pressure to work all the time. Living with a family of a different faith from us was a challenge, but I thank God because that was a great way of making our lives to be a testimony. When things were really bad I remembered my mother and grandmother's deep teaching, which emphasised maintaining a kingly poise when everything around says bring out the animal part of you. By the time I got accommodation close to university things had greatly changed and we were really like one family and many of the prejudices that had prevailed on both sides when I first moved in there had disappeared.

Working at BT and the Royal Albion exposed me to people from a wide variety of backgrounds. Almost all continents of the world were represented in those two workplaces. Similar to my workplaces, my church was very diverse. It was in that church that God provided me with sisters who lifted me up, making sure collapsing was out of question. Two of the sisters were also studying; one of them, Sister Sharayi was in her final stages of a doctoral degree and Masego was finishing an M Phil program. We prayed and even experienced miracles together.

Sister Sharayi became a mentor me in that season of my life and it was through her that I fully discovered academic qualifications do not interfere with who people really are. Sharayi was a very humble woman and through her mentorship I learnt that sometimes in order to go up we should not be stiff, but flexible to the leading hand of God. I learnt that sometimes when God takes you up to greatness His pathway leads through downward and very lowly valleys. On the other hand, Masego, a fanatic for the Lord was like a baby sister to me. When with Masego, the young girl part of me came alive and we listened and danced to Benjamin Dube's praise songs. Our favourite track at the time was *Humble yourself in the sight of the Lord, He will lift you up* and *Dance, dance, dance, all night long.* I had known and sung the 'humble yourself' song as a chorus back in Swaziland, but it took on a different meaning for me this time around, because when I spoke of 'humble' I then knew what I was talking about.

I learnt about the importance of being very patient and waiting upon the Lord who gives me what He has for me at His time. I realised that God is the one who knows people better than they know themselves and therefore I decided to spend good time in His presence, trusting Him to lead me through and I continually told Him I needed His guidance. It took me time to understand that what God was allowing to come my way as I obeyed the instructions He gave me was actually making me a spiritually well toned beautiful woman. I learnt to appreciate a lot of what I had taken for granted before.

In Swaziland I had more than enough of almost everything and as a result did not really appreciate all that the way I now know I should. Simple things such as good weather, friends and family began to have more value than ever before. I realised that if I had got to the UK with a full scholarship that would cater for all my expenses as is normally the case with most people who go to study abroad from my country I would not have appreciated His provision the same way. God led me all the way in His way through the valley called *Humble* for a reason. If I knew all this was going to happen before I left Swaziland I probably would have resisted.

I learnt to count every blessing and to receive my daily bread from my Heavenly Father in a way similar to the Children of Israel receiving their Manna when they were in the wilderness. In my wilderness I learnt to live one day at a time, depending entirely on God's daily provision. We scheduled prayer times with Sister Sharayi and rested our heads and hearts on Matthew 18: 18 and 19 in agreement:

"Assuredly, I say to you, whatever you bind on earth
will be bound in heaven,
and whatever you loose on earth will be loosed in heaven.
"Again I say to you that
if two of you agree on earth concerning anything that they ask,
it will be done for them by My Father in heaven.
(Matthew 18: 18-19 NKJV)

We would sit there, having already made two lists of what we were going to present before our Father's Throne of Glory and we dated everything. We always started with the longer list which was the list of praises. There were always many things we wanted to praise and thank our Father for. Some of those items had been in the request list before, but the majority of them were things our Father had done for us without even our asking. The list of requests was also long as the scripture confirms the immensity of our challenges:

Many are the afflictions of the righteous,
but the LORD delivers him out of them all.
(Psalm 34: 19 NKJV)

All those prayer items were answered fully. Praise God! Even as I am writing, I feel like shouting with joy at the thought of it! Our Father answered all our prayers! I even feel like jumping the gun and leaving out the rest of the story to tell you what has happened between then and now and tell you where I am now. It is difficult to share in one sentence what has happened over years. What I am pleased to announce right now is that Dr Sharayi Chakanyuka made it and returned to her country where she has a prestigious position. The experiences we had as students that year are a thing of the past and can be recited only for a laugh now, and a way of seeing further ahead with confidence in God, knowing that He who has done what is behind us will do what we believe Him to do for us in times ahead. Right now, I feel like David, the shepherd boy who remembered very well what God had done for him and through him and then had much confidence in God to help him bring down the giant before him. David boldly declared:

... "The LORD, who delivered me from the paw of the
lion and from the paw of the bear, He will deliver me
from the hand of this Philistine."

> ... *"You come to me with a sword, with a spear, and*
> *with a javelin. But I come to you in the name of the*
> *LORD of hosts, the God of the armies of Israel, whom*
> *you have defied.*
> *This day the LORD will deliver you into my hand, and*
> *I will strike you and take your head from you. And*
> *this day I will give the carcasses of the camp of the*
> *Philistines to the birds of the air and the wild beasts*
> *of the earth, that all the earth may know that there is*
> *a God in Israel.*
> *Then all this assembly shall know that the LORD does*
> *not save with sword and spear; for the battle is the*
> *LORD's, and He will give you into our hands."*
> *(1 Samuel 17: 37, 45 – 47 NKJV)*

Remembering all that God has done in the past makes me even confident enough to declare that the testimony I am relating now is a starter because God has set a table with a six-course meal ahead! I am aware that **victory is inevitable** when one continues in the walk of faith and continues **speaking** those things which one believes God for as though they are already there, for indeed in the Spirit realm they are there already!

I always thought that faith can be verified by how much our prayers have been answered. Having our prayer needs answered is part of the deal but, there is a part I would like to bring out now; that faith is a ***PROCESS***. The process is not very easy, but with God as the guide and following all the simple and a bit 'foolish' instructions we make it. I want to emphasize again that it is a walk because walking is a process. One of the simplest instructions that I have noted to be recurrent in all situations where faith is in action is ***TALKING***. God talked when He created the universe. He brought into being what was not there by only a word of mouth. In my walk of faith I have found myself **talking** more than just wishing.

My breakthrough was continually interconnected to the words I said out loud with my mouth. Those words were provoked by what I saw before me. Whenever I saw negative and hopeless circumstances I would then refer to the Word and find out what it says about me. My condition of combining parenting, work and studies the way I did in a foreign land was a huge challenge I had never seen before. I often felt like I was crumbling down, but as each challenge became overwhelming I cried out to God and then confessed each Word with a promise such as this one:

And the LORD will make you the head
and not the tail;
you shall be above only, and not be beneath,
if you heed the commandments of the LORD your
God, which I command you today,
And are careful to observe them.
(Deuteronomy 28: 13 NKJV)

There was a time when I was battling badly and did not even have money for transport, but as I was sitting right in church God urged me to encourage those who were battling with certain needs and tell them that He does not want us to limit Him. He said we should see Him as a Father who can actually do more than we can even imaging as the Apostle Paul states to the Ephesians:

Now to Him who is able to do exceedingly abundantly
above all that we ask or think, according
to the power that works in us,
to Him be glory in the church
by Christ Jesus to all generations,
Forever and ever. Amen
(Ephesians 3: 20 – 21 NKJV)

God made it clear to me that when we have limited thinking we limit Him of His glory too, because whenever He manifests in our lives He gets the glory. I stood up and spoke to the believers what God was saying to me, but it sounded a bit absurd to me to be the one to say these things when in the natural I looked like I was the least qualified. Whenever I obeyed His instructions to make confessions that did not really make sense in the natural He then started providing for me in a way that made me marvel such as the two occasions when I got money in the mail without stating where it came from. At that particular time I had not told anyone of my need except for my daughter. One of the envelopes was stamped Gatwick and I had no idea who could have sent me money from there. All I know is that God assigns His angels to do the incredible things we least expect.

Another peculiar thing about my experiences was my student status which was endorsed in slots. Each time I paid the monthly instalment I was registered for that month only and in order to have continuous access to all university amenities I had to have paid in full. Sometimes I was not able to bring the right amount of money because when we made our calculations we did not take taxes into consideration. The situation kept me on my knees and my mouth coughed out and breathed the relevant scriptures like daily carbon dioxide that we exhale. Whenever things seemed bleak I took a deep breath of 'oxygen' from the Bible and exhaled:

You are of God, little children,
and have overcome them,
because He who is in you is greater
than he who is in the world.
(1 John 4; 4 NKJV)

See, I have inscribed you on the palms of My hands;
Your walls are continually before Me.
(Isaiah 49: 16 NKJV)

I personalised these verses and said them like a crazy person, "greater is He that is in me than He that is in the world...I am His Princess and I will not lack...my Father will finish what He started in me...my face is engraved in the palm of His hand." The one of being engraved in the palms of His hands made me realise that I am what He wants to look at all the time. I imagined how He continually looks at His hand to see me like a lover always opens a locket with the photograph of a loved one just to have a glance at them. It realised that His difference is that lovers take a break from looking at their loved ones and they even sleep, but my Father does not:

I lift up my eyes to the hills—
where does my help come from?
My help comes from the LORD,
the Maker of heaven and earth.
He will not let your foot slip—
he who watches over you will not slumber;
Indeed, he who watches over Israel
will neither slumber nor sleep.
The LORD watches over you—
the LORD is your shade at your right hand;
The sun will not harm you by day,
nor the moon by night.
The LORD will keep you from all harm—
he will watch over your life;
The LORD will watch over your coming and going
both now and forevermore.
(Psalm 121 NKJV)

God likes it when we believe Him and stay obsessed with Him. When you do not stop talking about your trust in Him and the full assurance that He is going to keep His promise, He finds no reason to deprive you of the requested thing as the Psalm of the sons of Korah assets:

> *For the LORD God is a sun and shield;*
> *The LORD will give grace and glory;*
> *No good thing will He withhold*
> *from those who walk uprightly.*
> *(Psalm 84: 11 NKJV)*

My Father sustained me in that very uncertain situation of looking up to Him for each new day like the children of Israel experienced in the wilderness. I completely focused on surviving and did not even think of other things such as what to do next when I finish as well as where to get the ticket home if I was to go. God completely put me into a deep sleep about all other matters. I had even forgotten about the Commonwealth Scholarship application forms I had given to my spouse, when he called and told me he had been granted the scholarship. He was coming to pursue a Master of Science degree in the UK. He told me there was no need for us to return to Swaziland because we could stay on as his dependants. I had even forgotten what God urged me to say in my church about my whole family being in the UK the following year.

I received the news as a great breakthrough and looked forward to the family reunion. Without even being aware of it, the end of the academic year was approaching and I had to write my dissertation (thesis in the US). That was almost impossible to do with all three jobs. I had to make a decision. Although I badly needed the money, I realised in order to pass I had to drop the two less paying jobs and stay with teaching. The BT and Royal Albion people had become family to me, so it was with watery eyes that we said our 'good-byes' a I told them I was no longer going to work. I pushed myself with my reading and writing and sometimes had to cross night, but on the first week of September I miraculously completed my MA dissertation! When I dropped the two other jobs, the Finance office agreed that although I had not paid a substantial amount of money I could go ahead and submit my dissertation. He said they were going to withhold the results and transcripts until I had paid. What a relief!

Just before I left Brighton God connected me to MBE Heather Cowl. She was the one who led my friend Hailey to the Lord. I discovered that she knew the missionary who established my childhood church in Swaziland and she had even purchased some of the necklaces that my grandmother and other women made and sent abroad. MBE Heather connected me to her friends who were pastors of a church in Leicester where we were going to stay. God blessed us a lot through Pastors Richard and Rosie Jarvis. God used them to make my move from Brighton to Leicester comfortable. My young son came down from Newcastle and joined us with my daughter before we moved to Leicester.

When I moved to Leicester it was easy for Teaching Personnel to forward all my papers to the Leicester branch. In Brighton I had done very well even in the most difficult of schools where supply teachers are normally summoned to fill in for teachers. The good references landed me in the challenging schools of Leicester, but I was happy I had work because I wanted to pay off my fees at Sussex University and get my results. They had already told me I had passed, but in order to know the final grades as well as get the transcripts I had to pay. That was another challenge I had to present to my Father. I believed I was going to get my results. I had to get the transcripts urgently!

Holy Spirit talks and He designs the pathways upon which the righteous tread. When my walk of faith started I accustomed myself to obeying Him without analysis to a point whereby when He started using the very acts of obedience to bring by my breakthroughs, it all came as a surprise to me. I did not see the connectedness of everything until later. When Holy Spirit nudged me I was beginning to be content with my long placement at Rawlins 6th Form College. I was used to waking up early every morning to go to teach, when all of a sudden I remembered the words of the lady at the Ministry of Labour and Public Services in Swaziland.

The lady had told me that the Commonwealth Scholarship was competitive and I remembered that the Ministry of Education had actually given me a recommendation that I never took advantage of. It dawned on me that I needed to put in my application whilst there is time. Somehow, I felt like if I applied I could definitely get the scholarship for a PhD this time. In my spirit I was convinced that if my proposal and whole application pack could get to whosoever made the selection I was going to get the scholarship. However, there was a hurdle before me; I had no transcripts and I could not get them until I had paid what I owed the university. I had to do something and do it fast!

When God wants to bless you He whispers to you and if you are waiting for a screaming voice you miss His voice. I was still learning to heed His voice. I heard the words 'bank loan', but I thought that was out of question because I **could not** get any loan as I had just opened a checking account in my new bank and I was hardly two months with them. I also did not like having a debt. At the time I had not even know about Robert Kiyosaki's teaching in His ***Rich Dad World*** to understand more about leveraging as well as good and bad debts, but the inner voice about a loan insisted. Next, I had a debate within myself with the louder voice saying I should forget about the whole thing and just work to pay off the Sussex debt. God's whispers continued and He told me to just go and ask and not allow the voice that was already talking on behalf of the bank people saying I did not qualify to get the loan.

My appointment was only a telephone call away. I prayed before going there believing that if He had nudged me to go and apply for a bank loan He would not embarrass me. The attendant told me my case had to be referred to a manager because I had not been with the bank for even three months. I climbed up the stairs to the manager's office and we sat and talked. I told her the whole chain saga about wanting to pay off my tuition fees, to get the results and transcripts, to apply for a scholarship whose deadline was less than a month away. Also, I told her I needed just the amount I owed the university, which was a little more than £3 000. I had already been getting some steady income from my teaching, but the stumbling block was the limited period I had been with the bank. The manager looked at me for a long while and as I am writing it is like I can hear her voice, "I have never done this, but I can see your situation very clearly, so I will say go and pay that university and get your results."

That was a miracle. I did not say a proper 'thank you,' but I simultaneously thanked her and prayed to God right there in front of her with tears falling down my face praising God as well as pray blessings over her. I am just telling it as it happened. That bank manager was an angel assigned to fulfil a mission for God in my life. I called the university and paid by debit card that same afternoon. I do not need to even get into details, but by God's grace in less than a month, through DHL; my application pack had hopped from one place to the next starting from Leicester in England to the Ministry of Education and Ministry of Labour and Public Services in Swaziland and finally the Association of Commonwealth Universities in London, England! What I remember is that as I was putting my proposal together, I spoke like a crazy person, declaring that I was going to get the Commonwealth Scholarship!

God is faithful and what He says surely comes to pass. I love the song by Queen LaMbikiza of Swaziland, which she sings accompanied by the Courageous Group, "What goes says will surely come to pass!" What God said to me in 2001, as I obeyed His inner voice and stood up to speak about what I did not even know or understood at my church EBC, definitely came to pass. In 2002 my whole family was in England for Christmas and we were in Leicester, a place I had never even heard of whilst still in Swaziland.

Chapter 18

What is this now?

o o o o o o o o o o o o o o o o o o o o o o o o o o o o o o

As the year 2003 showed up its face I was eagerly waiting for it and more than anything else I was looking forward to my graduation ceremony at Sussex University. That was going to be a very unique ceremony for me because that was going to be where I celebrate God's faithfulness. I am learning every day, but I still see myself not having fully mastered the understanding of how God operates. When I felt like I was really on the edge in 2001, God told me to engage in a walk of faith with Him. As I have already said above, I knew He was going to provide for my studies, but I thought He was going to give me one fat cheque in the form of a grant, but He knew that giving me that kind of provision was not going to get me to where He is taking me, so He trained me by giving me what I needed, in His own way, one portion at a time. Well, the afternoon of 23rd February, 2003 was going to be the day I celebrate His providing for me 'in style!'

My sister Zanele and her husband took days off work to come and celebrate with me. MBE Heather Cowl, in Brighton was also going to put the day aside for me. She even offered to have us come to her house for dinner after the ceremony. She wanted me to bring all those celebrating with me. I was a little disappointed to go down to Brighton with only my daughter, but I was still happy there were a few others who planned to celebrate with me. Although my own ceremony was in the afternoon, the Sussex University Publishing Department people asked me to come early because they were going to do a special article about my achievement. The Argus Newspaper was also going to do an article. They all wanted me to share how I had managed to get through within the circumstances I had faced. As Lord Attenborough shook my hand on the stage, I felt like screaming 'Hallelujah, Praise the Lord!' right there. Amazingly, in his speech he made reference to my country and another neighbouring one, emphasising how women in that region value education for their children. As I posed for photographs I could not help it, but lift up my hands and bless His name with no shame!

After the graduation life went back to normal, but once again, there were some abnormalities in my life. When I took the bank loan I thought I would pay it easily because I knew I had survived in Brighton, a more expensive city than Leicester, but my nasty past caught up with me. I realised the money I got from teaching was not enough to feed the family and pay the rent plus the loan. Things became harder than they had been in Brighton where we lived our simple life with my daughter in order for me to pay my fees. This time around with a man in the house I had to prepare descent meals which my shallow pocket could not afford. I had always done that and there seemed to be no way out. I tried to seek help, but when I got none, in my troubled mind I had to come up with something quick and I decided to take two jobs. I taught during the day and in the late afternoon had to wait at the library for a car to take me to another faraway place where I worked in an industry lifting heavy metals and all those kinds of things. I was not the only woman, but it was honestly a tough job.

In my abnormal living, I got home after midnight and managed only three hours of sleep and I soon tuned my mind to think it was all right. My body complained, saying it was too much, but I did not give any voting right to the body, so three hours-sleep stayed on. I was depriving myself of sleep, something important, which God gave us for a reason:

> *It is vain for you to rise up early,*
> *To sit up late,*
> *To eat the bread of sorrows;*
> *For so He gives His beloved sleep.*
> *(Psalm 127: 2 NKJV)*

Looking back at this whole confusion, I wonder how I did not crumble then. The reason is that I was not alone. God was there with me as I said earlier. The situation resembled that of the Israelites in Egypt where Pharaoh raised up the demands by saying they should produce the same amount of bricks without the provision of straw. When they failed to produce they got their whippings for not meeting the demands, but for me the whippings were emotional. As I was quite skilled at concealing nasty situations, I continued to wear the 'make-up' I had worn for years, by showing a bright image to the world. However, some of the inner pain surfaces without any invitation.

In April, I got the good news from Swaziland that The Association of Commonwealth Universities in collaboration with The British Council had awarded me a full scholarship which came with allowances for a spouse and children! What a breakthrough at last! I did all the necessary paperwork and all our passports had a visa stamp that covered all my years of research. Although I had applied to some universities and I already had a prospective supervisor in one of those universities, my sponsors said they wanted me to go to the best university for my proposed area of study. They gave me three top universities to choose from. Listen to that; I had to choose!

I learnt a great lesson from God's provision of such a wonderful and comprehensive scholarship in 2003; God does not close doors when he has better ones only, but He also closes doors when He wants to open gates that lead to corridor doors whereby the opening of the gate automatically leads to the opening of every other door that follows thereafter! Another striking truth I have learnt is that when God opens a door or gate there is always a contender. Satan has been close to God before and he knows all the benefits that come as a package of that intimacy, so he does all he can to block anything good. My announcement, however, is that he was defeated long ago and all his attempts are a failure – if you kick him in the face in the name of Jesus of Nazareth like Jesus did. The best kick is found in the very story of Jesus being tempted by Satan. It is quoting the written Word:

> *Then Jesus was led by the Spirit into the desert*
> *to be tempted by the devil.*
> *After fasting forty days and forty nights, he was hungry.*
> *The tempter came to him and said,*
> *"If you are the Son of God, tell these stones to become bread."*
> *Jesus answered, "It is written: 'Man does not live on bread alone, but on*
> *every word that comes from the mouth of God.*
> *Then the devil took him to the holy city and had him*
> *stand on the highest point of the temple.*
> *"If you are the Son of God," he said, "throw yourself down.*
> *For it is written:*
> *"'He will command his angels concerning you,*
> *and they will lift you up in their hands,*
> *so that you will not strike your foot against a stone.*
> *Jesus answered him, "It is also written: 'Do not put*
> *the Lord your God to the test.*
> *Again, the devil took him to a very high mountain*
> *and showed him all the kingdoms of the world and their splendour.*
> *All this I will give you," he said,*
> *"if you will bow down and worship me."*
> *Jesus said to him, "Away from me, Satan! For it is*
> *written: 'Worship the Lord your God, and serve him only.*

Then the devil left him, and
angels came and attended him.
(Matthew 4: 1 – 11 NIV)

Right in the midst of my great breakthrough I saw the enemy sneaking in like a snake. I thought things had changed, but nothing had changed. I saw what I will call 'troubled water' stirring up from nowhere. I became determined in my heart to fight for my family like I had always been doing even in my earlier years of marriage. When my sponsors asked me to choose a university I chose The University of London – School of Oriental and African Studies. My spouse did not want to move to London so I decided I was going to commute by train or coach from Leicester to London on the two days I had to be there in order to save my marriage. My sponsors and the university were concerned about my plan to stay so far from London, but when I told them my main reason was to save my marriage they allowed me to commute.

Very soon, in August I had to go for my orientation in London and that was when it became clear that I was back to square one with my 'troubled waters'. The situation got worse such that I could not even start writing the very first part of my proposal. My sponsors had told all of us new award holders that if we did not perform well they were to withdraw the award. I found myself trapped and needed help. As the case was in Swaziland where I desperately needed someone to turn to for help, I felt a great need for a counsellor, or a church pastor. Back in Swaziland I had my pastors at church, but the only help they could give was pray for me because they could not talk to us as a couple. My spouse said he did not need any counsellors.

I feel very strongly led to interject a special word into my narration. It is for any person wanting to get married whether young or old, male or female. I have hinted on this earlier, but I cannot stress it enough: It is very important to know what you are getting into and with whom you are doing it before you marry. Please hear me well I am not implying that marriage is an easy-go institute, although it can be. Marriage is something you grow in and it is something you work on together and develop as a couple. Therefore, in order for that to work the people getting married should be people who will struggle together or pull toward the same direction. One vital element is that God really has to be the central person; the pillar of the marriage:

Unless the LORD builds the house,
They labour in vain who build it;
Unless the LORD guards the city,
The watchman stays awake in vain.
(Psalm 127: 1 NKJV)

You can get my point very well if you imagine a lizard and a fish planning to get married. Fish thrive in water, but lizards thrive on dry land. Imagine the chaos that would result from the marriage of these two. First of all they may find it hard to agree on where to live and what to do for a living and definitely, the one with an upper hand may decide what happens, but the other one will just die. Sometimes death takes a long time such as when someone has got some slow slowly poisoning substance. It may take a long time to happen, but death eventually results. The main reason why I am including this bit in my testimony is that I do not want any other believer to experience what I experienced. As one of the ministers of the gospel says, 'there is no better teacher than those who have gone before you'. You can learn from those who have been successful and emulate them, but you can also learn from those who have made mistakes like me and avoid their mistakes thus avoid the immense hurt.

My supervisor became concerned that I was taking long to write the research proposal and I was even more concerned because I knew if my sponsors did not get good progress reports they were going to keep their word and withdraw my funding. My supervisor reminded me of the counselling services that students were entitled to and I made an appointment to go there. When the day came, as I sat there I remembered so vividly one of lecturers who taught us when I was doing the counselling course as part of the Bachelor of Education Degree package. Back then I had never imagined myself sitting on the side, as the recipient of help, but then it happened and found myself sitting there for help. As the counsellor asked me questions I knew where the real issue rested, but I was in denial. I was so protective of my cherished marriage that I found it hard to openly admit it had crevices that occurred from its inception and I was warned about them before I even said 'I do'.

The month of September stood to be a significant month because it was then that I realised what I had always thought was a moving car was an illusion. My counsellor had asked me questions which made me think very hard, but still I saw no way out of my problem because the only way out was what I dreaded the most. As said earlier on, God had used me to minister to other people who had problems in their relationships. This did not involve only women, but men as well. Some of the men were even respectable in society. I learnt from those experiences of ministering to people that God can use anyone like He used the servant girl to inform Namaan where he could get help with his leprosy.

I find it hard to simply carry on without warning you over and over again, because I know the repercussions of judging people who warn you and ignoring their words. One of my mother's sisters', Aunt Maria and her husband, Uncle Tom who was a finance specialist and was the Commissioner of Taxes in the country took their time to sit down with me before I was married and spoke about finances in marriage. I heard every word they said, but I spiritualised everything to the point of thinking that taking their advice would spoil my relationship. Right from the beginning I agreed to every suggestion my spouse made and thought that it was being more spiritual to do that. In the process of being a 'yes' woman all the time, I was ignoring the rich advice and in all my labouring had nothing of value under my name. It pleased me to realise that I was a Proverbs 31 woman who was bringing in the wealth:

Who can find a virtuous wife?
For her worth is far above rubies.
The heart of her husband safely trusts her;
So he will have no lack of gain.
She does him good and not evil
All the days of her life.
She seeks wool and flax,
And willingly works with her hands.
She is like the merchant ships;
She brings her food from afar.
She also rises while it is yet night,
And provides food for her household,
And a portion for her maidservants.
She considers a field and buys it;
From her profits she plants a vineyard.
She girds herself with strength,
And strengthens her arms.
She perceives that her merchandise is good,
And her lamp does not go out by night.
She stretches out her hands to the distaff,
And her hand holds the spindle.
She extends her hand to the poor,
Yes, she reaches out her hands to the needy.
She is not afraid of snow for her household,
For all her household is clothed with scarlet.
She makes tapestry for herself;
Her clothing is fine linen and purple.
Her husband is known in the gates,
When he sits among the elders of the land.
She makes linen garments and sells them,
And supplies sashes for the merchants.

Strength and honour are her clothing;
She shall rejoice in time to come.
She opens her mouth with wisdom,
And on her tongue is the law of kindness.
She watches over the ways of her household,
And does not eat the bread of idleness.
Her children rise up and call her blessed;
Her husband also, and he praises her:
"Many daughters have done well,
But you excel them all."
Charm is deceitful and beauty is passing,
But a woman who fears the LORD, she shall be praised.
Give her of the fruit of her hands,
And let her own works praise her in the gates.
(Proverbs 31: 10 – 31 NKJV)

I somehow felt a sense of worth from working hard to provide for the family as was expected and did not realise that it was reversing the order of things according to God's standards. Knowing that my marriage was the 'In Community of Property' type, where what is mine is my spouse's and what is his is mine I thought things would practically be like that. I was so wrong! I was busy 'bringing it in' and it made me feel even more secured and feel like the marriage was going to be for keeps as intended! During the months of September and October 2003 I was in tears all the time and there seemed to be no point to life. I do not want to relive the past because it was very nasty, but I stood there and watched everything I have valued so much in this world, apart from my God slip right between my fingers like melting ice cream.

The day my spouse left for Swaziland I had many questions whose answers I could only get by wiping the tears away, sitting in the presence of the Lord and His word as well as even putting food aside in prayer and fasting. God does not speak in a complicated way. He addresses us in a way we can hear and understand well. The only problem is that sometimes we are immersed within noisy crowds and as He speaks we confuse His words with the noise. I had been immersed in a noisy environment and whenever He spoke I would confuse His words with the noise, so my being in a posture of hearing Him and Him only, I heard clearly what He had always said. I had before me a situation I felt hopeless to change. I felt as someone who had been given a life sentence in prison. Actually in 1997 I even wrote a winning short story entitled "The Sentence". The story features a man, but I wrote it based on my own hopeless situation.

It was like Holy Spirit was the one probing and as if in a movie everything came so clearly. I did not need any external informant. Answers were right before me. Firstly, I got the answer to what confused me most at the time. The answer was that the United Kingdom was a country that did not take lightly the issue of abuse. Abuse is a reality and it is a term with meaning. In some cultures abuse is acceptable and it is actually perpetrated as part of the culture. God helped me replay my life story like a movie, from 1980 to that time, and making specific significant highlights all the way through. There were numerous rollercoaster kinds of experiences which I always denied, except for the fact that it was at those times that I almost took my own life. God had used so many methods of communication to wake me up, including dreams and direct scenarios which did not even require any interpretation, but each time the truth emerged I denied it.

My situation reminds me of a time when as young children we would climb into a wrecked car that had been abandoned for years and we called those cars *skorokoro*. Most of them did not even have wheels anymore. As we got into our *skorokoro*, one of us would sit on the driver's seat and the passengers in theirs too. We would then start making body movements as if our car was moving and sometimes wave hands to imaginary people walking by the road we were driving. Sometimes we would make jerks as if the driver had applied brakes on. Oh, we had so much fun as children, but the truth is that the whole thing was imaginary. We were not moving anywhere. The *skorokoro* was static.

As I sat in God's presence hearing no one else, but Him I saw things as if in a movie. I hated what I saw and wanted to play my old game of denial, but this time around Holy Spirit made me 'shut up!' and let Him continue showing me what I had to see. Having stayed there and not knowing what to do I decided to call my spouse and indeed his words confirmed everything Holy Spirit had been pounding in me for a long time and I never heard because of my immersion in noise. The words, "I have never changed" stamped the whole thing. The one who said them had no idea what they meant for me, but as I was the one who had been spoken to by the Lord I got it all so clearly. The biggest question I had and I loathed addressing was, "Betty, are you married?" The *skorosoko* imagery came again and I realised how I did the same thing in my life. When I did not get anywhere I would always cry, but Holy Spirit knew the truth.

Another question that had always bothered me was why my marital life had been emotionally strangling to me more than even marriages of some of the non believers I knew. The answer was so easy and I even realised that a majority of the non believers I knew were married indeed because they belonged to the same world with their spouses. The marriage of a fish and a lizard will never work no matter how good they are simply because they belong to different worlds. I also wondered why I missed this big issue when I had been so avidly involved in the work of the Lord.

I am aware that as you read this part of the testimony, it is easy to miss my point about difference in people. I do not imply the two parties in a marriage have to be the same. Differences in people are good and I have actually observed in people that opposites attract and they even complement each other. By using animals that thrive in opposite environments such as the water and land animals to illustrate my point here I want you to see that my concern is not even about the differences, but it is about the total survival of the animals. If one of the parties celebrates when the other is drowning that is not a marriage because one of them is actually dying. Also, if the other animal thinks it is fun for its partner to gasp for air and eventually collapse in death that is definitely no marriage. Having seen all these clarifications about relationships, I wondered how on earth I landed on this kind of situation and my answer was in the story of Samson.

I have mentioned earlier that if you are carrying some anointing within you, you need to take extra care and protect it. You cannot afford to go about playing and believe you will make no losses. I did not understand how I had been playing about with something important in my hand. As a young person I thought the main thing I had to do in order to preserve what God put in me was to avoid premarital sex. I made it on that side, but I was missing something crucial there. When you are a carrier of big things the enemy targets you more than anyone else.

You know in a ball game, once the opponents have identified who the dangerous player is, they tend to mark that one more than the rest. If you are right handed the enemy will target hitting you that right hand so that you are completely disabled and if you are left handed he will strike your left hand to do the same. The special anointing God had on my life in the area of relationships was evident to those who knew me well and the enemy knew that was exactly where he had to hit me hard. Speaking in tongues and all the rest of spiritual gestures we know does not make the devil tremble. He knows he wins if he makes believers not to pay attention onto what matters the most.

Taking the example of Samson illustrates this well. He was anointed, but he did not see its value. He sat anywhere and anyhow. He disobeyed his parents' words of caution. The book of proverbs is full of verses that address the subject of stupidity of foolishness. The biblical meaning of foolishness is different from the one average people have. The so-called clever people are the foolish ones biblically. Biblically, anyone who ignores the word of God is a fool, regardless of who they are. I will not go any further there, but as I pondered on all those things my stupidity stared me right in the eyes.

I felt shattered and the truth became very clear that as long as I was busy turning an imaginary steering wheel, making body jerks and waving my hand to imaginary people walking by my imaginary road, I was always going to come back shattered and wanting to die. Divorce had been out of question for a long time because I knew God hated it, but the big question was whether or not I had been really married in the first place. I knew there had been a wedding but I was not really sure about marriage, where the two become one. When growing up I thought being one was just about sex, but I later learnt that sex was part of the deal and its being sublime depended on the real oneness, which is a spiritual thing too.

As I sat there I knew death was staring me right in my eyes. I had also realised that the thing I had called marriage had never been marriage as God designed it. All along I had been very concerned about people, but as I saw the reality of the matter I had to choose between my life and death; life became my choice. I became grateful to God for just making me alive. I decided to go back to where I missed it and start living the life He designed for me before I was even born. The road I took was clearly marked in bold letters, **LONELY ROAD**! As I studied it I recognized that the loneliness was only according to people's standards, just like the life of an eagle that is normally a loner as it soars high in the skies. Down below, by the park there is comfort from pigeons chipping and perking on the ground. In the chicken run there is also comfort from the company of other chickens doing the normal everyday things. The good news is that lonely as the life of an eagle may look to birds that fly in mobs, there are other eagles that an eagle encounters as it soars higher and higher.

Making the decision to be loosed and live the life God initially meant for me was not very easy, but with tears flowing down my eyes more than ever before I sat and it was like I could hear the words of Jesus, "Go and never sin again." Somehow, that baffled me because I did not regard myself as a sinner. I saw the revelation so clearly, I was a sinner as long as I did not heed the voice of Holy Spirit. My decision from then was to heed His voice, as the book of Revelations repeatedly says "He who has an ear, let him hear what the Spirit says to the churches." I knew I had to go forth and never sin again. Now I know better, sin is not only committed, there are also sins of omission. I can only avoid the latter by completely relying on Him and leaning not on my own understanding (Proverbs 3: 5).

God brought his angels to hold me up. I believe that the financial help The Association of Commonwealth Universities and The British Council give scholars is amazing on its own, but seeing them 'mother' me and pull me all the way through when I was literally crumbling down and did not even know where to go and what to do has left a mark up to today! My pastors, Richard and Rosie as well as the church family supported me in an amazing way. Bitterness overwhelmed me and I threw many 'pity-parties' for myself and those who had the time to listen, but the Healers of healers touched me. My healing did not come instantly. It took time because there were numerous legalistic voices that kept coming and questioning me even when I did not have both time and energy to answer. I was still in a shock of material loss and yet I had to be focused and do justice to the amazing scholarship offer God had given me. I had believed him for an 'egg' in 2001, but in 2003 He gave me not just an egg, but a hen that unendingly lays **golden** eggs.

When I got the scholarship I had thought, 'what a rest!' Having gone through my Sussex University unique experience I thought my PhD pursuit was going to be easier, but I soon realised that I had challenges of a different nature. The wonderful remaining thing that makes me say I would not trade the horrible experience I went through for any other is that, looking back to the whole thing, now I take it as childbirth. The labour pains were horrible, but the outcome is glorious and I cannot trade it for any other thing on earth. I saw myself going back to where I lost my freedom in worshipping and serving the Lord and started all over again.

Within a short span of time I found myself connected to many men and women of God who had always been there, but I did not even know them and their ministries because I was living in my small closet. We had Sky TV with many channels, but I could not watch the Christian channels. God selected one of His special servants, Dr Joyce Meyer to hold me by her hand and walk me through the healing process. She was not even aware of it, but I sat at her feet and bought every teaching material she had from the time I discovered her. I listened to her daily television program so many times as she featured on different channels. Her *Emotional Healing Pack* did it for me. In my cell group people told me they had noted I was always 'Joyce-Meyering'. All the time I was Joyce Meyer this, Joyce Meyer that! I had drunk from her cup and I literally had a cup from her ministry written something along these lines, although I may not be precise, "**I am not where I have to be, but I thank God I am not where I used to be.**"

There came a time when God released me to tap into other ministries such a Bishop T.D. Jakes' whose anointed edition of the Bible, *Woman Thou Art Loosed* is my all time favourite with all the special articles that remind women they have to always look at themselves the way their Father looks at them and reject the demeaning world view! Bishop Jakes later became the reason why I discovered the International Gathering of Champions in London. I had never heard of Pastor Matthew Ashimolowo and Dr Murdock who were later to be my pastors in England and later America respectively! I did not understand what was going on, but some of Dr Murdock's Wisdom Keys explained the whole thing within moments:

When God Wants To Protect You
He Removes A Person From Your Life
(Wisdom Key Number 354)

When God Wants To Bless You
He Brings A Person Into Your Life
(Wisdom Key Number 347)

The Most Important Person In Your Life
Is The Person Who Unlocks Your Faith
(Wisdom Key Number 359)

As I make a small quick review of the events of my life, I find that the enemy meant to make 2004 the worst year of my life as I officially lost what I valued the most, my marriage, but God has turned the same year into a blessing because it was the year I started reclaiming what matter the most in my life. It was the same year I encountered most of the men and women of God I strongly believe are in my future.

The testimonies of two special men of God in America where they relate what God did in their lives made me realise that God is just starting with me. The very part where the enemy struck me the hardest is where God is going to strike him the hardest through my life. I do not doubt that I will love again because the Bible tells me so clearly, He will restore all the years that were eaten away:

So I will restore to you the years that the swarming
locust has eaten,
The crawling locust,
The consuming locust,
And the chewing locust,
My great army which I sent among you.
You shall eat in plenty and be satisfied,
And praise the name of the LORD your God,
Who has dealt wondrously with you;
And My people shall never be put to shame.
Then you shall know that I am in the midst of Israel:
I am the LORD your God
And there is no other.
My people shall never be put to shame.
(Joel 2: 25 – 27 NKJV)

197

The Word of God is not silent about past and future events. To those who have some undesirable past experiences, but fully trust Him He has wonderful promises. The promises come along with orders. Similar to what Abraham's relatives were told when they were escaping from the doom soon to strike Sodom and Gomorra, God tells those who have escaped from the sword of death to run and never look back. The order He states before the promise in these verses is one of **not looking back to the past** and I have learnt to be swift when He speaks:

> *Do not remember the former things,*
> *Nor consider the things of old.*
> *Behold, I will do a new thing,*
> *Now it shall spring forth;*
> *Shall you not know it?*
> *I will even make a road in the wilderness*
> *And rivers in the desert.*
> *(Isaiah 43: 18-19NKJV)*

> *I will open rivers in desolate heights,*
> *And fountains in the midst of the valleys;*
> *I will make the wilderness a pool of water,*
> *And the dry land springs of water.*
> *I will plant in the wilderness the cedar and the acacia tree,*
> *The myrtle and the oil tree;*
> *I will set in the desert the cypress tree and the pine*
> *And the box tree together,*
> *That they may see and know,*
> *And consider and understand together,*
> *That the hand of the LORD has done this,*
> *And the Holy One of Israel has created it.*
> *(Isaiah 41: 18 – 20 NKJV)*

You may wonder why I have such confidence to speak of things to come as though they already were, but I think by now you will understand me. I know my Father way too much to play hide and seek, doubting Him. I have read in the word what happened to those who doubted Him and also what happened to those who believed Him, such as the story of the twelve spies who were sent to survey Canaan land:

> *Of the men who went to explore the land,*
> *only Joshua son of Nun*
> *and Caleb son of Jephunneh survived.*
> *(Numbers 14: 38 NIV)*

Apart from the experiences of the people we read about in the Bible, I have personally walked with my Father and I know He keeps His word. As I take you to the next part to show you how He has kept His word beyond what I have said so far, I want you to go on with the amazing truth about God that we find in the book of Numbers:

> *God is not a man, that He should lie,*
> *Nor a son of man, that He should repent*
> *Has He said, and will He not do?*
> *Or has He spoken, and will He not make it good?*
> *(Numbers 23: 19 NKJV)*

Chapter 19

Aftermath and Restoration

o o o o o o o o o o o o o o o o o o o o o o o o o o o o o o o o

The sun will shine again
Oh the sun will shine again
Dark clouds will fade a new day will break
Just like God promised to send
There's a rainbow on the other side
The storm is going to end
Midnight is almost over
The sun will shine again
(Dr Mike Murdock - The Sun Will Shine Again)

I like the above song and studying the lyrics deeply reveals that it may be a time of dark clouds, a storm and midnight, but the sun will shine again. Here, I want to clarify a lot in order for this testimony to make sense and help somebody who may need it badly, or help those who know others who may need this. The aim here is to lay on the table what may not be easy to discuss under normal circumstances. This testimony is not meant to follow a specific set trend, but it is a step of obedience to God so that His church may get something to help them avoid some of the pitfalls that have destroyed millions of believers. It is also meant to help those who are swimming through similar challenges and they have no idea what to do because they have never heard of anyone who went through the same and survived to talk about it.

I know how it feels like to sit all alone feeling like a branded animal that should be avoided by all means because it has a contagious disease that could contaminate the flock if the shepherd is not careful. Here, as a way of bringing this testimony to a close or a pause since there is more to come, I want to talk about some of the serious battles that are part of the aftermath of divorce and how I dealt with them. I do not exhaust them, but I have selected the deadliest ones. The menu that divorce serves you with includes among many things, guilt, bitterness, a feeling of rejection, resentment, unforgiveness which comes with its twin, blame, loneliness, self pity and even lack. This may not be the case with every person, but when the enemy put a tray full of these before me I had a sip and a quick bite from all of them.

Firstly, I want to point out that these emotional battles do not come in isolation. Sometimes they come one by one and at times they occur simultaneously. Most of all, they may concurrently attack during moments of celebration. For instance the whole saga of my divorce came at a time when I thought I had hit my great breakthrough of financial provision and an opportunity to pursue my PhD research without worrying about funds. When this thing hit me I realised that what I thought was going to be the easiest academic endeavour was actually the hardest ever, because of factors outside the study itself.

Children

When my divorce took place we lived in West Knighton, one of the posh areas of Leicester and the main reason being that it is a watch neighbourhood area and I felt that was the best for the children who had the kind of background they had. I could have moved to an area with more affordable rent, but that came as a package too, because as a mature student who had to be in London and get home by train in the late evening the children had to be in a secure place. I also felt like a change of life would exert too much pressure on the children yet they were already in trauma as a result of the family breakdown. I remained in the same house, but the challenge was that, with the limited stipend I got I could not make ends meet. This took me back to combining work and studies. It was hard, but God pulled me through.

I soon realised that this thing was affecting the children's self esteem. I also saw that my name change from their surname to my maiden one would have negative effects on them, but I could not play with that on my side too. My name meant a lot because using the name from my painful past would be like walking about dangling my shackles along. Also, I realised that it was hard for the children to feel positive about themselves when they knew they are a product of a marriage that has not worked and it is easy to feel like they are a mistake or unwanted. It was this realisation that made sit down with the three young people and have a thorough talk with them.

Dealing with children from a divorce and helping them stay with high self esteem is not easy. What helped me more than anything is that when this thing happened, my Christian life rocketed higher. Most of the time I took days of prayer and fasting and the Lord would specifically speak to me and reveal whenever there was a problem. So in this regard my point of starting off is, Godly solutions emerge when you spend time in God's presence, by reading His word as well as prayer and fasting for those who can fast. The Lord showed me that I had to talk to the children and tell them where they feature right now.

I am very grateful because God provided me with the Kurt family in Leicester and Sister Kate had walked the same road before. She was actually called to minister in relationships. God used her to wake me up on the issue of children, so one good evening I sat down with them and explained why I had changed my name whereas all their lives they knew me bearing their father's surname. I also explained to them that to me they are not scars from my past as the case may be in other instances. I announced to them that they are actually **my stars** and I do not imagine myself without them. I went into a lot more, making them aware how much I valued them and will continue as long as I live because it was God who chose me to be the woman to mother them on earth. I told them how committed I was to do all in my might to provide for them.

The truth is that a mother is not enough to parent a child alone. There is a need that can only be met by a father whether the child is male or female, so I told my children that I wanted them to be connected to their father. I also did all I could to make the connection happen by giving room to provision to take place. I did what I could, but when it did not happen, I realised that the children were suffering because of me. Whenever they needed to be provided with certain supplies which I could not afford as a student, I recognised the effect it had on them, then I gave them a special word of truth; that God was their true Father. That was a word that one of my aunties gave me at my father's funeral and a word that my mother always said to me whenever I was crying because I felt like certain things were happening to me because my father had passed on.

At my father's funeral as I was collapsing my auntie told me that God was then taking over in fathering me. She explained that initially God had always been my father and the father I knew Cwatha James Dlamini, had only been a steward, doing the job for God. This stayed strong in me and my mother practically demonstrated her having God as a husband after my father's death. She addressed God as her children's father in a way that could sound crazy, but it went a long way on my side.

I made my children aware that there was a Head and Father-figure in our house, God. I told them that I had multi-relations with God as He is my own father and husband. I also emphasised that Jesus is the Firstborn brother for those going to heaven one day, so He is my brother and a Friend. I told them that in God they had everything, ranging from a reliable father, uncle granddad, family friend and all. Each time I brought supplies into the house I told them they were from God. Things became worse when time for my funding to stop came before I had completed my thesis (USA dissertation) writing fully. Those were very testing times when I did not know exactly how and when the next supply would come, but my faithful father always provided. The family was always filled with joy as we received supplies from God.

I became transparent to the children and sometimes involved them in prayer and fasting for shorter periods on their side. I would inform them about the challenges such as rent or bills and provision of supply teaching work. Everyone would be excited during our daily evening prayer whenever I informed them of my long term placement in some of the colleges. They knew that meant a normal life for them. Looking back at the time I realise it was all training for all four of us. We were trained to stay in continuous dependency on and expectancy toward God our sole provider. I made it very clear to the children that God does discipline His family when they disobey. I knew that I had to teach them and leave the rest to them to decide whether to obey or not and the strict and very clear order I got from God was that I had to live an exemplary life before these young people. I will not say I am perfect, but I am pressing in and pressing on toward the mark continually!

Loneliness and hurting

Although I would not say I had experienced a very romantic kind of life in my 'marriage' whilst it lasted, when it eventually dismantled completely I was attacked by a devastating wave of loneliness. I would sit there all alone and feeling sorry for myself and I needed to have some kind of comfort. I had experienced loneliness even whilst married, but the difference was that it only occurred at certain times. When I was at work teaching or when I was in my business I always forgot and had fun with other people. A lot occupied me and made up for the void that only an intimate relationship could fill. This time around things were really bad because I was in a different place with not much to offer a person of my calibre. To clarify, I mean that with the kind of life I live I could not go clubbing or go out for a drink as other people could do.

The enemy knows the right time to attack, so whenever I had strong feeling of loneliness he would tell me that all that was my choice and I could instantly stop it if I wanted. As he whispered all that to me there would be somebody interested in dating me. As warned by Sister Kate about the phases that one goes through when in my position, I was still profusely hurting. I decided I did not need any extra baggage in addition to the heap already before me. I was also aware I could jump from the pot right into the fire if I was not careful, but the loneliness was not about being careful. God Himself had to intervene. I would not just invite God to intervene if there was no real challenge before me. Twice, at different times I encountered men who were 'written *eligible husband* all over their faces' and I was almost taken into accepting even the date, but I heard so clearly from God that dating was out of question. Oh my! That killed me because I wanted to be like other people too.

God spoke to me privately and confirmed it through two other women that it was not time for me to date anyone at all. Megan, whom I called my baby sister who just had a different colour spoke words that really sunk in me: "my sister, yours is not an ordinary man. God is bringing you a *Jesus Man*." That was very deep and somehow prophetic. The other sister was Lorna. We were praying in her car and without even asking for my permission, she prayed for God to shut my heart and feelings until the right person God has for me comes. Lorna may even have forgotten, but that was powerful. God used it to keep me focused. The words of both of these women of God aligned with what God had said to me personally. God had shown me clearly that my focus was supposed to be on three main areas: Him, my children and my studies. After I had said yes to that He started bringing out numerous ways of having fun without dating any man. It was at the same time that I managed to demonstrate my love and care to the children.

Having fun inside God's House

After saying 'yes' to God a lot of things which I did not see whilst still throwing a big pity party for myself became illumined. Whilst still hurting, I had been crying a lot and making a lot of noise showing my wounds to those who were eager to sympathise and fiddle with the wounds that could never heal that way anyway, but with the new focus on God things had to change. God taught me that the phone was not the first thing to pick up whenever I had a problem or hurting in any way. He reminded me of a song we used to sing from when I was young:

> *Central never busy always on the line*
> *You may hear from Heaven almost anytime*
> *It's a royal service free for one and all*
> *When you get in trouble give this royal line a call*

> *Telephone to glory oh, what joy divine*
> *I can feel the current moving on the line*
> *Built by God the Father for His loved and own*
> *We may talk to Jesus through this royal telephone.*

This song is very powerful except for that it has a limitation of saying **'almost** anytime'. The line to my Father is **always open** and my pastor in London (Pastor Matthew Ashimolowo) even says we actually have a specific number to dial which is 5015, taking it from the following verse:

Call upon Me in the day of trouble;
I will deliver you, and you shall glorify Me
(Psalm 50:15 NKJV)

After I had made the new resolution at God's guidance, my emails took a different shape and my list of telephone contacts went drastically down as a lot of numbers had to be deleted. Amazingly, most of the names to be deleted were for women, because in the first place I did not have that many male contacts. God helped me in weeding my garden of relationships. As he removed some He brought in new ones of a different calibre. Before then, I did not know that it is possible to have a wrong relationship with a Christian woman. God was changing the way I speak and anyone who spoke a different language that was to plant wrong thinking and wrong confession had to go. I still loved people, but some friendships can pull you down rather than you pull them up if you are not careful.

With my list of contacts dwindling, one would think that loneliness was going to attack more, but on the contrary it did not happen. I was learning new things. I was learning also that time was the only currency God has ever given us humans and it is what we do with it that eventually makes a difference to determine the poor and the rich. My vicarious connection to the Woman of God, Dr Joyce Meyer and other servants of God taught me that there was more to do than there was time to do it. I started going to the gym from Monday to Friday and occasionally go to watch a movie with a sister who felt I was her mentor in the Lord. Sometimes I would go swimming or go to the park. There was more to do than there was time, and I honestly do not remember when the kind of crazy loneliness that had been 'biting' me left, but it left.

All along I had thought there was not much for a believer to enjoy as there is outside Christ, on the contrary I realised that real joy was in the House. With my new freedom to worship and go wherever I wanted at anytime as long it was not ungodly, I recaptured all that I had lost years ago. I started going to church even in the evening and attended prayer meetings. I enjoyed going all the way from Leicester to London for the KICC seasonal 72 hours of prayer as well as the monthly all night long prayer meetings. It was also in the all night long prayer meetings that the man of God, Pastor Biodun Yola used to crazily make prophetic proclamations. I received them and **I am seeing them come to pass**. In his special way, as he led his part of the prayer session he would say "**you shall be discovered!**' I could not be elsewhere outside that kind of a prayer meeting. Those were prayer meetings that eventually brought manifestations.

Whilst still in Swaziland I would listen as some of the teachers excitedly talked in the staff room about some of the gospel concerts they attended occasionally where local and as well as outside singers featured and wish I had been there too. It was only during my healing up time in England that I actually saw live some of the South African singers such as Lundi, Vuyo and Benjamin Dube in places including Leicester, Birmingham and London. In such concerts I danced before my Father like nobody's business, in a way that makes me imagine King David dancing when the Ark of Covenant was returned from the enemy! I could not see anything better than the freedom of worship I had.

Once I was blessed in one concert featuring the acclaimed American gospel artist Karen Clark-Sheard and her daughter Kiki, where Karen had a special T-Shirt she threw at the audience and it came my way and I caught it. I got my message from God right there, which was a confirmation of a prophetic word I had recently received from a sister who did not know anything about my singing at all. God somehow grew my 'wings' because at the very financially challenging time of my life I flew to from England and America four times in a single year and attended five conferences, two of which were consecutive. All those trips were divinely orchestrated and miraculously provided for, by God Himself as you may already be aware that everything about me was His business.

Feelings of rejection

As God was walking me through the valley of transition from misery to exhilaration I realised that something about me had changed. For many years I had involuntary twinges accompanied by cringing that always happened when I was approaching our house. This thing had happened even in Leicester the first and second year I lived there, but without any warning it vanished. Whenever I approached the house I had feelings of joy and security. The kind of belly laughter that I used to have as a young person, that even made me shed tears and sometimes roll uncontrollably returned to me. It was all amazing. In the midst of this beautiful picture I am giving you here, something painful happened. I experienced a very strong sense of rejection from the people that mattered most to me such as my blood relations.

Apart from my family I sensed a rejection from some of the believers I had thought to be close to me. They did not understand how on earth I could do this horrible thing **to them**. I battled with this thing, not really getting an understanding of what was behind their behaviour toward me. I wanted them to have pity with me and be a source of comfort. To me their reaction toward me resembled the reaction of the Pharisees when Jesus had healed people on the Sabbath. They did not care about what the person had been going through in their sickness. What mattered most to them was keeping the Sabbath. It was my research supervisor who gave me a little bit insight into the whole thing by telling me all those people felt like I had wronged them and I had stripped them off something they had valued. She explained a lot urging me to understand their stand point.

As I was asking myself questions I could not answer regarding the rejection, I realised that Jesus was rejected too and He had a special way of dealing with it. When they crucified Him on the cross and divided His clothes by casting lots, He said, "Father, forgive them, for they do not know what they are doing" (Luke 24:34). He set an example for us to follow whenever we have our own little 'crucifixions' which are not even a small version of what He experienced. The example was to forgive those who wrong us. I began to understand it well. It was not easy, but I became honest before God, telling Him exactly how I felt, which in addition to feelings of rejection, was a development of deep bitterness. God's Word speaks clearly about bitterness:

Let all bitterness, wrath, anger, clamour, and evil speaking
be put away from you, with all malice.
And be kind to one another,
tender hearted, forgiving one another,
even as God in Christ forgave you.
(Ephesians 4: 31-32)

In my prayer, asking for a forgiving heart, I clearly stated to God that I was bitter about the situation at hand. God is faithful and He helped me forgive the people I was bitter against. I think the key to my breakthrough and ending the turmoil within me was my truthfulness and not denying the reality before me. Paul's words to the Philippians also helped me where he tells them, "Finally, brothers, whatever is true, whatever is noble, whatever is right, whatever is pure, whatever is lovely, whatever is admirable—if anything is excellent or praiseworthy—think about such things" (Philippians 4: 8). This made me purposely decide to occupy my mind with the good things I knew. This was not an instant thing. It was a matter of daily endeavour, like someone who engages in daily physical work out to tone the body. It goes hand in hand with self discipline. I think that is what we develop as we pray and fast. That way, we bring our bodies under our control and refuse to be controlled by them.

As I trained myself and brought my body and mind to be Spirit controlled I saw God eventually helping me understand that indeed my friends and relations did not know what they were doing. Not knowing what one is doing is not just an adage; it is a reality! People talk a lot just because they do not know. Sometimes they do it thinking they are doing the best. A deeper interrogation of my situation also helped me realise that my family back home was reacting to what they were being told. I prayed to God against the wrong voice or voices feeding them with what resulted in the dissention.

I prayed, asking God to restore the relationship I had with my mother and sister, because these were people who loved me and had been very close to me. God promises us that He will restore everything that the enemy has stolen from us as the verse mentioned earlier states. I knew that soon I was going to recover all that the adversary had stolen. Whilst waiting for my restoration I had to make a significant difference and maintain the kingly anointing bestowed by God! There were numerous provocations that could easily trigger me to react, but Holy Spirit was already on the His seat and He ordered me to be still and quiet like a dead person.

Completely forgiving and letting go

I did not feel rejected by my family only. The worst feeling of betrayal I ever experienced which resulted in the worst level of bitterness in my life was surrounding my spouse. As said earlier, when I was hurting the most, I made a lot of noise, crying for help even where there was no help. This happened before as well as after the divorce. May be you would think that immediately after the divorce I instantly became free from all ties, but as a matter of fact, I did not. I was like a little girl on a swing or a pendulum going back and forth. Someone on a swing does not progress. The swinging back and forth kind of behaviour is deadly because it has to do with looking back when you have to look forward. The main force that caused me to often look back was surrounding finances and my all my life time labours. I strongly felt robbed. No one could help me on this issue, but God.

Whenever I sat down to think over and over again about my past, that gesture allowed the adversary to have conversations with me. He would therefore, sympathise with me and throw a pity party for me, also asking me questions such as, "What are you going to do about the twenty years of labour, believing that you are building up for your future only to see it all slip through your very fingers?" It is so shocking, how the enemy attacks us and also swaps roles to talk into our spirits as if he is on our side. He has never stopped his old game he started in Eden, when talking to Eve and demonstrated later, as he tempted our Saviour, when He had fasted for forty days and forty nights. So, he did the same with me and whispered that I had been robbed a whole lifetime. Satan is such a liar!

We really need to detect the adversary's lies. Who says what was stolen from me is **a lifetime**? The bible reveals a promise for long life, "Honour your father and mother, so that you may live long in the land the Lord your God is giving you" (Exodus 20: 20). This same promise is repeated in other Old Testament books as well as the New Testament in reference to the old. The promise for long life comes again where the Psalmist lists the benefits of dwelling in the presence of the Most High God:

> *He who dwells in the shelter of the Most High*
> *will rest in the shadow of the Almighty,*
> *With long life will I satisfy him*
> *and show him my salvation*
> *(Psalm 91:1 & 16 NKJV)*

When reading the scriptures I recognised that the enemy was lying to me because the long life benefit promised to those who honour their parents as well as those who dwell in the presence of the Most High God is definitely mine! God keeps every promise He makes. I have learnt that I developed the strong sense of loss which led to bitterness whenever I looked back to my past. God's word has many examples of people who made losses and He Himself multiplied the little in their hands to make it bigger than even the losses. The story of Jacob in Genesis 29 and 30 demonstrates this truth so clearly where we see God blessing Jacob amazingly after he laboured for nothing in his father-in-law's household:

> *Thus the man [Jacob] became exceedingly prosperous,*
> *and had large flocks,*
> *female and male servants, and camels and donkeys*
> *(Genesis 30: 43)*

God has already shown me clearly that what is in my hand now is far greater than what I think I have lost. All I have to do is surrender into His care what I have as the song in Chapter 3 of this testimony states '...how your little becomes much when you place it in the Master's hand...' Having discovered all those biblical truths I wanted to release and completely let go of my past hurt, but my pendulum kept swinging back and forth with my bitterness and feeling a strong sense of betrayal and loss.

In 2005 April I had to move from the house which had memories of my past. Within the same West Knighton area, God provided me with a better house for the same amount of rent as the former one. It was in Number 47 Hylion Road that my life took on a new move in most things. I felt the presence of God in an incredible way and I had 'speaking wall pictures,' which continually told me of my future. It was in that house that I experienced what I regard as my breakthrough from my past hurt and bitterness. In 2006 I obeyed God and designed a special place in my room, which I dedicated to God. I called it my Secret Sacred Place (SSP). Although I had been spending time in God's presence before, after having the SSP, I developed the habit of starting each day with quality time in God's presence. It was the same new habit that I regard as the secret key to what became my breakthrough in my hurt and bitterness. The breakthrough happened in June.

On Saturday, June 17, 2006 I read three chapters from the book of Joshua, but chapter 9 stood out to me where Joshua made a mistake by making a treaty with the Gibeonites. Later that day I had a strong sense of loss as I reflected on my past. The 'pendulum attack' of a sense of loss I have mentioned above came in a mighty way that day. I pitied myself for having nothing in the name of wealth and riches under my name on earth. I knew the wealth I had helped accumulate was still there and having nothing to do with me anymore and it hurt. It was then that God corrected me and reminded me that all my life I had been an industrious woman, working hard and earning a lot of money and general wealth because He was behind it all. He blessed me so that I prospered in everything I touched as promised in Deuteronomy 28. He also spoke clearly, telling me to let go of my past and remember that, as the Bible says, He will restore to me all I have lost as reflected in Joel 2.

Later that day, as I was praying, God gave me a picture. It flashed as if I was in a dream. In the picture, I was walking in town (Leicester), by FENWICKS Department Store opposite the Central Lending Library. I saw a young woman carrying a big and heavy bag. She was struggling with the stuff she was carrying. I hurried to help her because I felt I could carry her bigger bag with ease than she could. As I rushed to do that I came back to consciousness and realised I had just seen that picture. I tried to get the message from this and at first I thought God was saying, "Betty be helpful to those who need an extra helping hand", but the more I prayed over this I heard God was saying 'Betty I see the heavy stuff you're carrying and I am now picking it up from you so that you walk with ease". I thanked God and I later went to sleep.

On Sunday, June 18, 2006, I was led to call my Spiritual Father, Dr C.P. Gumedze in Swaziland. He prayed for me and blessed me over the phone. Later I went to church, at Leicester Christian Fellowship (All Nations Centre) where I was one of the worship team (singers). God's presence was incredibly rife that morning. Pastor John Webster was preaching and he read from Joshua 9, the same chapter that I had read the previous morning. The main message was the importance of getting confirmation from God, the Holy Spirit before making decisions. Right away, I knew God had something special for me there.

As Pastor Webster preached on, God gave me a picture of a road behind me and thickets before me. He said 'Betty look at the road behind you, and remember that before you walked through it, it was all thistles and a thorny bush. As you walked through, it cleared. Even now whatever you have before you will soon be like that road behind you. I quickly wrote this on my memo book. When I got home, that afternoon I watched Bishop T.D. Jakes on the TBN television channel, which is what I used to do every Sunday afternoon. Bishop Jakes mentioned the same illustration I got at church. This kind of confirmation really blew my head off.

Whilst still at church, after the service, one of the sisters had asked me where my husband was and getting that question really hurt. I was tired of answering the same question, which I had been asked so many times even when I was married. I got this question in church settings in Swaziland, such as when we had a combined service in my church, EBC and as we had our potluck lunch and mingled, other believers would ask this question. The question revived a wound that had not healed **at the time**, because I knew my case was different from that of women who had given their lives to God and their husbands were not believers. I was already born again when I got married. Having an absent husband really hurt. That special Sunday of June, 18th I went to God asking the old '**WHY**' question. I wanted to know why He allowed this to happen to me. It is incredible how I feel like I can visualize God smiling at me even now as I am writing. He answered by giving me Joshua 9, the scripture I read on Saturday, which Pastor John Webster read on Sunday too. God spoke to me like He was a person with a physical body staring at me. I was in my SSP.

God showed me that when, as a young person, I made my choice before marriage, I did a similar thing to what Joshua did when he made a treaty with the Gibeonites. I realised that the commitment Joshua made cost him a lot as Pastor John Webster had emphasised that Sunday morning. For the first time ever in my life, I realised that I had no one to blame, but me. It became very clear that if Joshua had refused to get into covenant with the Gibeonites they would not force him at all. They would have gone their way. Similarly, if I did not consent to the relationship my ex husband would not have forced me at all. He would have gone to someone else. Oh my Lord! That crushed me. As if that was not enough, I started seeing before me like a movie all the events leading to my commitment in the early eighties, which I have already related earlier in chapter seven.

Before that Sunday afternoon, I had never ever viewed things that way. I had been pushing the blame on my ex husband. I felt a strong sense of guilt and felt like I owed the people who warned me an apology. The great news is that God is unlike us humans. He does not ask us why we faltered. When someone has realised their mistake and come asking for forgiveness, God accepts that person. That is why even the thief on the cross got instant forgiveness of sins and was promised entry into Paradise right away. That Sunday afternoon I cried like a baby. I felt like I had to do something such as going back to all those people who warned me and say I am sorry I did not take their word, but God told me there was no need for all that. He said words similar to those Jesus Christ of Nazareth said to the woman who was accused of committing adultery by the teachers of the law and Pharisees, **"Neither do I condemn you; go and sin no more"** (John 8: 11 NKJV). Instantly, I got my freedom!

Looking back at the experience I had on both Saturday and Sunday, at home and at church, I saw God's orchestration of my final freedom from the heavy load. He had foretold me the whole thing in the dream-like picture when I heard Him tell me "Betty I see the heavy stuff you're carrying and I am now picking it up from you so that you walk with ease", but I did not know it at the time. To completely claim and enjoy my freedom in Him, God gave me an order through His word, to **FORGIVE my ex husband FULLY** for anything I had been holding against him. I surrendered. A series of verses showed me that by holding things against my ex-husband I was blocking my own forgiveness, because this is not an issue of just spoken words; it goes deeper as a thing of the heart. God is a God of hearts. I sought His help to help me forgive and He did.

Satan never gives up. He tried many tricks to take me back to unforgiveness, asking me how I can forgive someone without repentance and restitution. In response to that I told him that the forgiveness was focused on my getting rid of my bitterness and I do not have to depend on someone else to get my own help. I had to decide and claim my freedom from the **self inflicted** hurt and bitterness. As for repentance and restitution, that is now God's business. Vengeance is His. I am not involved. I told the enemy and I still tell him whenever he brings such thoughts. The great news is that there is no need for such things as vengeance as long as each individual decide to claim their true and deep freedom from God.

Satan, the adversary did not stop there. He sometimes twisted the truth and asked me to prove my forgiving heart by going back to my past. To that one, I thank God He has provided me with His faithful servants, mothers, fathers, shepherds and all the spiritual carers who opened my eyes by teaching that forgiving someone does not mean that you have to be in covenant with that person. Discovering this truth removed another heavy rock that Satan had placed on me to carry, through feelings of guilt. What I have now is true freedom; freedom that does not depend on any third party, but one that has been determined by my own decision before God!

I experienced another mighty wave of liberation when as I was having my morning devotion, Holy Spirit reminded me of a conversation we had with my mother before I was married in the early 1980s. I had just told her I was going to be married and her reaction to my 'good news' was that I was still too young to get married. She even mentioned another young woman in the area who was much older than me, but still unmarried. Holy Spirit showed me how He did not like the way I reacted to my mother those many years ago. My mother did not argue with me and I had my way. I got married and my parents gave me their blessing. Holy Spirit showed me how I had to go back to my mother and ask for forgiveness for my reaction to her. I felt like it would be weird for me to do that because my mother never held anything against me. However, I heard clearly what His instruction was and, yes, this very year, 2009 I had to pick up the phone very early in the morning and with waterfalls from my eyes I recalled what she had forgotten. She remembered very well and the results of that obedience were amazing. That posture of **repentance** and then **obedience** started fast-tracking my blessings right away!

Chapter 20

Restoration, soaring higher and looking to the future

o o o o o o o o o o o o o o o o o o o o o o o o o o o o o o o o o o

I am moving forward; I am following the Creator
I am moving forward; I am following Holy Spirit
Along the way (3X)
There may be challenges; there may be obstacles
But I am telling you, yes I am moving forward
I am following Holy Spirit
(Moving Forward – Betty Dlamini)

Dumping the heavy burden of unforgiveness enabled me to lift up my once 'frail wings' and fly freely like the eagle mentioned earlier in Dr Aggrey of Africa's story. Flying up and soaring higher and higher is a natural thing for eagles, but there are times when the natural ability is used up. We get a clearer picture of this from Dr Munroe's seventh of the Principles of An Eagle. It states that as the eagle gets older, it goes through a phase of life which apparently appears to be a phase of rejection, loss and loneliness, yet taking a deeper and closer look reveals that it is a phase of restoration. The seventh principle states:

When the Eagle grows old
His feathers become weak
And cannot take him as fast as he should
When he feels weak and about to die
He retires to a place far away in the rocks
While there he plucks out every feather on his body

Until he is completely bare
He stays in this hiding place
Until he has grown new feathers
Then he can come out
(Principles of an Eagle by Dr Myles Munroe)

The image I get from this principle is similar to that of a chicken that has just been killed and then plucked off all its feathers ready to roast or cook in any way the cook wants. Such a chicken no longer lives and its own life is laid down for the good of the cook and those who will enjoy the meal. The Apostle Paul understands this and says it about his own life stating that he no longer lives, but Christ lives:

I was put to death on the cross with Christ,
and I do not live anymore—
it is Christ who lives in me
I still live in my body,
but I live by faith in the Son of God
who loved me and gave himself to save me
(Galatians 2: 20 NKJV)

The kind of dying that Apostle Paul refers to here is not necessarily a loss, but gain because it is through dying to the 'Self' that an individual actually gets empowered in Christ. This also means dying or passing away of old things. Losing the old things is similar to the eagle's plucking off all the old feathers, beak and talons. The process appears to be loss, but it is gain in that new feathers, beak and talons can only grow after the old have been removed completely. This is also similar to what a gardener or a vineyard dresser does when s/he prunes the plant. Pruning appears to be a reduction, yet it is the gateway to greater productivity. The removal of the old excessive *baggage* intensifies productivity and recharges the organism at hand.

In order for an eagle to get rid of the old and get the new it draws itself away from the mundane life of eagles and stays in seclusion, in far away rocks. This process and principle of eagles reminds me of the powerful Psalm 91 scripture earlier quoted:

He who dwells in the shelter of the Most High
will rest in the shadow of the Almighty
I will say of the LORD,
"He is my refuge and my fortress,
my God, in whom I trust."

215

Surely he will save you from the fowler's snare
and from the deadly pestilence.
He will cover you with his feathers,
and under his wings you will find refuge;
his faithfulness will be your shield and rampart.
A thousand may fall at your side,
ten thousand at your right hand,
but it will not come near you.
With long life will I satisfy him
and show him my salvation."
(Psalm 91: 1-4, 7 & 16NIV)

The Psalm 91 chapter signifies the benefits of a life of full reliance on God. This is a life of finding refuge in Him and trusting in Him. It is a life of realizing that there is no hope on one's own abilities, so the individual entrust herself/himself in the care of the almighty. Dwelling in the shelter of the almighty requires retiring from the everyday fast life and hiding oneself under the 'wing' of God. The whole chapter lists the benefits of finding refuge in God, but the sixteenth verse brings out the benefit of long life. This is similar to the eagle that extends its life by losing its dear old valuables: wings, beak and talons to grow new and more durable ones.

There is a phase of **waiting** between the removal of the old and gaining the new, but when the new comes, the person who has been patiently waiting experiences something more exhilarating than ever before! I can associate this with the period of nine months pregnancy. The last days of carrying that baby, waiting for the delivery day are taxing and not pleasurable at all. Also, just before the birth of the baby, the horrible experience of labour pains attacks the expectant mother, but having said all this, when the baby cries out, immediately after its birth, all the pain vanishes and all the mother can see is the new born baby. The pain of waiting for nine months and stinging labour pains becomes completely forgotten! The prophet Isaiah analogises this splendour very clearly:

But those who wait on the LORD
Shall renew their strength;
They shall mount up with wings like eagles,
They shall run and not be weary,
They shall walk and not faint
(Isaiah 40: 31 NKJV)

My understanding of these elements of the truth helped in changing my attitude. Instead of mourning and always magnifying my losses, I started looking at the future and celebrating the new thing that God is doing in and for me. At the very time when people looked at me and thought I had made losses I began to see all my gains. It was at a naturally challenging time that I wrote my song "celebrate" Which we later sang with my dear friend Peppy:

Every day is a celebration!
Every hour is a celebration!
Every minute is a celebration!
Every moment is a celebration!
***

Celebrate the air I breathe
Celebrate the water I drink
Celebrate for the food and sleep
Celebrate everything I've got
***

Thank you God for all these blessings
Thank you Lord for all these friends
Thank you Lord for the smiles I get
For the 'hellos' and the 'thank you s'
***

Thank you God for all these blessings
Thank you Lord for all these friends
Thank you Lord for the smiles I get
For the 'hellos' and the 'thank you s'
***

Celebrate the name of God
Celebrate the name of Jesus
Celebrate the Holy Ghost
Celebrate God three in one
We bless the name of God (3X)
Hallelujah, Hallelujah!
('Celebrate' in the album 'Faithful God' -Betty Dlamini)

My change of attitude literally made me thank God for what other people who have not been where I have been may not necessarily deem as worth making a lot of noise about. As the lyrics of my song express, I started seeing the beauty of living life! I could only do this because I had uncluttered my life and detoxified my life in and out! My period of seclusion and loss meant that even my phonebook became slim and ran down to almost nothing and then my Father helped me build up everything anew. He started bringing new people into my life one at a time.

The elimination of people including those I had held so dearly happened through obedience. I obeyed Holy Spirit without analysing situations and my language changed. I did not have to say good bye to anyone, all that happened was a change of language and lifestyle and then I became boring to those who were used to the language of 'sister, we are just hanging in there'. I boldly refused to 'hang in there' and I did not waste time to correct it because the Bible tells me what is contrary to the survival mentality. This may sound a bit pompous, but beloved, if you have been 'hanging in there' for a long time, as I have done, you cannot afford to continue 'singing that same old chorus' even after you have been loosed.

The Bible states that I am blessed coming in and blessed coming out! Now I have learnt to make the confession "I am blessed and highly favoured" without feeling guilty or haughty. When I started doing this some of my old associates felt uncomfortable and expressed that this was being arrogant, yet making positive confessions and declarations is nowhere near arrogance, but a way of agreeing with what God says about us instead of what the adversary says. Where I would see loss before I started seeing gain, restoration and longevity!

Beloved, please understand me well and know that I do not imply that the rugged roads of life suddenly became levelled and all tarred up. Challenges still come and obstacles are still there, but I have learnt to use them as my stepping stones as my song *Moving Forward* states. Also, each time a challenge comes, I realise that Father Himself is always with me and it is like I can hear Him whispering to me in the midst of challenges telling me to relax in His loving arms and know that the phase I am in is one where I am restored and being renewed in order to soar even higher than ever before. Actually, renewal is not just about soaring higher and higher or about one aspect of life, but it is about total renewal and restoration. It is a total lifestyle makeover. An eagle that is going through the restoration and renewal phase may even look like a stupid bird because it does not soar like those with wings and it does not do any of all the activities of eagles, such as nest building, hunting, and a lot more eagle fun things, but it just rests by the rocks and gets restored. How does this go then?

Restoration requires the eagle to **wait**. Waiting is not the easiest thing to do, but in order for the eagle to be renewed it has to do it. The verse in Isaiah 40: 31 sums up the whole story as it states, 'those who wait upon the Lord shall renew their strength, they shall mount up with wings as eagles, they shall walk and not be weary, they shall run and faint. Outwardly, the eagle's renewal is noted through the new wings and new beak, but the real renewal cannot be seen because it is internal. The strength of the eagle is renewed, so that there is increase in everything it does. This could be in terms of a variety of effects such as its altitude, energy, velocity and a lot more. The main point here is that before the restoration, renewal and increase take place there is the undesirable phase of waiting lonely and nakedly on the rock.

In my seclusion and waiting posture I began hearing Holy Spirit talk to me better and clearer, showing me truths that I had never heard anyone say before. Amazingly, after He started showing me what I regard as new revelations of His truth I began hearing other men and women of God pronouncing the same. This is still going on right now. He continually speaks and even tells me what I need to correct in my life. I have to move swiftly and do what He says. Sometimes He gives me instructions such as asking for an apology from even my children as He shows me where I had taken things wrongly. Naturally this is difficult to do, but obeying that inner voice is rewarding and leads to restored relationships. In my waiting I did more introspection than judging others and suddenly there came an amazing restoration of what I had lost.

Relationships

There is no greater loss than that of relationship with loved ones such as family. Amazingly, after my waiting period I started seeing 'the feathers, talons and beak grow'; my relationship with my family got restored. The strong bond I have always had with my two siblings Busisiwe and Zanele became restored. Zanele, my baby sister has always been my fun friend to whom I logon whenever I need real belly laughter. The two of us just click and always find fun in unusual stuff. After each conversation we have, every cloud that has been lingering disappears. I missed that kind of connection a lot. Now it is back full force. My sister who comes after me has her own special attributes which I really missed badly. In her unique persona I get what no other person could give me. As for my mother, I now enjoy her counsel more than ever before, because in her I see a woman of virtue who took her assignment of bringing us up seriously. I can now enjoy the embrace of this very first human I had contact with on this earth. Although my mother lives thousands of miles away from me, technology has made it easy for me to tap into that reservoir of wisdom anytime I want!

Ministry

Apart from the restoration of my relationship with my family, that is my mother and two sisters, the Lord began to gradually restore numerous other aspects of my life. The restoration began internally. I became more loosened and as I drove my car daily between Leicester and Hinckley in England I listened to CDs and tapes and sometimes sang as loud as I could without having to worry about the neighbours I had in my semi detached house. Sometimes as I worshipped in the car the Lord would clearly speak to me giving me a personal Word or led me to pray for other people. There were days when I would start praying and end up preaching to an audience I did not see with my naked eyes. At first I did not understand what was going on regarding the preaching part of it, but it helped me to hear the testimony of my mentor, Dr Joyce Meyer who had a similar experience when her ministry started.

This restoration happened when I was still pursuing my PhD at The University of London. Over the long vacation I could take on full time work. In Hinckley, I worked with teenage girls who had behaviour problems. Most of the girls continually physically harmed themselves. That was a very challenging job, but as I worked with them I began to see the Lord marking a clear difference in the way I dealt with the girls. One of them, whom I will call Miss S had a very serious problem and I had to work with her one on one. The Lord led me to pray for the youngster and I asked my son, Sibusiso to give me some of his music suitable for rap to use as I worked with this girl. I discovered that Miss S had a talent. She stopped harming herself and we rapped together, although I was nowhere near what she did. It was sad when I had to stop working with her because of my studies, but I left a completely different person from the one I had found there. That encounter and numerous other ones made me realise that I may be a teacher, but right inside me there is a minister who needs to come out of the closet soon.

The Lord started doing something which I regard as not really conforming to the expectations of society. He started using me to minister to people who had marriage problems. I praise God today because **ALL** those marriages are still going on right now, and I believe they are godly marriages. God rekindled my passion for healthy relationships. I never lost this, but I felt like I was not the right person to be involved in helping. I did not advertise anything to anyone. I simply lived and portrayed outwardly, the person I was inside, then like a magnet, people who had challenges in their relationships started approaching me for help. There were times when I could get a telephone call and had to drive across town even after midnight. In other instances, I had to spend hours ministering over the phone. Some of the calls were international. In one instance a woman had decided she was packing her bags and God showed me so clearly how that marriage could be salvaged. He gave me clear instructions to give to the woman and I did.

I spent days of prayer and fasting and what a joy it was to get the reports from two different women whose husbands were preachers. There had been cases of infidelity, but the two men asked for forgiveness. These women were in the same country, but did not even know they were in the same position. Both of them had followed the instruction God gave me to give them separately. This was a great breakthrough to me, but amazingly both sisters had a new problem of forgiving their husbands who had actually done what was rare among men from that country, to admit and ask for forgiveness. Again, God gave me a strict order to be stern and speak the truth to His daughters without mincing words. By the time I came out of the situation we were continually praying for complete healing and forgiveness.

In another instance, God had brought into my life an orphaned young woman who had come from a country in Southern Africa and was dumped by her husband who ran away with a nurse in London. This woman was over ten years younger than me and I heard clearly that I had to pray for her problem like it was my own and be there for her whenever she needed someone to talk to. As I prayed and read the word, I had such great confidence that God was going to restore the relationship. I actually started praising Him for the miracle before it happened. God ordered me to pray for the young husband over the phone where he was with his nurse in London.

You know beloved, there is nothing like obedience. I could not have done anything like that if not told clearly by God. I spoke to the man and he started crying, telling me that he loved his wife and their two young children, but he was trapped and could not leave the other woman. This was a man I had never seen in my life. God is not a man that He should lie. Right now the couple has been reconciled. They now have two more children following their family reconciliation! Hallelujah! You know beloved walking with God takes you where you cannot go on your own. I do not see myself doing anything like that on my own right now, but the one who knows what He put in me when making me is restoring His anointing and it is working. There are many more other relationships which were restored in the UK through God's sending me and telling me clearly what to do, but in order not to make this testimony monotonous I will not divulge more.

When you spend time in God's presence, He can do to you what He did to Peter as he was praying in the afternoon and fell into a trance. One night as I was about to sleep, the Lord led me to call a Woman of God whom I regarded as someone having no challenges at all. I was led to call her and pray for her over the phone. I obeyed God and called her although I had no idea what I was going to pray for, exactly. She answered the phone and she was really down in spirit. She told me that both of them with her husband were really down because they had tried all they could to convince her son's girlfriend not to abort her pregnancy. The minute she said all that, my spirit just got 'excited'.

I became very bold and I told her we were going to approach our Father's throne and report this thing in all boldness right away! We did. Actually I prayed over the phone. I remember clearly, I was like a possessed person. Indeed I was possessed by the Higher Ones from Glory land. When I finished praying the Woman of God told me she had amazing peace! In a few days my phone rang to tell me the good news. The girl was already in the hospital room where the 'murder' was going to be exercised, but something made her walk out and tell them she was keeping her baby! Praise God our pretty girl **Olivia** is alive. That is her true name! Praise God!

When you are in ministry you do not always do what is normal according to human standards. God often tells you to do what is contrary to the socially expected behaviour. Right in the middle of my serious focus on writing my thesis (USA dissertation), I had an urge to call one of the sisters who went to the same church with me in 2001/2 when I lived in Brighton. I had not spoken to her in years. I looked up her number from my old telephone book, got it and called her. She was very down in spirit and sounded very weak. She told me she had been ill for a long time and all hope for life was gone. Right now she is already up yonder at home, but God brought me into her life at the point of departure from this world so that she could enter home victoriously and not as a dejected person.

After being reconnected to Sis BM, I specifically remember two special days when I wanted to work on my studies so much, but I had a strong feeling to call her and speak words of encouragement into her life. She went home feeling special. She told me she understood why other believers had given up and they were no longer there for her; she had been ill a long time. I was in the East Midlands of England and she was in the South part of the island. I thank God I seized the moment to lift up the spirit of a soldier that was about to enter Home!

The home going of Sis BM felt like deep loss to me, and the enemy told me my prayers had been fruitless, but Holy Spirit spoke clearly that I had fought a good fight because BM could have gone home feeling neglected and not needed by anyone anymore. In the same year of Sis BM's home-going, one Friday afternoon a friend I had worked with in the same college in Leicester invited me to go shopping with her and her children in one of the neighbouring towns of Leicester. I did not want to go because I had studies to focus on, but Holy Spirit whispered, "you go!" I went. Later that Friday night we had supper in my house. That supper will stay vivid all the days of my life.

Later, that Friday night Sis JT left with her two daughters. My car was in the garage that weekend, so Sis JT offered to take me around town looking for the leather sofas I wanted to buy. When I wanted to go back to my house and work on my research, JT would not easily release me. We spent the whole day together, and she kept asking me questions about God and I remember like it was only yesterday how we prayed as we talked about so many things ranging from how to bring up our children and how to focus more on pleasing God than people. I did not realise the role God had placed me to play, but I poured out my heart the way God led me to. Sis JT continually said "Betty, there are friends and then friends – You are the friend that I do not have fun with, but I when I am with you I am my real self. You help become the person God wants me to be. You tell me the truth." Although she repeatedly said these words, I did not really take it in that much.

When we parted after 3:00 pm she had encouraged me to do so many things and I had mentored her on so many spiritual principles. We had been together since 9:00 am. In the evening, I was speaking to my baby sister, Zanele from my house phone when Sis JT called me on my cell phone. All I heard was 'hello Betty'. I did not let her speak. I told her I was talking to my baby sister and was going to get back to her as soon as I finished. I tried to call her a few minutes later after winding up with my sister. She did not answer on both cell and house phone. It was on the next day, Sunday that the police came to my house to tell me of her demise. They said my cell number was the last one she had called as she was brutally murdered by her ex husband.

I did not understand the whole thing, but reflecting on it now, I know if I had not spent that Friday afternoon and the whole Saturday morning and afternoon I would have missed the opportunity of stuffing her spirit part with what she needed the most that day. Thinking of the numerous prayers we uttered together in her car that Saturday gave me peace during a time and scenario that were not peaceful at all. God handpicked me to be the auntie that was to wipe tears from the young girls who saw their mother slashed to death. There were times when I could not talk about this. The pain I felt was very deep and actually deeper than any loss I had ever experienced in my life. The healer has healed me and now I appreciate the call into ministry He has bestowed in me rather than the comfort I so much desire.

My value system rocketed immensely as I saw God take me from one level to the next. I have learnt to obey God even when I have no idea where my obedience of what He says will lead to. When I moved to Leicester Christian Fellowship (LCF) at the All Nations Centre, I had no idea that it was there that God was going to restore yet another aspect of my life. As said earlier, I used to minister through singing whilst still back in Swaziland. God had already spoken about the restoration of my singing through a sister who came to me one Sunday morning and told me what she dreamt about me and my daughter. She did not know anything about us. The dream was actually a reality in our lives. That sister even gave me an electric piano/organ music instrument to revive our singing ministry.

One Tuesday evening as I went for the membership class at LCF, one of the men in my class asked me if I sang and I told him, yes. He said he knew it, but I had never sung with him hearing me. He said he knew I sang before I even responded. That was yet another way of God talking to and through people, but out of that conversation days later I had to meet the Man of God and Worship leader David Hadden. That was yet another beginning of God manifesting Himself in a marvellous way in my life. The presence and move of God was rife every day of my life and Sunday services were all uniquely a portrayal of His presence among His people. It was at LCF that I saw what I had never seen anywhere before. Those pastors were uniquely obedient to God. There was a set routine like all other churches I have seen, but there were days when God would come down and speak in very peculiar ways other than preaching. Sometimes the whole program would be altered completely. That was a home of miracles.

When the Man of God Ian Andrews had come to our church, God used him to unleash a part of me that was still budding. I was sceptical of laying hands on someone with a distinct illness or disability, but God spoke clearly that it was time I come forth boldly. In the year 2007 things escalated more than ever before. Sometimes God would order me to pray for someone over the phone and lay hands on myself where the person on the other end was ill. Sometimes he would tell me to call someone because they were ill and as I did I would find that indeed they were ill and as I prayed and laid hands on myself I literally shivered and shook.

The same year, 2007, at Dr Morris Cerullo's Missions to London, I was one of the ushers and at the end of the meetings we ushers had to minister to those who had given their lives to the Lord. On one of the nights a woman from North London, who happened to be in my group of people asked me to pray for her. One of her eyes was covered with cataract and she could not see at all. The way I was focused and confident in God made me not to even analyse what the nature of the problem was. I asked her if she believed God could heal her. She did. As I prayed for her I first of all bound the spirit of illness, and then claimed her healing with her. I was still praying when the lady screamed, "Oh! My eye can see! Oh! It's gone! The cataract is gone!" She shouted with joy and continued to check her healing by covering the previously seeing eye. She showed me and the others there that she could see everything perfectly. As I saw God's faithfulness manifest, my eyes just started watering and I stood in awe of Him who was, is and is to come! God did not stop then. He is still at work. He continually moves and does miraculous things of all sorts.

The one who revealed secrets to the Prophet, Elisha and told him what was being said inside the house of the king of Aram so that Elisha could warn the king of Israel is still at work. He reveals His secrets and gives words of knowledge in an amazing way. I used to be scared whenever I saw God move, but now I know better, such anointing is supposed to be protected more than one would protect billion dollar cheque. King Saul had an anointing and could prophesy, but his disobedience led to God deserting him. I am aware that disobedience can strip off what God has laid in me, so my aim is to stay in alignment with Him. This has caused me to lose some of the human connections, but what better experience is there on earth than to be obedient and do what the Father says?

Restoration of order in my family

It is not enough to celebrate external manifestations when internally there is turmoil. When my marriage came apart I realised I was left with a huge assignment of singlehandedly bringing up my three children and teaching them more about God's principles. God immediately corrected me and told me that I was not going to do anything singlehandedly because I did not even have that kind of ability. He told me He would never ever leave me and so He was going to do it Himself as long as I obeyed whatever He told me to do. I found my task to be very tough, but whenever I forgot about what everyone else was doing and focused on what I was told to do things became better. I would be lying if I would say things became easier. Naturally, it is more appealing to do wrong than right, so whenever I had to teach my children the Wisdom of God, I experienced some difficulty. God's word as well as the testimonies of other men and women of God in Ministry told me clearly that I had to be firm like Daniel and not waver from what God had ordered me to teach and expect from my 'Three Stars," as that is what I call them.

Today I can openly say I have not hit the winning point as the Apostle Paul also said, but I know I have fought the good fight (2 Timothy 4: 7). I am saying this because looking back I know the 'thickets and bushes' that we cleared together with My Father holding my hand. Seeing my daughter grow in the love for God and having passion for the Ministry has been the world to me. She did well in her A' levels, but could not go to university because I was still studying and could not pay her university fees. All over her bedroom walls she put self-made posters with Faith-focused scriptures. The scriptures gave her hope that God was going to provide for her soon. Whilst still believing God, she focused on dance worship and youth ministry.

I had seen Nqobi excel in her performance and stand as the main dancer during the Young Americans UK performance in Leicester and I had also seen her wow us as parents as she sang with her friends at Sir Jonathan North Girls Community College, but when I got the invitation to come when she received her award as the Number One UK worship dance group of three (Taome -*Apple of God's Eye)* I saw God being a faithful Father as always. Ministering with the Shekinah Glory Ministry group from the US was an encouraging experience for my daughter.

During the worst testing times, my daughter stood by me and encouraged me like a sister when God was the only person who could really stand by me. As I paid her university accommodation fee in 2009, I did so with tears gushing down my eyes remembering those days when we stood with nothing, but faith, believing that God would make a way. God has now given us more than what we asked for; Hallelujah! To me it is a great blessing that she is pursuing courses related to her passion of youth ministry. My expectancy is great and I know God is just beginning with this young woman.

My younger son has been the one who gave me the greatest challenge, but I thank God because in him I see a strong willed person, whom I believe and continually confess, is going to give Satan a hard time. When he decided on his own to take his acceptance of Christ further to be baptized in water at LCF I blessed the name of the Lord. In the same year, 2007 when I went to grace my daughter as she received her Gospel Star award in Birmingham, I was invited to be there as my son Mazulu received his award as the youngest counsellor to have contributed an idea that positively affected Lancaster Boys' College for better. I further got the blessing of being one of the parents of the boys who participated in the UK BBC choir 'Boys don't sing'. Although we left Leicester just before the final performance in London watching my son do his be-bopping as part of the choir was a thriller to me. The first time he performed at LCF at one youth evening I just cried and realised that God is bringing beauty from what Satan meant to be ashes.

Sibusiso, the big brother of my house has been a blessing indeed as goes the meaning of his name. God used him to launch me into singing again. He gave me and my sister-friend Peppy music to use for our ministry. In 2007 God gave me a song which portrayed the picture of marriage according to His design and we started singing this song and other ones in weddings across the UK. Following what Sibusiso gave us, we later worked on a project with another producer in London.

Sbusiso has been a very strong force of encouragement, telling me in his very calm way, 'Mum I always knew you would do it'. Whenever I compared myself and feel like singing is not my thing, this young man always encouraged me to release what God uniquely put in me and not compare myself with other singers. The music he has produced for me has made me minister in numerous scenarios in the USA, as I sing and sometimes dance through my praises for God, the King of kings. The project, *Moving Forward* would not be there without his major contribution.

God finishes what He starts and in the year 2007 I completed my PhD research, but due to other commitments of my examination board, I had to wait and have may oral examination in January 2008. The night before my viva I had VICTORY ringing all over the place. I prayed and sang about victory and God granted me the victory I believed for. I passed my exam and had to wait for the July graduation. I instantly got a job with the University of Landon to teach isiZulu in the Languages Centre. Through the university I also got another part time job to work on a translation for Rise Films in collaboration with BBC Channel 4.

From April to June 2008 God miraculously did for me what normally takes many years to happen. I will not even start to mention that testimony because it would require its own special testimony. As I was getting ready for the graduation ceremony I got a job in Indiana University, USA and had to start working on the necessary documents. God proved His faithfulness again. On the same week that I graduated I got an urgent message that my SiSwati novel, *UMsamaliya Lolungile* had won the Macmillan Grand Prize of 2008! God literally restored what the enemy had stolen!

Before I left London for the USA, God provided me with special accommodation as I prepared for my move. I had to get rid of most of my possession and it was all a blessing because of God's promise for more and better things ahead. Although it was parting time, we celebrated being together as family once more in my Loveridge Flat in London. During those last moments together, Sibusiso helped us record a song which I cherish to this day, because it is a portrayal of our heartfelt gratitude to God. Due to the delay of our British travel documents and visas I left the UK on the last day of September with my son Mazulu to begin a new life in the USA. I regard this move as yet another move of faith because I completely had no idea what exactly the future held for me there.

The reception I got at Indiana University (IU) was quite good. Most of all the students I had come to teach were excited to finally see the long awaited professor arrive. My enthusiasm to work at IU was augmented by my students' reception. It was a great fulfilment to work with people who were keen to receive what I offered them. As part of the practice I started doing outreach work in neighbouring schools. I spoke about and demonstrated Gumboot Dance. God started opening numerous avenues where I could mentor younger women as well as make speeches to encourage other women both within the Christian life and in general life. One thing that stood prominently was that even if I spoke outside a Christian setting, the Christ message always emerged spontaneously.

Working in the USA, especially at IU made me appreciate more who I am because they have a very strong foreign language teaching and learning environment and the people there are eager to learn from other cultures. Teaching courses related to my culture broadened my own outlook to life as I identified some useful cultural practices that even people from outside my own culture could learn from. I taught a course in Gumboot Dance as a vehicle that could move someone from pain to pleasure. I also taught a course about the Southern African Culture of Song and Dance and the Reed Dance of Swaziland and KwaZulu Natal. That was a personal restoration and empowering venture and it also impacted on those who participated in my courses. One student did a documentary on my Gumboot Dance Course and hearing the testimonials of students from across the globe excited me incalculably.

Moving from the UK to the USA with my son was similar to our 2001 departure from Swaziland. England had proved to be home for us, but then God spread our wings and helped us adapt to the new life and a new variant of the English language altogether. Mazulu found a home in the Salvation Army Church where he worked together with the pastor in fund raising campaigns and played drums for the church worship service. It was a motivation to him to be in his school's football team.

Before I left London many prophetic words were given to me. I lived to see some of them come to pass and at the point of writing this testimony, more is manifesting. My pastor Yemisi Ashimolowo gave me her send off blessing and I know that was a very rare opportunity in a church of thousands like my London church, KICC. One of the deacons told me not to worry about anything for God's angels had already gone before me. During the very first week in Bloomington I saw everything happen as God divinely connected me to a church I would not have chosen on my own considering my background, but I know He took me there for a purpose. I fellowshipped with the Bethel AME church and became one of the worshippers there. I only left Bethel AME because I was then connected to what I believe to be my permanent home church in the USA and in life generally.

The transition God took me through was very taxing and led me into a more secluded pathway than ever before, but in my spirit I enjoyed every bit of it because I knew the end. What made Father Abraham persevere in faith was that he had already seen the land God promised him and he already had imagined the numerous children as sand and stars. Once you have seen your promise, you need to stay focused and not waver.

As I waited for more manifestations God opened more doors of opportunity and some of them did not really look like doors of opportunity at all. I only walked into those kinds of doors at the prompting of my Guide, Holy Spirit because He is never wrong. It was a blessing to sing at the 2009

Juneteenth celebration as well as share the stage with the acclaimed Gary Hines of *Sounds of Blackness* who has a string of awards hanging from his name. What encouraged me most was not the fame of this man of God, but his passion to build up the morale of children from disadvantaged backgrounds. It was a great blessing for me to support Mrs Boddie's work for the Lord and be part of the Cry of the Children campaign in July 31, 2009.

Seclusion and hearing His voice better

My period of seclusion and drifting away from the busyness that used to arrest me trained me to rely more on what God says than people. He speaks to me through His Living Word. I feel like I am in Joshua's position as he was told to meditate on the Word:

> *This Book of the Law shall not depart from your mouth,*
> *but you shall meditate in it day and night,*
> *that you may observe to do according to all that is written in it.*
> *For then you will make your way prosperous,*
> *and then you will have good success.*
> *Have I not commanded you?*
> *Be strong and of good courage;*
> *do not be afraid, nor be dismayed*
> *for the LORD your God is with you wherever you go*
> *(Joshua 1: 8-9 NKJV).*

Joshua took Moses' word seriously and also started commanding the officers of the children of the people to prepare provisions for themselves as they were going to cross the Jordan within three days. Provisions could have been food such as bread, but Jesus Christ spoke clearly to Satan when he tempted Him that "***it is written 'Man shall not live by bread alone, but by every word that proceeds from the mouth of God***" Learning about all these facts of Life from God propels me to perpetually make a decision to live by His Word, which is the Bread of life. This kind of lifestyle that I have developed through waiting upon Him gives me the power to move forward without fear although I may not always know where I am setting my next footstep.

My bag of provision is full of explosives which I use to demolish whatever positions itself as a foe to me as I move forward. His word states that, "You, through your commandments, make me wiser than my enemies; for they are ever with me (Psalm 119: 98). "You prepare a table before me in the presence of my enemies; You anoint my head with oil; my cup runs over (Psalm 23: 5). In Hebrews, He promises He will never leave me nor forsake me (Hebrews 13: 5-6). Also, He is able to do exceedingly, abundantly above all that [I] ask or think, according to the power that works in [me] (Ephesians 3:20). The Psalmist reminds me where to look for help and that is up to the "Lord who made heaven and earth. He will not allow [my] foot to be moved; He who keeps [me] will not slumber. Behold, He who keeps [me] shall neither slumber nor sleep. The LORD *is* [my] keeper; The LORD *is* [my] shade at [my] right hand. The sun shall neither strike [me] by day, nor the moon by night. The LORD shall preserve [me] from all evil; He shall preserve [my] soul. The LORD shall preserve [my] going out and [my] coming in from this time forth, and even forevermore. (Psalm 121: 2-8). His law is my delight and therefore I know He will give me the desires of my heart (paraphrased Palm 119: 77).

When challenges show up my body may sometimes feel weak and my eyes still shed tears, but my Spirit is adamant, and like the Apostle Paul, I perpetually declare, "...I am more than a conqueror through Him who loved me. For I am persuaded that neither death nor life, nor angels nor principalities nor powers, nor things to come... shall separate [me] from the Love of God which is in Jesus our Lord" (partially paraphrased - Romans 8: 37 – 39). With my Father doing all this for me I am determined to walk until I enter what He has set to be my Canaan and as He commanded not to forget Him when already entered (Deuteronomy 8: 2) I know He will help me remember Him.

His Word promises that soon there shall come a time when He will bestow a crown of beauty instead of the ashes and the oil of gladness instead of mourning. He has put aside a garment of praise instead of desperation. Morning will be replaced by dancing (Paraphrased Isaiah 61:3). Every moment I am getting excited, because His word promises these things. He actually says what He has prepared for those who love Him is far beyond what eyes have seen, what ears have heard as well as what hearts have conceived (1 Corinthians 2: 9). These promises blow my head off and I am learning to stop playing false humility and boldly approach My Father's throne and receive what He is giving me.

Beloved, let us receive this amazing promise from our heavenly Father:

> *"Thus says the LORD to His anointed,*
> *To Cyrus, whose right hand I have held—*
> *To subdue nations before him*
> *And loose the armour of kings,*
> *To open before him the double doors,*
> *So that the gates will not be shut:*
> *'I will go before you*
> *And make the crooked places straight;*

I will break in pieces the gates of bronze
And cut the bars of iron.
will give you the treasures of darkness
And hidden riches of secret places,
That you may know that I, the LORD,
Who call you by your name,
(Isaiah 45: 1-3 NKJV)

***

So the people went in
And possessed the land;
You subdued before them the inhabitants of the land,
The Canaanites,
And gave them into their hands,
With their kings
And the people of the land,
That they might do with them as they wished.

And they took strong cities and a rich land,
And possessed houses full of all goods,
Cisterns already dug, vineyards, olive groves,
And fruit trees in abundance.
So they ate and were filled and grew fat,
And delighted themselves in Your great goodness.
(Nehemiah 9: 24-25 NKJV)

I have given you land for which you did not labour,
and cities which you did not build,
and you dwell in them,
You eat the vineyards and olive groves
which you did not plant
Now therefore fear the Lord,
Serve Him in sincerity and in truth
and put away gods which your fathers served
On the other side of the River and in Egypt
Serve the Lord
(Joshua 24: 13 – 14 NKJV)

If my heavy use of Scripture has felt too much, I would like to clarify, that I could not have done better and reduced anything because this is the way I live. The word tells me in Proverbs 18:21 that what I speak has the power of life and death, therefore I deliberately choose to declare life because for many years I used to speak death into my own life. Now I speak life and I know the declarations always yield results. God's word and my Spiritual fathers, mothers and mentors have demonstrated to me that if I decree a thing indeed it shall be established!

This testimony has left out a lot more that God has already done and I believe that by the time you hold this book in your hand more would have already happened, so I would like to cordially invite you to look out for my next testimony which is already in the pipeline. Also, if you like, please take your time to visit the website www.drbettydlamini.com as well as Best Brand Ministries to see what God is doing in our lives! You may also join us for a discussion of real life issues in the blog, Dr Betty's Lounge. Avalanches of blessings!

A Final Word and Invitation

Finally, I would like to ask you a few questions that I regard as very important. Why do you think you are still alive? For those who have felt desperate, what do you think kept you from committing suicide? Why are you holding this book of my testimony in your hand today? Think deeper about the things I have written about and you will realise they are not really exciting. They are nasty experiences, which have been turned into something fantastic. May be, you may not have seen anything fantastic in that testimony, but there is a lot that has happened which I have left for the next testimony. Now the big question is why do you think I am hanging my 'dirty linen' for the world? Do you think it is just for fun? Not at all! The answer to all these is the same. God loves you. He has a wonderful plan for your life. He wants you to enjoy life, not just in heaven, but starting here and now in this land of the living. He sent me to share this testimony so that you may see that He is real and you can go beyond 'hopeless hope' and actually experience your breakthrough in life. For some, He wants you to wise up and prevent pain rather than put energy in healing what could have been avoided.

You may not realise, but I feel like you can use my experience and my shared testimony as a way of barring away pain that could come your way if no one had told you what I just told you. Count yourself as blessed for even taking your time to read the testimony. I would also like to extend my invitation to those who completely have no relationship with Jesus yet. Jesus is yearning to have a relationship with you. He says,

Here I am!
I stand at the door and knock.
If anyone hears my voice and opens the door,
I will come in and eat with him, and he with me
(Revelations 3: 20 NIV))

As you have heard me several times referring to religion, there is a difference between Christianity as a religion and having a personal relationship with Jesus. The first is about going to church or having a church you belong to, with its man made doctrine, and several rules and regulations, constitution, or whatever they call it in that particular church denomination. Amazingly,

Jesus does not advocate for any special denomination, but He wants to have a personal and intimate relationship with you. This is not a myth. It is real, like I have just related above.

The invitation is for everyone. Your suffering has to stop. You do not deserve it because your case was settled long ago when Jesus cried out "It is finished" on the cross. God does not want anyone to suffer. He sent us His only Begotten Son to die for us because He wanted us to escape the pain and suffering. The only mystery that has made many people miss out on such grace and love is that God is not forceful as our earthly authorities can be. He allows us to decide willingly. If you want Him to come into your life please say this prayer:

Thank you Jesus for dying for my sins on the cross of Calvary and please forgive my sins. I invite you into my life so that I may have an intimate relationship with you. Thank you for receiving me into your family. In the name of Jesus Christ of Nazareth I pray. Amen.

If you have prayed this prayer, believe that Jesus Christ has already answered your prayer and He is in your life now. Make it your habit to talk to Him through prayer. By prayer, I mean simply talking to God like you talk to the people you see with your naked eyes. Just talk. Just open your mouth and say what you want to say to Him in simple everyday words. You do not need to speak in a special tone or phraseology. Where there are things you do not understand, just ask Him in simple language and tell Him what you do not understand. I personally have learnt to talk to Him in a way some religious people may not even think is prayer at all. My prayer is stuff like this:

- Jesus, please help me. I am stuck and I do not know how to start writing this next chapter. I believe you are helping me even now. Thank you Lord. In the name of Jesus Christ of Nazareth I pray. Amen;

- Lord, I just want you to know that I am hurting right now because So-and-so * has taken my books and she does not want to return them, yet I need them badly. Lord I am very bitter with So-and-so right now. Help me to forgive her. I need my books though. Please let me have them back Lord. I pray believing you will do this for me. In the name of Jesus Christ of Nazareth. Amen;

- Lord, I know I said I wanted to forgive So-and-so, and thought I had forgiven her, but this thing she did to me keeps coming to me. Please teach me how to forgive her completely. I have no joy now because of this thing. Help me God. I trust you. Thank you Lord. I pray in the name of Jesus Christ. Amen;

- Oh God, thank you for the new skirt. Jesus the skirt is so beautiful and dear to me. I love it. Thank you for even leading me into this shop at the right time. Amen;

- Oh, thank you Jesus for such a great day today;

Friends I could go on and on, but I think already you have got my idea of prayer. God has weaned me from the lengthy, carefully phrased, religious prayers. I still have lengthy prayers, but I do not plan it to be long. I just talk to my God. God's Spirit leads me to say what I have to say. When praying for my children's lives, now and their future or praying for other people I sometimes have lengthy prayers. Sometimes I just tell Him how much I love Him without even asking for anything from Him. Since this is my testimony, if I happened to confuse you as you were reading or I aroused some questions, do not hesitate to contact me by email. I promise to respond to your questions through God's Divine guidance. God bless you all.

Betty Dlamini

Email: **drbetty@drbettydlamini.com** or
check the updated contact details on Google or visit
www.drbettydlamini.com

(Endnotes)

1   Dinah went outside the camp to where she was not supposed to be, and was raped by some of the young men of the area. The story is in Genesis 34:1

2   It does not really matter how far away you are from where you need and want to be. What matters most is the willingness and determination to get there. You may be from the South East of the globe, but within a tick you may get to its North Western part!

3   Dr Mike Murdock's Wisdom keys –key number 14

4   Many Swazi men regard themselves as childless if they have girls only and this mindset is also instilled by Swazi culture into girls. It has been through mental battles and serious debates and discussions that the Swazi girl child is accorded value.

5   In Swazi culture elderly women become heads of the families when their husbands die.

6   Widows in Swaziland are expected to wear black clothes for a period of two (winters) years as part of mourning their husbands. Mourning a husband comes as a package with many rules and regulations the culture imposes on widows, making their loss even worse.

7   King Somhlolo of Swaziland was laying down asleep and he had a dream where although he had never seen a white person in his life, he saw a vision showing these people with a pale colour different from his own skin colour, and with her similar to the whisky part of cow tails. In his dream he was shown these people bringing a button and a book; representing money and the Bible. He was told both were good but he was advised to choose the book…

8   *Gogo* is a SiSwati term for grandmother. Young people address adults who are their grandmothers' age as grandmothers too.

9   *Make* is the siSwati term for 'mother'. In siSwati culture women are respected as 'Mother' so and so as opposed to 'Auntie' so and so.

10 My daddy called me Bongiwe which is one of the numerous short versions of my SiSwati name Sibongile.

11 Ladysmith Black Mambazo is a famous group that has toured the world. The group was established 48 years ago and is still on the move.

12 *Mkhokheli* is a special term for a pastor's wife which means the one who gives counsel.